WITHDRAWN

D1544373

Music *Musique*

Music *Musique*

French & American Piano Composition
in the Jazz Age

Barbara Meister

INDIANA UNIVERSITY PRESS

Bloomington & Indianapolis

This book is a publication of

Indiana University Press
601 North Morton Street
Bloomington, IN 47404-3797 USA

http://iupress.indiana.edu

Telephone orders 800-842-6796
Fax orders 812-855-7931
Orders by e-mail iuporder@indiana.edu

© 2006 by Barbara Meister

All rights reserved

No part of this book may be reproduced or utilized in any
form or by any means, electronic or mechanical, including
photocopying and recording, or by any information storage and
retrieval system, without permission in writing from the publisher.
The Association of American University Presses' Resolution
on Permissions constitutes the only exception to this prohibition.

The paper used in this publication meets the minimum
requirements of American National Standard
for Information Sciences—Permanence
of Paper for Printed Library Materials,
ANSI Z39.48-1984.

Manufactured in the United States of America

Library of Congress Cataloging-in-Publication Data

Meister, Barbara, date
   Music musique : French and American piano composition in the jazz age /
Barbara Meister.
      p. cm.
   Includes bibliographical references and index.
   ISBN 0-253-34608-8 (cloth : alk. paper)
   1. Jazz—History and criticism. 2. Music—France—20th century—History and criticism.
3. Music—United States—20th century—History and criticism. 4. Piano music—History and
criticism. I. Title.
   ML197.M244 2006
   781.6'8165—dc22

                                                                        2006004443

1 2 3 4 5 11 10 09 08 07 06

To the memory of my parents

Just as my fingers on these keys
Make music, so these self-same sounds
On my spirit make a music too.

Wallace Stevens, "Peter Quince at the Clavier"

It don't mean a thing if it ain't got that swing.

Duke Ellington

Contents

Acknowledgments

I should like to thank the editors at Indiana University Press, Gayle Sherwood and Suzanne Ryan, who helped formulate and define the scope of this book. I should also like to express my appreciation to Caitlin Greer Meister, whose computer skills and intelligent overview of the information and style of the text were invaluable to me.

Music *Musique*

1

Introduction

wo disasters struck France in 1870. The first was the Franco-Prussian War, a catastrophe whose effects on European geopolitical balances were felt for generations. Under Napoleon III and his ravishing redheaded empress Eugénie, France enjoyed glittering balls and apparent prosperity. Paris was gradually being transformed into the city of broad boulevards, gracious parks, and elegant buildings we know today. The haute bourgeoisie enriched itself by way of land speculation associated with the reconstruction of the city, while the less fortunate were crowded into undesirable areas. The gap between rich and poor, always enormous, continued to grow. The military seemed to be at the height of its power and glory, but magnificent uniforms and splendid parades only masked the essential weakness of French forces.

In 1867 Offenbach's *Grande Duchesse de Gérolstein* mocked the pretensions of the large number of heads of state who had flocked to the Paris Exposition. Only one visiting dignitary was neither amused nor fooled: Chancellor Otto von Bismarck of Prussia. A recent turn of events alerted Bismarck to the cracks beneath the French surface. At the urging of the ardently Catholic Eugénie, Napoleon had sent the Austrian Maximilian along with his wife, Charlotte, to rule Mexico as a puppet emperor. In a particularly bizarre instance of colonial hubris, Eugénie was convinced that the Mexicans would welcome the foreigners as their sovereigns and convert to their religion. The Mexicans themselves felt differently about their new ruler, however, and Napoleon was unable to send enough troops across the Atlantic to save the hapless Maximilian from execution (this tragic dénouement was captured in a remarkable painting by Manet). Bismarck recognized France's baseless bravado for what it was, and advised his Kaiser accordingly.

Bismarck cleverly manipulated the French into attacking Prussia, thereby rendering any mutual-aid treaties it had signed with other European countries null and void. Within six weeks the entire French army had capitulated, and Bismarck won an easy victory. Only Paris, besieged by Prussian troops, held out until the entire populace was in danger of starving to death. Napoleon and his empress went into exile, and the party was over.

The second cataclysmic event that marked the year 1870 was nature's own contribution: a plague of the dreaded vineyard-destroying *Phylloxera vitifoliae;* its effects were equally felt in the United States. The earliest wines produced in North America came from vines indigenous to the territories that eventually became the New England states. Like the settlers of this rocky, only partially arable area, these vines were certainly hardy, but the grapes they brought forth seemed unsuited to the production of the finest wines. In the second half of the eighteenth century, Franciscan monks from Spain, seeking a way to make their tours of missionary duty a little less ascetic, brought European grape-producing plants to San Diego. This was the beginning of a flourishing California wine industry, which soon incorporated the finest stock from France.

And then along came phylloxera. This tiny insect, with its fly-like transparent wings and voracious appetite, relished the taste of the roots of the California and European vineyards and soon demolished every last one. Fortunately, the roots of the New England plants did not appeal to the fussy phylloxera, and so these aboriginal vineyards remained alive and well. The roots of a vine do not affect the taste of the grape it produces, and so these roots were bought by vineyard owners in France and California alike. Onto these strictly American roots wine producers were able to graft the branches of their own plants, thus saving the wine industries of both continents.

As we shall see, the Franco-Prussian War had a direct effect on the development of French music. Composers of that humiliated nation, determined to shake the influence of the great German masters, began to forge a distinctive French style either by returning to their own Lully-Rameau-Couperin roots or veering in new idiosyncratic directions. This surge of patriotic pride was but one manifestation of the spirit of nationalism that swept nineteenth-century Europe, leading to Czech, Finnish, Russian, Spanish, and other folk-based, easily identifiable alternatives to the Germanic tradition.

The United States in 1870 was far too preoccupied with the aftereffects of its own Civil War to worry about internecine European squabbles. The sorely buffeted Union had its own reasons for wanting to create discernibly American styles in the arts, owing to its sense of inferiority in the face of long-standing European culture. America either had to compete with the music of the canonical European masters, or create something entirely new out of its own indigenous spirit and experience.

The phylloxera story is analogous to the world of music, in which influences fly freely from place to place and cross-fertilization is vital to production. From the 1920s onward, France has been wild about American jazz, much of which had been created by New Orleans musicians of

Creole origin. These jazz players in turn often used Debussy-like augmented chords and unresolved sevenths and ninths in their riffs. Did these musical ideas come from France, or were they independently conceived in the United States? Melodic and rhythmic elements may have been derived from the African music in the backgrounds of so many of these musicians; harmonic innovations were European or homegrown.

We begin our discussion of the development of French and American styles of music in France in the early 1870s, when French composers like César Franck and Vincent d'Indy, both of whom leaned toward the German Romantic tradition, held sway. We continue with explorations of the music of such transitional composers as Bizet and Chabrier, moving through Fauré, Chausson, and others to the culminating achievements of Debussy and Ravel. We then turn to the United States in the post–Civil War years, which saw the gradual awakening and blossoming of musical activity. Original composition was, of course, the last step in the slow march to a distinctive American style, with jazz and minstrel-show music playing significant roles.

After a brief discussion of the history of jazz in the United States, composers important in France and America in the 1920s and 1930s are given individual attention, with leading jazz innovators awarded full consideration. Emphasis is placed on those composers who experienced musical life on both sides of the Atlantic: Aaron Copland, Virgil Thomson, and many others who studied with the famed French pedagogue Nadia Boulanger; Darius Milhaud, who spent over a year in Brazil; Louis Armstrong and Duke Ellington, who toured France; the Harlem Hellfighters, who fought and played for the French armed forces during World War I; and Edgar Varèse, George Antheil, and many others who were truly Franco-American in spirit.

The social, economic, and political aspects of the times are also considered as they had significant impact upon the development of the music and musical culture of the period. The "Great Migration" of African Americans from the South to New York, Chicago, and other northern cities, the Harlem Renaissance, the Parisian African American community established after World War I, the stock-market crash of 1929 and the ensuing depression, and the creation of the WPA—all these nonmusical events are important to our story.

Throughout the study we shall concentrate on music composed for the piano, touching also on a few landmark orchestral, operatic, and chamber works, and exploring the rich and rewarding relationships among French and American composers as they moved in and around the jazz phenomenon.

The Formation of a French Style of Composition

he end of the Franco-Prussian War brought with it the end of both monarchy and empire as viable forms of government for the French. Despite the upheavals of World Wars I and II, the concept of republic, although not the newly formed Third Republic itself, was permanently established in France. The First Republic had been created after the 1789 Revolution and dissolved when its elected head, Napoleon Bonaparte, disenchanted with dependence on popular favor, declared France an empire and crowned himself Emperor Napoleon I. The Second Republic was proclaimed after the overturn of a monarchy that had been disrupted by the Revolution of 1830 and finally deposed after the revolutionary year 1848. The Second Republic was in turn negated just as the first had been, on December 2, 1851—the fiftieth anniversary of the first Napoleon's coup—by his nephew, Louis Napoleon, or "Napoléon le petit" (the little Napoleon), as Victor Hugo dubbed him. As the title Napoleon II had been retired when Napoleon I's son, "*l'Aiglon*" (the little eagle), died too young to cause any mischief, Louis Napoleon styled himself Napoleon III.

Among the first acts of the Third Republic was the foundation of the Société Nationale de Musique (National Society of Music). In the words of *The New Grove Dictionary of Music and Musicians,* the purpose of this addition to the centuries-old Paris Conservatoire was "to restore French music to a position worthy of rivaling the masterpieces of victorious Germany."[1] Illustrative of the enduring power of the new chauvinistic attitude was the fact that even decades later Debussy was signing his compositions *Claude Debussy, musicien français.*

One of the principal factors in the ability of the French to create a truly national idiom in a relatively short time was the intimate connection between French art song, or *mélodie,* and the great French poetry of the nineteenth century. In the first half of the century, composers such as Charles Gounod (1818–1873) and Hector Berlioz (1813–1869) had begun to choose important texts and give them settings in which the words retained their original cadences. Although composers may prefer to use poetry in their native languages, the poetry of such masters as Victor Hugo,

Théophile Gautier, Alphonse de Lamartine, and other great Romantics seemed tailor-made for reinterpretation into French song. The next generation of song composers, the most renowned of whom are Gabriel Fauré (1845–1924), Henri Duparc (1848–1933), Ernest Chausson (1855–1899), and Claude Debussy (1862–1918), were even more fortunate, as they continued to draw on the Romantic poets while also having at their disposal their choice of the more contemporary Symbolists and Surrealists like Charles Baudelaire, Paul Verlaine, and Maurice Maeterlinck.

Even in ordinary prose, the French language is an exceptionally good foil for music. Because so many letter combinations produce the same or very similar sounds and only the letters c, f, l, and, in some instances, r are pronounced at the ends of words, there are many more natural rhymes in common French speech than in most other languages (e.g., *son, sont, sent, vont, paon, lent,* and *avant* all rhyme). In addition, French is an essentially unaccented language; there are no meters—no iambs, dactyls, or the like—in prose or poetry because the only stressed syllables are those at the ends of isolated words or phrases. It is no wonder then that several French composers have set prose passages, especially the "prose poems" favored in the 1850s and 1860s, to music (Ravel's song cycle *Histoires naturelles* is a particularly delightful example).

The poem-manifesto of Paul Verlaine (1844–1896), clearly Debussy's favorite poet, best explains this fortunate affinity between French poets and musicians:

Art poétique
De la musique avant toute chose
Et pour cela préfère l'impair,
Plus vague et plus soluble dans l'air
Sans rien en lui qui pèse ou qui pose.
. . .
De la musique encore et toujours!
Que ton vers soit la chose envolée . . .

Music before all else
And for that prefer the uneven,
Vaguer and more soluble in the air
With nothing in it that weighs or imposes.
. . .
Music again and always
Let your verses take flight . . .

It would be hard to imagine a more explicit invitation to a composer, and many accepted. Some, like Debussy, developed their unique styles of keyboard composition in large part through setting poetry. Indeed, the piano parts of the late-nineteenth- and early-twentieth-century songs of Debussy, Duparc, Fauré, Chausson, and others form an indispensable aspect of French pianism. Since comprehension of the words was so important to French composers, the vocal lines were often relatively simple, with many lines of text sung on a single repeated pitch. The piano thus carried much of the melodic as well as the harmonic content, making the so-called accompaniments viable pieces in their own right. They are often technically challenging and invariably rewarding.[2]

Not all French poets were pleased about their verses being set to music. Victor Hugo is said to have scrawled on the manuscript of one of his collections, "Défense d'afficher de la musique sur cette poésie" (It is forbidden to post music on this poetry), and in another context the poet Stéphane Mallarmé was said to respond to Debussy's announcement that he was going to set the former's "L'Après-midi d'un faune" to music, "I thought I had already done that." The stories may be apocryphal, and composers helped themselves to Hugo's and Mallarmé's texts with or without their blessings. *Prelude à l'après-midi d'un faune* is, of course, a tone poem in Debussy's setting, but in the case of a song setting some problems arise for the author of the text. When the rhythm of the music does not match that of the poem, the music always imposes its will. One example of this is the beautiful Debussy setting of Baudelaire's "Harmonie du soir"; the poem is in alexandrines, the characteristic twelve-syllable line of classical French poetry. Baudelaire follows the dictum that the twelve syllables should be evenly divided by a pause after the sixth; the first line of the poem reads

Voici venir le temps où vibrant sur sa tige

Now comes the time when trembling on its stem

There is no punctuation, but it is natural to pause slightly after *temps.* Debussy changes this by having a musical pause after *Voici* and none for the rest of the line. The effect of the music's rhythm on the listener is so much stronger than that of the words that it prevails. Despite issues such as these, poets like Pierre Louÿs were more than willing to work with composers, in Louÿs's case specifically his friend Debussy, and many others were so closely allied to the musicians of the day—and the visual artists as well—that their various forms of expression blended naturally.

We have already encountered some of the great composers of the second half of the nineteenth century who were so influential in forming a distinctive French style. Naturally these giants stood on the shoulders of the giants who preceded them, by whom they were taught and influenced. A brief overview of the best known of these composers, with emphasis on the music they created for piano, is in order.

One of the most vociferous advocates of recognizably French music was Camille Saint-Saëns (1835–1921). When, in 1886, the Société Nationale de Musique, obeying the wishes of Vincent d'Indy and its other conservative members, voted to allow the performance of non-French music, Saint-Saëns severed his connection with the organization, and during World War I he pushed for a ban on the operas of arch-German composer Richard Wagner. Paradoxically, the most enduring works in Saint-Saëns's catalog, which is enormous, are those in the forms most successfully exploited by the Viennese masters: concerti and symphonies.

By and large Saint-Saëns's piano works are lightweight, with many a mazurka, waltz, "album leaf," and the like. That he had a wonderful sense of humor is obvious to anyone who has heard his *Carnaval des animaux* (Carnival of the animals), in whose menagerie one finds, with the other birds and beasts, a pair of pianists obsessively practicing their scales. Also very amusing is his little piano four-hand piece *Pas redoublé* (Double time), which lurches from key to key like a drunken conservatory student. Saint-Saëns was a superb pianist and organist as well as one of the most prolific composers on record. (Debussy, after hearing *Les barbares* [The barbarians], one of Saint-Saëns's thirteen operas, wrote in his critique, "Why then this sickening need to write operas?"[3] Saint-Saëns never forgave him.) Saint-Saëns was a child prodigy and a formidable polymath. If his compositions did not really do much to further the development of a strictly French idiom, his polemics and personal choices certainly did.

There were some major composers in France at the time who, despite a general reaction against things German after 1870, continued to write in their accustomed Germanic style. To some extent their music became more French almost in spite of themselves, as the spirit of the times changed. Preeminent in this apolitical group was César Franck (1822–1890). Franck was born in Belgium, but he spent most of his creative life in Paris. As well as being a fine pianist and outstanding organist, he was a most revered pedagogue, influencing many of his pupils, including d'Indy, in the direction of German Romanticism.

Musicologist Wilfrid Mellers has called Franck "a myth which modestly parallels the Wagnerian legend." Mellers goes on to describe the composer as hampered by his father, "a not less monstrous wife, the bad taste of his time, the adulation of his disciples, and possibly an innate lack of intelligence."[4] If this assessment is even partially true, it makes the man's achievements all the more remarkable, for politically incorrect as they might have been, he composed some marvelous works for piano. His most often-performed solo piano piece is his *Prélude, chorale et fugue* (Prelude, chorale, and fugue) of 1884, a masterwork of majestic proportions. The fugue is particularly compelling, a brilliant combination of Baroque-inspired counterpoint and passionate Romanticism. The falling figure in the fugue's theme is characteristic of the composer, heard in his ever-popular Symphony in D, his Sonata for Violin and Piano (now, there's a marvelously difficult piano part!), and so many other works. The solemn chorale, with its religious overtones, is nonetheless clearly the product of a Romantic sensibility. (The French have always loved the juxtaposition of the sensual and the religious; Baudelaire's "Harmonie du soir," for instance, whose first line, "Voici venir les temps où vibrant sur sa tige," was quoted above, continues, "Chaque fleur s'évapore ainsi qu'un encensoir"—Now comes the time when trembling on its stem, / Each flower sends forth its fragrance like a censer.)

Franck's *Danse lente* (Slow dance) of 1885 is an interesting contrast to the massive *Prélude, chorale et fugue.* Only about three minutes long, it is both charming and melancholy. His Piano Quintet and *Symphonic Variations,* the latter a piano concerto in easily penetrated disguise, provide plenty of room for virtuosic pianism. The element that strikes the listener as particularly French in this wonderful music is the lush sensuality Franck evidently struggled to squelch all his life. How fortunate that he lost the battle over and over, especially in his later works.

The F-minor Quintet, composed in 1878–79, was the real breakthrough for this hitherto repressed sensuous element in Franck's nature. A seminal work, it adumbrates the shimmering texture of so much of Debussy's music, validating its composer's place as a participant in the development of distinctly French music. Again according to Mellers, the Quintet was thought to be so overtly sensual that "the respectable Saint-Saëns objected to playing it in public and it even brought a blush to the cheek of so experienced a sensualist as Franz Liszt."[5] Mellers offers no documentation for this startling statement, and it is hard to imagine anything making Liszt blush, but it complements the accepted wisdom that Saint-Saëns was embarrassed by his own *Carnival of the Animals* and did not want it played in public until after his death.

One of Franck's most devoted students was Vincent d'Indy (1851–1931). D'Indy fought bravely against the Prussians in the Franco-Prussian War, and so it was fitting that when the war was over he should be named one of the first and youngest composers on the faculty of the newly formed Société Nationale de la Musique. However, despite his fierce patriotism, d'Indy was ambivalent about German music. After all, the masterpieces of Bach, Beethoven, Brahms, Schubert, Schumann, and Mendelssohn could hardly be ignored. D'Indy felt compelled to pursue musical experience and inspiration in the lion's den—Bayreuth—site of the idiosyncratic opera house Wagner had constructed to suit his theories (the orchestra plays from under the stage, for example). There he had the overwhelming experience of hearing Wagner's *Ring,* and he never quite shook the mesmerizing effect it had on him.

After receiving an instructive critique of his early compositions from Franck, d'Indy became a member of the so-called *bande à Franck* (Franck band). He was not alone in worshipping this august figure—Duparc, Chausson, and many others became Franck's devoted disciples—but d'Indy's Germanic proclivities seemed to be stronger than most, and, especially in his operas, he sounded unacceptably Wagnerian.

Around 1880 d'Indy decided to change his musical direction by seeking inspiration from the folk songs of a rough, sparsely populated area of France known as Les Cévannes. The conscious effort brought forth a spate of folk-song settings for voice and piano and d'Indy's most popular and lasting work, *Symphonie cévanole* or, as it is better known, *Symphony on a French Mountain Air* (1886). Although written a few years later, his magnum opus, the opera *Fervaal* (1895), was still accused of echoing Wagner, specifically *Parsifal*. Others, in the meanwhile, had gone on to compose more easily identifiable *French* music, and d'Indy's influence was by and large limited to his role as a fine teacher of the technique of composition.

A strangely underappreciated French Romantic of this period was Georges Bizet (1838–1875). Several of Bizet's works are staples of today's concert and opera repertoires, among them his delightful First Symphony, the orchestral suite known as *L'Arlésienne*, the twelve-part cycle *Jeux d'enfants* (Children's games), originally composed for piano duet and then orchestrated, and, of course, that perennial favorite, *Carmen*. It is said that the cool critical reception that greeted *Carmen* at its premiere was a principal cause of Bizet's premature death just a year later. One wonders if the relative lack of success his major work garnered was not in part due to the continued preference among French audiences for the Germanic style. Bizet was not completely ignored, but he did not have the recognition posterity has judged him worthy of.

Of the Bizet works mentioned above, the most interesting to pianists is the cycle *Jeux d'enfants*. This is one of the many works intended for piano four-hands and later orchestrated (to those pianists who have played them in their original form, the orchestrations seem overblown, less fresh, less intimate, less successful). *Jeux d'enfants* begins with *L'escarpolette* (The see-saw), in which *primo* and *secondo* exchange rising and falling arpeggios to vertiginous effect. Next comes *La toupie* (The spinning top), the spinning effect created by trill-like sixteenth notes for *secondo*. *La poupée* (The doll), which follows, is sweet and tender; the horses in *Chevaux de bois* (Merry-go-round) gallop at full speed, while *Le volant* (The badminton ball) flies on *primo*'s thirty-second-note runs. *Trompette et tambour* (Bugler and drummer) shows toy soldiers at their bravest, while *Bulles de savon* (Soap bubbles) float away in three-note phrases. And so it goes, with *Les quatre coins* (Puss in the corner), *Colin-maillard* (Blindman's buff), *Saute-mouton* (Leapfrog), *Petit mari, petite femme* (Playing house), and the runaway *Le bal* (The ball) for a rousing finale. The technical demands of the cycle are just enough to keep the pianists hopping, and the musical fare is not just for children. In their original four-hand version *Jeux d'enfants* represents what French composers most valued in their music—wit, brevity, and charm.

More intimately linked to the work of the post–Franco-Prussian War generation was Emmanuel Chabrier (1841–1894), whose compositions are so accessible that his importance is often overlooked. Chabrier was born in the Auvergne region of central France, and—a typical Auvergnat—he was fiercely independent. Largely ignoring the hegemony throughout Europe of Brahms, Schumann, and Liszt, he was nevertheless caught up in the Wagner frenzy current in the avant garde of the day, even belonging to a Parisian group called *Le petit Bayreuth* (Little Bayreuth). Wagner's Teutonic axioms proved for the most part uncongenial to the fun-loving Chabrier. They rear their heads primarily in his opera *Gwendolyn,* whose libretto deals with the conflict between paganism and early Christianity and manifests discernable echoes of *Parsifal.*

Despite this one compelling influence, Chabrier generally went about composing in his own, delightfully spontaneous way. His *Dix pièces pittoresques* (Ten picturesque pieces), extremely varied short piano pieces composed in 1881, show a lightness and absence of bathos more closely aligned with the aesthetic of François Couperin than with that of any German master. This sort of insouciance and lack of pretension would mark the works of Erik Satie as well as Francis Poulenc and others of the group Les Six (The Six) who flourished after the turn of the century. The key word in the title of this group of pieces—not really a cycle since each of its ten vignettes can stand on its own—is *Pittoresque,* for although the titles were supplied by the publisher rather than the composer, each does seem to evoke a setting or situation. *Danse villagois* (Village dance), for instance, has alternating passages of rustic simplicity and slightly off-kilter references to Baroque dance forms. While only one of the ten is actually titled *Improvisation,* the feeling of improvisatory spurts of inspiration suitable only to short pieces pervades the set. Like Schumann, about whose shorter compositions much the same might be said, Chabrier often chooses arpeggiated figures instead of solid chords as accompanying figures. This preference adds to the lightness of the music.

Chabrier loved playing the piano, performing wherever anyone was brave enough to let this famously piano-destroying firebrand near an instrument. He also liked playing with other pianists, and his *Valses romantiques* (Romantic waltzes) for two pianos was a smash hit when first performed. The repertoire for two pianos is sparse indeed, and it is surprising that this work is so seldom heard.

Bourrée fantastique (Fantastic bourée) of 1891, one of Chabrier's last efforts, is another attractive solo piano work. Its plethora of repeated notes makes agile fingers and a fast-action piano an absolute requirement. A feeling of wildness lurks behind its playfulness, but a certain natural elegance prevents its sometimes vernacular material from descending into vulgarity. In this, too, Chabrier is typically French.

Like his dear friend Manet, Chabrier was fascinated by all things Spanish. The distinctive dance rhythms and folk melodies of that exotic land, not to mention the seductively undulating bodies of its flamenco dancers, which Chabrier described as "Andalusian bottoms writhing like snakes in the mating season,"[6] proved a fruitful source of inspiration for his music. According to his wife, Chabrier preferred to do his research in situ—that is, in the cafés of the region. He was especially fascinated by the way the dancers instinctively clapped off the beat while the guitarists kept up a steady $\frac{3}{4}$ time.[7] The *Habañera* for solo piano and the ever-popular *España* (Spain) for orchestra are the best illustrations of this imported flavor in his music.

Chabrier was certainly not alone in seeking inspiration in Spain. One often hears the bromide that French composers have written the best Spanish music. Certainly Bizet's *Carmen*, Edouard Lalo's *Symphonie espagnole* (Spanish symphony, for violin and orchestra), Maurice Ravel's *Bolero*, *Alborado del gracioso* (The fool's dawn song, from *Miroirs*) and *Rhapsodie espagnole* (Spanish rhapsody), as well as Debussy's *Iberia* (Iberia) and *Sérénade interrompue* (The interrupted serenade, from book 1 of his *Préludes*), to name some outstanding examples, constitute a convincing argument. While not the first, Chabrier's work in this style belongs in the forefront of the trend. Central and South American music, particularly that of Mexico and Brazil, would later influence Aaron Copland and Darius Milhaud, respectively—in Milhaud's case adding to his interest in nontraditional non-European rhythms, as evidenced in his receptivity to jazz.

While none of his works justifies putting Chabrier in the first rank of composers, he had an enormous influence on the next generation of French musicians. Among his seminal innovations was his interest in and acceptance of the popular music of the day, an area later mined by French and American composers. In fact, he was the first French composer to bridge the divide between highbrow and bourgeois tastes. Among his vast circle of friends was one Charles de Sivry, the brother-in-law of poet Paul Verlaine. De Sivry played piano at Le Chat Noir (The black cat), a favorite watering hole for artists of all genres. Not only did Chabrier frequent the cabaret, he and de Sivry often played piano four-hands for its delighted customers. Of his published works, *L'étoile* (The star, 1877), a light-hearted comic opera that was his first success and made him an instant star, was not so far from musical-comedy entertainment. Direct links from this work to Jacques Ibert's *Divertissements*, Poulenc's *Les mamelles de Tirésias* (The breasts of Tiresias), much of Satie's piano music, and Gershwin's *American in Paris* are not hard to discern.

Ernest Chausson and Gabriel Fauré have already been mentioned in connection with the *mélodie,* to which genre both contributed many small masterpieces. Of the two, Chausson seemed less attracted to the piano as a solo instrument, and his most important writing for keyboard is to be found in his Concerto for Violin, Piano and String Quartet (Opus 21, 1890–91). This unique work begins with three single notes boldly played on the piano, an attention-getting summons that becomes the material for the entire movement. The structural unity this repeated three-note motif provides, combined with the free-flowing Romanticism of the rest of the music, gives a particularly French intermingling of the logical and the sensuous.

The second movement of the concerto is a charming *sicilienne* with a mildly antique flavor, while the third is tender and melancholic. The passionate outburst toward the end of this latter section is soon subdued, and the Finale, a cousin to the last movement of d'Indy's *Symphonie sur un air montagnard* (Symphony on a mountain air), is lively and rhythmically incisive. Throughout the work the French virtues of balance and decorum are in evidence, with the piano figurations, no matter how busy and virtuosic, never allowed to overpower the violin, and all passion eventually contained.

There are many significant pieces for piano solo in the oeuvre of Gabriel Fauré—nocturnes, ballades, impromptus—and many of them are lovely. In general, although there is an occasional outburst of passion, these works are quiet and intimate. Like many of Fauré's song settings, they often resemble comparable works of Debussy in their ability to create atmosphere through evocative harmonies. (For poetry aficionados or pianists who like to accompany singers, it is interesting to compare settings of the same poem—Paul Verlaine's "Il pleure dans mon coeur" [There is weeping in my heart], for instance—by these two composers.) To exemplify the difference between the aesthetic of Fauré, the majority of whose works have fade-out endings rather than bang-up applause getters, and that of most late- and post-Romantic composers, one need only listen to his Requiem and those of Brahms or Verdi. One of his signature devices that had a major influence on later French composers, especially Ravel, was his habitual avoidance of the traditional V–I cadence during or at the ends of compositions. The substitution of a whole step for the usual half-step leading tone before the end of a final cadence is what often lends an antique quality to his music.

Of Fauré's many piano compositions, none better exemplifies his style than *Dolly*, a six-part suite for piano duet (the title refers to a woman of that name, not to a toy). Like Bizet's *Jeux d'enfants* and so many other French works for piano four-hands, this suite exemplifies prime elements of the Gallic *esprit*. Aside from Franz Schubert, who takes the prize for both quality and quantity, no one enjoyed composing for two people at one piano than the French. Comparing Schubert's works in the genre to those under discussion in this study, one hears in microcosm the vast difference between the Teutonic tradition and the emerging French style. With a few exceptions the Schubert pieces are grand in concept, long, serious, often symphonic in scope. The French works, on the other hand, are brief, aiming for—and achieving—charm rather than profundity (exemplifying Ned Rorem's much-quoted remark that the French are profoundly superficial while the Germans are superficially profound).

The Fauré suite begins a *Berceuse* (Lullaby), which makes an ideal piece for beginning adult students: the *primo* is quite simple, but the harmonies are gratifyingly sophisticated. The second piece, *Mi-a-ou* (Meow), although written in straight $\frac{3}{4}$, has some unexpected rhythmic quirks. The third, *Le jardin de Dolly* (Dolly's garden), is a treasure house of harmonic inventiveness. Fauré begins conventionally enough with an E-major arpeggiated chord, but by the second measure we are off and running through a kaleidoscope of modulations. *Kitty Waltz* has scales that begin in *secondo* and conclude in *primo,* always a challenge for the ensemble. *Tendresse* (Tenderness) lives up to its title, which does not prevent it from being harmonically rich. *Le pas espagnol* (in this case "Spanish dance step," but punsters might choose "Not Spanish"!) completes the set in a lively fashion, with typical Iberian rhythms and even a hint of a plucked guitar in its staccato notes.

Debussy added the *Petite suite* (Little suite), his own contribution to the very limited repertoire of piano duets, and Ravel and Poulenc continued the tradition in the next generations, composing *Ma mère l'oye* (Mother Goose) and a short three-movement sonata, respectively. Several French composers—Debussy, Poulenc, and Milhaud among them—have also written works for two pianos, an even less common genre; these too tend to be light and witty, owing little if anything to the German Romantic tradition.

Most musicologists agree that the formation of the quintessentially French style of piano composition is completed by the work of Claude Debussy. Virgil Thomson, an American composer and music critic who lived and studied in France and who knew French music intimately, wrote:

> Historically viewed, Debussy is the summit toward which, during the two centuries since Rameau's death, French music has risen and from which, at least for the present [1950], it seems to decline. . . . Just as Beethoven, not Bach or Mozart, really summed up the German temper—all emphasis and ordered planning, jollity and private meditation—so Debussy, not Berlioz or Bizet, encompasses most fully the French, with its dramatic contrasts of reason and sensuality, of irony and tenderness, stiffness and grace.[8]

Among Debussy's distinctive additions to the idiom that had gradually developed since the 1870s was an emphasis on whole-tone scales and the augmented chords derived from them. These unstable and enigmatic scales and triads had been used *en passant* at least as far back as the Baroque; Debussy was the first to make them a focal point of his style. He also stressed unresolved sevenths and ninths and unprepared modulations within a composition, usually, however, returning to a traditional tonic chord for the end (later composers like Poulenc dared to end compositions on unresolved dissonances).

Debussy was equally uninhibited in his use of rhythms that blur both the bar line and the essential meter, as any piano student proficient enough to tackle his *Clair de lune* (Moonlight) can attest. This too is a characteristic found in the works of other composers, but seldom featured in Debussy's fashion. (Only Johannes Brahms takes as much delight in polyrhythms, hemiolas, and other such performer-bedeviling concoctions!)

Debussy's characteristic combination of harmonies and melodic lines unassignable to any given key with rhythms that defy the bar line has led to the description of his music as "Impressionistic," attempting to do in music what visual artists like Claude Monet did in painting. He rejected this rubric as he rejected all schools and categories: "I belong to no school and have no disciples," he declared.[9] His very nature "compelled him to define himself against the norm,"[10] whatever that norm happened to be, and he refused to be boxed in by the expectations of academics or critics. In turn-of-the-century Paris the norm was so free, so varied, that it was hard to be iconoclastic unless one pitted oneself against conservative institutions like the Académie française (French Academy), which preferred to admit nonentities rather than the literary geniuses who were available; the Salon, which rejected the Impressionist painters in favor of the academic painters of the day; or the Conservatoire, which wanted contemporary composers to stick to the time-honored rules of composition.[11]

While modern musicologists agree with Debussy that the label "Impressionism" is not suited to his or any other music, it was, and often still is, the term commonly used to distinguish his music from other styles. Pianist Marguerite Long, one of the few interpreters trusted by this crotchety and highly critical composer to introduce his works to the public—after he had coached her, of course—wrote, "the only word that could apply to such disturbing harmonies and scattered tonalities was 'impressionism.'"[12] It is not hard to understand why Debussy's oeuvre is seen as parallel to the works of the Impressionist painters of his day. In an Impressionist painting the shape of the object portrayed is often suggested by colors and brush strokes rather than outlined as it would be in an academic work. In other words, color takes precedence over form. In Debussy, the texture and atmosphere created by his evocative harmonies and innovative rhythms may obscure the underlying structure of a work, but underlying structure there inevitably is. The primacy Debussy assigned to harmony is summed up by his instruction to Long, "never sacrifice the harmony for the melodic line."[13] (So much for always bringing out the melody, as pianists are usually taught!)

Fundamental to Debussy's style is a love of a beautiful sound for its own sake, or what Mellers calls "the isolation of the sensory moment."[14] The famous story of Debussy's reply to a Paris Conservatoire composition teacher who demanded to know why the fledgling composer had used a certain chord in a certain place when the rules of harmonic structure did not call for it—"Because I like the way it sounds there"—sums up both his iconoclastic nature and his pet modus operandi.

Another Debussian—and hence French—characteristic is a preference for music that conveys feeling rather than action. This is apparent in his choice of texts, both for songs and for his only completed opera, *Pelléas et Mélisande* (Pelléas and Mélisande), in which inscrutable characters of unknown origins and unstated desires wander through mysterious forests. The vague atmosphere thus created stands in stark contrast to, let us say, Wagner's vociferous (and noisy!) heldentenors and Amazonian sopranos. Mélisande herself is a wisp of a girl, fragile, unknowable. Instead of broadcasting his love for her at full *forte* and over an extended aria, Pelléas whispers almost inaudibly, briefly and utterly believably, "I love you."

Despite the fact that Debussy did write three sonatas toward the end of his life, his distrust of the sonata form is well known. Apparently he had planned to compose six sonatas, but ill health limited the project to the three for violin and piano, cello and piano, and flute, viola, and harp. The reason for Debussy's lack of enthusiasm for the form is clear: sonata form involves considerable repetition, as the first subject or theme of the exposition must be repeated in the same key at the beginning of the recapitulation, and the second subject—first stated in a contrasting key—must be transposed into the original tonic and repeated to complete the recapitulation and the sonata-form movement. This kind of predetermined repetition, exploited so magnificently by Haydn, Mozart, and Beethoven and then gradually transformed into somewhat freer structural versions by those Romantic composers who chose to use it (Schubert, Brahms, and others), ran counter to the ideals of spontaneity and economy of means espoused by Debussy. Lully, Rameau, and Couperin, the holy trinity of early French music, lived and worked before the establishment of the sonata form as the norm for at least the first movements of long and complex compositions, and hence tended to use dance forms instead. In truth the French canon holds relatively few major works in the form, most French composers eschewing it as essentially Germanic. (Wonderful violin-piano sonatas by Franck and Fauré, and of course the three by Debussy himself, are exceptions that perhaps prove the rule.)

An excess of intellectualism was another of Debussy's pet peeves, causing him to criticize the output of d'Indy, for example, although he did express his appreciation of d'Indy's technical skills in his critical writing. Debussy considered head-over-heart (or perhaps "ear" would be the better choice!) to be a Teutonic characteristic—one to be avoided by those wishing to compose truly French music. His admiration for the operas of Jules Massenet, for example, is based primarily on that composer's charm, lyricism, and intimacy, characteristics Debussy valued over the heroism of Wagner or Beethoven.

Among the most characteristic and idiomatic of Debussy's many key-board compositions are his twenty-four *Préludes*. The second of the twelve preludes in Book 1, *Voiles* (*voiles* may be translated as "veils" or "sails," which has led to two very different "explanations" of the piece but changes the music not a bit) has no key signature. The C–E interval on which it ends is blurred by the whole-tone scales, sustained by the pedal through the final measures which precede it. It is possible that C major is the designated key, but since no hint of C major is heard until the final interval, that prem-ise is unlikely. With the exception of two repeated appoggiaturas, there are no half steps in the score; the major third is the prevalent interval, with major seconds also featured. The absence of minor thirds precludes either the major or the minor triad, and all triads are augmented. Debussy had no trouble sustaining this strict absence of tonic-dominant reference throughout the little prelude; in longer works lack of dissonance coupled with withholding of the sense of completion conveyed when a composi-tion returns to a previously established tonic might prove wearisome. In any case this shimmering work is a gem. It is possible that Gershwin had this or some similar Debussy work in mind when he began *Summertime*, the beautiful blues lullaby from *Porgy and Bess* (1935), with parallel augmented chords.

So many of Debussy's twenty-four preludes are favorites—*La fille aux cheveux de lin* (The girl with the flaxen hair), *La cathédrale engloutie* (The sunken cathedral), *Les pas sur la neige* (Footsteps in the snow), *Feux d'artifice* (Fireworks)—that it is tempting to discuss them all. I have chosen two that provide interesting contrast to *Voiles: Minstrels* and *La sérénade interrompue* (The interrupted serenade). *Minstrels* shows the composer's ability to have fun with popular material. African American minstrel shows, imported from the United States, some performed by blacks and some featuring whites in blackface, were very popular in France in the early days of the twentieth century. Debussy captures in this prelude the jaunty rhythms and insouciant esprit of the genre. *La sérénade interrompue* comes as close to telling a story as abstract music is likely to do; as its title suggests, a strum-ming would-be serenader is frequently interrupted in his attempts to woo with his music. His rage at these interruptions is funny, and the Spanish flavor is charming.

Another of Debussy's best-known short piano pieces, *Golliwogg's Cake-walk* from *Children's Corner*, fits neatly into our discussion. Like *Minstrels* it is partially based on African American musical performances seen in Paris, especially those featured at the Exposition of 1900, which started a veritable craze for the strutting dance whose name it bears. The little piece has an even earlier connection to American music, as its particular kind of syncopation abounded in the works of Louis Moreau Gottschalk (1829–1869), the first American pianist-composer to make a triumphant tour of Europe. Jacques Durand, Debussy's publisher and friend, also published the works of Gottschalk, and Ernest Guiraud, one of Debussy's teachers, had been mentored by Gottschalk in their native New Orleans. Debussy most certainly would have known Gottschalk's music and incorporated its rhythmic verve into his musical vocabulary.[15]

Golliwogg's Cake-walk is a perfect example of the blending music of the New and Old Worlds. The outer sections of its ABA form are pure ragtime. This precursor of jazz, in which a syncopated melody is supported by a steady $\frac{4}{4}$ bass, is the typical accompaniment for the cakewalk. Indeed, cakewalk and ragtime were such a common combination that the two were often used synonymously. The cakewalk was a creation of black Americans from New Orleans, many of whom had French as well as African ancestors; Debussy captures its spirit with great élan. The Old World element in the little piece is heard in its middle section, which mocks the love music from Richard Wagner's *Tristan und Isolde* with typically Gallic wit. (Debussy was no fan of Wagner, calling him "a beautiful sunset that has been mistaken for a sunrise.")[16]

Not only is *Golliwogg's Cake-walk* a reflection of the American music that preceded it, it presages the last of Gershwin's *Three Piano Preludes*. The Gershwin prelude, in the same key, with the same ABA structure, and with similar chord progressions and rhythms, was written some fifteen years after the Debussy. The two are alike enough to make practicing them at the same time more than a little confusing, but one is discernibly American, the other decidedly French.

To round out our picture of the development of a French style of piano music, the composer Reynaldo Hahn (1875–1947) was as at home in literary circles—he was friends with Marcel Proust—as he was in the world of music. A lifelong and prolific songwriter, he was attracted to all sorts of poets, from the sixteenth-century Lazare Baïf to his own friend and contemporary Paul Verlaine. Hahn used their words not only as texts for his song settings but as an inspiration for his *Poèmes pour piano* of 1912, a collection of fifty-three short pieces recently recorded by Earl Wild for Ivory Classics (2001, #72006). These little musical sketches, known collectively as *Le rossignol éperdu* (The bewildered nightingale), show the influence of Hahn's principal composition teacher, Jules Massenet, as well as that of Gounod, Saint-Saëns, Debussy, and Ravel.

While making use of some of the harmonic innovations of Debussy and Ravel, Hahn was never a path-breaker. His music is gentle, pleasant, nostalgic, and conservative. He seems most distinctive when looking backward to the Renaissance and Baroque, but the touches of Impressionist harmonies he incorporates in his antique-oriented works give them a flavor that is strictly his own. A good example of this, and one of the most attractive of the fifty-three *Poèmes*, is *Le réveil de Flore* (The awakening of Flore [Spring]), a charming evocation of that season's early delights. Because of their unique mixture of the old and the new—but not too new—these pieces and others by their composer have earned their niche in the story of the development of French piano music.

With the ascendancy of sound and atmosphere for their own sakes, with the chord established as "an emotional experience in itself,"[17] with the deliberate downgrading of harmonic progression as a focus, with emphasis on the static moment and shifts of perspective, the works of Fauré, Chausson, Chabrier, and Debussy bring to its culmination the creation of an idiomatic French style.

There were, of course, other ways to compose and still be recognizably French. Erik Satie (1866–1925), a close friend of Debussy's until an unfortunate feud interrupted their friendship toward the end of Debussy's life, went his own idiosyncratic way from the beginning to the end of his creative career. A student first at the Paris Conservatoire, where his talents were not much appreciated, and many years later, when he was forty years old, with d'Indy at the Schola Cantorum, Satie was an anomaly no matter what the current Zeitgeist. Called by Debussy "a fine medieval musician who has wandered into this century,"[18] he was involved with the Rosicrucian movement (a throwback to a fifteenth-century society of philosophers, alchemists, and metaphysicians that attracted many late-nineteenth-century mystics and poets) and had a strong predilection for plainsong and organum. Nevertheless, in the 1920s he was considered the guru for two groups of young composers, L'Ecole d'Arcueil (The School of Arcueil—Arcueil was the lower-middle-class, industrialized suburb of Paris in which Satie lived for many years) and the far better known Les Six.

Satie's output before 1900 consisted largely of solo piano works, many of which are still very popular, especially with admirers or practitioners of minimalism. Among these early compositions are *Sarabandes* (1887), *Gymnopédies* (1888), and *Gnossiennes* (1889–1897). *Gymnopédies,* the most frequently encountered of these pieces, is a group of three remarkably similar sketches characterized by the same set of simple chords underlying a fluid melody. The rhythm, a slow waltz, is unvarying—a quarter note followed by a half note in the bass for each measure. The tunes of the second and third *Gymnopédies* are actually slight variations of the first, which makes the essential—and obviously deliberate—monotony of the work its salient feature. Debussy was very fond of these pieces, as his orchestral setting of the third and the first, in that order, attests. Naturally some interest is created by Debussy's varied instrumentation, but the hypnotic monotony of the concept remains evident.

There is more movement and variety in some of Satie's other early piano compositions, especially in those that use music-hall cadences and oriental intervals, but by and large simplicity, repetition, and a static quality mark his oeuvre. His lack of concern for conventional modulation, except when it is used in a deliberately banal "pop" manner, and his essentially nondramatic style fit the Debussy aesthetic, but the music of one composer sounds almost nothing like the music of the other. We shall see that Maurice Ravel "borrows" some of Satie's trademark features in a few of his own important keyboard works.

The absence of drama and a certain cool detachment render the title of Satie's *Pièces froides* (Cold pieces, 1897) more descriptive than most of his famously zany appellations, among the most enigmatic of which are *Embryons desséchés* (Dried embryos), *Sonate bureaucratique* (Bureaucratic sonata), *Trois morceaux en forme de poire* (Three pieces in the form of a pear), and *Croquis et agaceries* (Sketches and provocations). While such épater les bourgeois antics may account for some of Satie's fame, he definitely had a serious effect on twentieth-century French music.

In one Satie work, the ballet *Parade* (1916), we see coming together the efforts of representative figures of virtually the entire Parisian avant-garde. Commissioned by impresario Serge Diaghilev, who wanted something "delicious and shocking" for his Ballets Russes (Russian Ballet),[19] it had a surrealistic text by Jean Cocteau, cubist sets and costumes by Pablo Picasso, impertinent program notes by Guillaume Apollinaire, anticlassical choreography by Léonide Massine, and the requisite scandal-producing premiere in May 1917. The music Satie wrote for this Dadaist parade of circus characters constitutes a satirical look at early American jazz as then encountered in French music halls. The orchestration, sparse as it is, includes whistles, typewriter, and piano. The composer was doubly prescient in the piece, parodying music whose full impact on audiences and serious composers was not to hit France until after World War I and anticipating the inclusion of nonmusical paraphernalia as used by later composers such as George Antheil and Edgar Varèse. Like most of Satie's oeuvre, the score is deliberately banal and monotonous, but the piano rag fragments remain catchy and fresh.

When asked whether there was such a thing as national character in music, Nadia Boulanger, the famed Parisian teacher of many French and American composers, replied, "Can you imagine Mozart a Norwegian?"[20] Nor could one imagine him French. Mozart's love of symmetry, of the four-bar statement and its "response," his preference for large-scale works in which at least the first movement is in sonata form—these make Mozart the perfect example of a Germanic genius. His own clarity and wit (was there ever a wittier opera than *Le nozze di Figaro?*) notwithstanding, he was the German classicist par excellence.

Having followed the development of a French style from César Franck to Debussy, we assume that the differences between *le musicien français* and Mozart are clear. And so, with the great French pedagogue's implicit blessing, we shall now turn from our consideration of the formation of a distinctly French style of composition to the parallel forging of an identifiable American musical voice.

The Formation of an American Style
of Composition

ike France, late-nineteenth-century America was consciously trying to forge a national cultural identity.[1] No war with a foreign
foe precipitated this quest, but as France was emerging from its defeat
at the hands of the Prussian army, America was recovering from the far-
bloodier Civil War that had brought with it fratricide and the assassination
of one of the most beloved presidents in its history. The appalling events
of the 1860s had deepened America's sense of inferiority in relation to
European civilization, particularly its art, literature, and music. This lack of
cultural self-confidence was, perhaps paradoxically, coupled with a desire to
break free of European influence in the arts.

There had been, of course, indigenous music in North America long
before there was a United States. A chronicle written in 1670 by the French
Jesuit priest Claude Dablon talks of Indian music used for various rituals
and specific functions. The good Father, a missionary whose purpose was
to convert the "savages" to Christianity, was most impressed by music designated to be sung by brave warriors as they were being tortured to death.[2]

The earliest French and English colonists brought with them the sacred
music, dance tunes, and marches of their countries of origin, adapting
what they had grown up with to whatever means they had at hand. Differences in religious outlook led to different musical developments: Roman
Catholic communities were willing to undertake the expense of import-
ing organs and organists as soon as their congregations were established,
the Pilgrims opted for unadorned and unaccompanied hymn tunes. To
ensure "disciplined" singing, even these more Spartan groups were willing
to support singing masters and organized choirs.[3]

The first truly American musical statement took the form of a hym-
nal, William Billings's *The New England Psalm Singer* of 1770. Billings was a
Boston-based tanner and singing master—the latter was rarely a full-time
occupation—who deliberately Americanized sacred music, brushing a-
side many of the Puritans' restrictions.[4] Richard Crawford, author of the
exhaustive study *America's Musical Life*, astutely notes that this newly

expressed musical independence was a symptom of the general feelings leading up to the beginning of the American Revolution in 1775–76.

By and large, classical secular music in eighteenth-century America was confined to the large Eastern-seaboard cities of New York, Boston, Philadelphia, Baltimore, and Charleston. Boston was the first of these to have a public concert (1720) and the first to provide a proper venue for concerts (1754). Like their European counterparts, eighteenth-century American concerts were a potpourri of short pieces or movements of longer works. If an ensemble large enough to be called an orchestra were on hand, it was used to open and close the two halves of a standard performance, with soloists filling in the rest. Almost all the performers and the music performed were imported from Europe; with no state-supported institutions to promote native performers or composers, the demand for homegrown talent was slim indeed.[5] Even the musical theater, which was to become the outlet for some of America's most original artists, consisted almost exclusively of imports from London (*The Beggar's Opera* was a big hit from the 1720s on). Perhaps the earliest truly American theater was the minstrel show. Rapidly developing from the early nineteenth century, these popular shows featured white performers in blackface using African American–inspired material. Neither these shows nor the later versions featuring actual black players appeared in major theaters until the early twentieth century.[6]

Although classical concerts and musical theater were largely European imports to the United States all through the eighteenth and well into the nineteenth century, amateur music making was enjoyed in many American homes throughout the period. Many households had keyboard or string instruments, and many immigrant professional musicians who were slowly spreading out through the United States were available to provide lessons. It was thus inevitable that some genuine native talents should eventually appear.

And suddenly one such genius did. A composer, conductor, and piano virtuoso par excellence, he leaped from America to Europe's musical center stage as if to prove single-handedly that America was not devoid of musical ability. This phenomenon was Louis Moreau Gottschalk (1829–1869).

Gottschalk was born in New Orleans, which until twenty-five years before his birth had been the property of France (President Thomas Jefferson bought the entire territory of Louisiana from the financially strapped Napoleon I, who had recently acquired it from Spain, in 1803). Gottschalk's mother was the daughter of the French count who had been governor of Santo Domingo, and his father was a professor of science in Cambridge, Massachusetts. Obviously blessed with extraordinary musical talent, thirteen-year-old Gottschalk was sent by his parents to Paris for higher study, but the stuffy Conservatoire rejected the "barbarian" without a hearing. Undaunted, Gottschalk studied privately in the City of Light, becoming a pianist who could rival—at least in technique—such luminaries as Liszt and Sigismund Thalberg.[7] His European tours, which invariably featured his own finger-bending pieces, were huge successes, as were his subsequent tours of the United States and Latin America. A truly international figure, Gottschalk picked up folk tunes and rhythms wherever he went, incorporating them into charming and exciting compositions which now strike the listener as slight, salon-type music. At the time, however, they were taken much more seriously—the first American "classical" music to be applauded by European cognoscenti.

Despite his international background, Gottschalk was a fervently patriotic American. Among his most flamboyant keyboard compositions is *The Union*, a celebration of the reunification of North and South after the Civil War. It boasts spectacular octaves in rapid scales, and—anticipating Charles Ives—full treatments of *The Star Spangled Banner* and *Yankee Doodle*.

In a different vein, Gottschalk wrote the jolly *Banjo* with a strummed bass and energetically leaping treble. The banjo was one of the preferred instruments in blackface minstrel shows, and Gottschalk exploits both its delicate plucking sounds and its ability to raise a considerable uproar when its strings are vigorously struck. In sections of *Banjo* one can hear references to *Camptown Races*, a well-known song by Gottschalk's contemporary Stephen Foster. The resulting music is an interesting confluence of the two most influential American composers of the era. While the original song remains simple and folklike, Gottschalk's instrumental version ends in an awe-inspiring burst of virtuosity. Even in gentler works like *Creole Eyes*, Gottschalk makes sure that there are Lisztian figurations with which the pianist can impress the listener; in *Bamboula, Tournament Galop,* and *Midnight in Seville,* infectious rhythms set the feet to tapping.

One of Gottschalk's uncharacteristic descents into sentimentality is *The Last Hope,* a ballad that comes complete with a maudlin anecdote and moved countless young women to tears. The story was a supposedly true confession of a romantic, but not erotic, nature: an older woman, very attached to the young composer, is dying of a painful disease. She asks him to write a tune to ease her agony, which he does, but then he must leave for a concert tour. When he returns, he hears church bells tolling her demise.

The reaction of mid-nineteenth-century French composers to the music of Gottschalk foreshadows the ecstatic reception granted to African American jazz in the 1920s by Maurice Ravel, Darius Milhaud, and other Parisian musicians. Georges Bizet incorporated Gottschalk's *Le bananier* into his repertoire, never tiring of performing it; Jacques Offenbach, a virtuoso cellist as well as a prolific composer of operettas, wrote an arrangement of the piece for cello and piano. Hector Berlioz analyzed the peculiar appeal of Gottschalk's music as a mixture of Old World sophistication and New World naïveté, a blend that afforded him the instinct to go just far enough in his fantasy-creating music.[8]

Although Gottschalk wrote symphonies, cantatas, and the like as well as countless piano pieces, none of his works is now ranked with the output of his more "serious" European contemporaries. While Continental critics and composers were by and large enthusiastic about his compositions—everyone loved his piano playing—not all American cognoscenti were impressed. After one concert featuring his own works Gottschalk may have read this acerbic comment by Boston critic John Sullivan Dwight: "Could a more trivial and insulting string of musical rigmarole ever have been offered to an audience of earnest music lovers?"[9] Among his music's perceived deficiencies was an inattention to structural balance, a key characteristic of Germanic classical compositions. This was undoubtedly a deliberate decision on Gottschalk's part, for he obviously was more concerned with sound and special effect than structure. Even if nowadays Gottschalk's output turns up only, if at all, as an occasional encore, his place in the history of American music is secure. Like fireworks exploding in a dark sky, he made a spectacular effect, planting—to mix metaphors—an American flag on what had been exclusively European territory.

As Gottschalk toured Europe, a few brave European pianists began to give recitals in the United States. Among the first to wow American audiences was the sensational Sigismund Thalberg (1812–1871),[10] Franz Liszt's only serious rival in the keyboard battles then all the rage on the Continent. Judging from contemporary reviews, Thalberg set extremely high technical standards but played primarily his own showy, yet rather vapid, compositions. Like Gottschalk, he occasionally offered a movement of a Beethoven sonata—the *Appassionata* or the *Moonlight* perhaps—but these standard works did not afford him the opportunity to display his favorite trick, which was to play the melodic line in the middle of the keyboard, mostly with his thumbs, while liberally sprinkling arpeggios above and below the tune. This rather obvious device, which demands astute pedaling, led to hysterical excitement from the spectators, who were certain they were hearing three hands at work.

Thalberg first toured the United States in 1856. He and Gottschalk met and together performed a program of two-piano works which included a *Fantasy* on themes from Giuseppe Verdi's *Il trovatore*. The enormous success of these two virtuosi, similar receptions for Jenny Lind on her landmark tour (choreographed by circus impresario P. T. Barnum in 1850–51), and well-received performances by German pianists Leopold de Meyer and Henri Herz proved that there was an interest in, even a thirst for, music in America in the 1850s and 1860s. The audiences may have been naïve, the programs lightweight by today's standards, but people—many people—wanted to hear these artistic luminaries.

Missing from this spate of virtuoso-oriented concerts was an appetite for the longer, more difficult orchestral works of Beethoven, Haydn, Mozart, and the other masters, but even in this more intellectually demanding sphere, progress was being made. As early as 1815, the Handel and Haydn Society was formed in Boston, with the aim of making the sacred music of these and other "serious" composers known to the public. It was the first American organization to stress the composer over the performer.[11] In 1841, again in Boston, an orchestra performed an entire symphony— Beethoven's First—for a paying audience, and the following year the New York Philharmonic Society, a cooperative and permanent band in contrast to the prevalent, mostly pick-up, ensembles, played Beethoven's Fifth in its entirety. Obviously, since ticket sales had to support these institutions, there was an audience for this more sophisticated fare.[12] Many of the performers in these new orchestras were Americans, but very little of importance was still being composed at home.

Far from the formal concert scenes in Boston, Philadelphia, or New York, a quite different kind of genuinely American music was achieving popularity—the songs of Stephen Foster (1826–1864). Where native-born Gottschalk and the visiting Thalberg were all flash and fire, Foster's music was gentle and homespun. Uninterested in technical virtuosity, Foster kept the piano accompaniments to his songs simple enough for the barely trained amateur to enjoy reading through them.

Born and raised in the Pittsburgh area, Foster nevertheless captured the sound of the plantation blacks. He wrote almost all his own texts, often using the black vernacular in his lyrics, and his original melodies conveyed the flavor of plantation songs. Foster's songs are often thought of as folk music, although clearly, since they were all actually composed by a professional, they do not fit that definition. Critical evaluation of his songs changes from generation to generation, but no one doubts their place in American cultural history: his 250-plus songs are America's own national music, the first large body of secular work that sounds distinctively American.

Are Foster's songs "art" or popular music? In the 1850s, when his most successful songs were composed, the distinction was far less important than it is today. Schubert's songs and Verdi's arias were whistled by much of the general populace of their respective lands, and the latter was regarded as a national hero. Foster did indeed write for the man in the street, or more accurately the woman at the parlor spinet, but his songs appealed, and still appeal, to classical artists. Singers like Jenny Lind, Adelina Patti, Paul Robeson, and more recently Jan de Gaetani and Marilyn Horne have recorded them and included them in their recitals. The Commonwealth of Kentucky adopted Foster's *My Old Kentucky Home* as its official state song, and Florida did the same with his *Old Folks at Home*. Musicologists have heard his tunes sung in places as far off as Tibet, and Japan included them in its prescribed "Western Music" curriculum.

None of Foster's songs boasts the technical or emotional complexity of Schubert's *Winterreise* (Winter journey) or *Erlkönig* (Erl-king), but many of them delivered a potent message to pre–Civil War Americans. As Foster explained to Edwin Christy, white founder and leader of the Christy Minstrels, in a letter of May 1852:

> I find that, by my efforts, I have done a great deal to build up a taste for the Ethiopian [a term often used for black music in the late nineteenth century] songs among refined people by making the words suitable to their taste instead of the trashy and really offensive words which belong to some songs of that order.[13]

Christy may not have been happy to read the composer's letter, which found fault with the often grotesque caricatures of blacks that made up the lyrics of so many songs featured in minstrel shows of the era, including Christy's own. Foster's lyrics never descended to that level and often deliberately portrayed blacks in positive ways. His *Nelly Was a Lady* described the monogamous conjugal love between a black man and woman when black slave families were still being arbitrarily pulled apart by owners who maintained that the race was incapable of valuing such relationships. As the title makes explicit, Nelly is a lady, a status rarely granted to black women at the time.

Both Gottschalk and Foster died young—Gottschalk at forty, exiled in Rio de Janeiro to escape legal action for his seduction of a young woman, and Foster at thirty-eight, after much dissipation. Fortunately American classical music had two vital centers, Boston and New York, where activity of a more traditional, more conventional nature was thriving. The New York scene was vastly enhanced in 1885 when Jeanette Thurber, a wealthy and powerful patron of the arts, founded the American National Conservatory of Music. This institution, the ancestor of the Juilliard School of Music, was a curious mixture of the derivative and the unique: on the one hand, its curriculum was patterned on that of the venerable, classical Paris Conservatoire, and many of its most prestigious teachers were well-known Europeans. For example, Hungarian pianist Rafael Joseffy (1852–1915), whose devilishly difficult exercises have consumed thousands of hours of pianists' practice time, and Hungarian conductor Anton Seidl (1850–1898) were among its forty original faculty members. Also on board was the equally famous Victor Herbert (1859–1924), then regarded as the finest cellist in America as well as a writer of irresistible operettas.

On the more adventurous side was the school's admission policy. All talented students were welcome, and that meant blacks and women too. Tuition, low for all, was waived for the talented and needy. It may have been unduly optimistic to train blacks or women for careers in music in a society where neither group were welcome in most symphony orchestras or on faculties of music schools and conservatories, but many applied and were accepted. A few blacks, like William Marion Cook (1869–1944), who was a violinist in the Boston Symphony Orchestra, did actually have satisfactory orchestral careers, but were stymied when it came to solo appearances; conversely, women were always accepted as soloists, but not as orchestral players.[14]

In 1892 Thurber decided to invite Czech composer Antonin Dvořák (1841–1904) to teach at the American Conservatory. His acceptance was a real coup for the young institution, where hopes were high that Dvořák, who had so eloquently expressed the essence of Czech folk music in his classical compositions, could somehow achieve or inspire something similar in an American idiom. At this time the question of nationalism versus universality in music was of great interest to most composers. As Dvořák had done in his homeland, Edvard Grieg (1843–1907) had succeeded in giving a distinctly Norwegian flavor to his music. Liszt had done the same in his *Hungarian Rhapsodies*, as had Chopin in his mazurkas and "Revolutionary" Etude, yet all of this music had universal appeal. Could the same be done in America, and if so, how? Dvořák was clearly prepared to try.

Soon after his arrival at the school, Dvořák was introduced to a young black student, Harry T. Burleigh (1866–1949). Burleigh was at the time a voice student, but he had dreams of becoming a composer. Music critic James Huneker introduced the young man to Dvořák, who listened to— and was absolutely fascinated by—his renditions of plantation songs. When the Czech master heard *Go Down Moses* and *Nobody Knows the Trouble I've Seen*, he said, "Burleigh, that is as great as a Beethoven theme!" Later, in a much-quoted interview, he stated, "In the Negro melodies of America I discover all that is needed for a great and noble school of music."[15]

Burleigh went on to arrange many spirituals and traditional songs for concert presentation—*Little David Play on Your Harp* and *I Stood on de Ribber ob Jordan* are particularly beguiling examples—as well as compose some charming if rather slight original vocal works. Compared to many, if not most, of the art songs being written in the late-nineteenth-century, Burleigh's arrangements and songs stand out for their dramatic and impassioned accompaniments. Dvořák, with his superior compositional mastery, incorporated the cadences he had heard in the songs of Burleigh and other African American students into his beloved *New World Symphony*. It is easy to forget that the *Going Home* theme of that familiar composition was not actually a folk song—it was composed by Dvořák in the style of the authentic spirituals he had heard.

Despite the flavor of Czech music permeating his oeuvre, Dvořák wrote essentially in the Germanic symphonic tradition; his music was highly respected and championed by Johannes Brahms. In retrospect he seems to have taken from indigenous American music at least as much as he contributed to the nascent American classical style. His recognition of the innate value of African American music at a time when blacks were generally regarded as incapable of great art was, however, a great service both to the black community and to the development of serious American music.

Typical of the path taken at this time by composers who were actually born in the United States was that of Edward MacDowell (1860–1908). MacDowell's family, a familiar American mixture of Scotch, Irish, and Quaker backgrounds, settled in the States around the middle of the eighteenth century. As a boy, Edward studied at home with Cuban, South American, and Italian-born musicians, but eventually he went the obligatory European route. For about three years he studied at the Paris Conservatoire, but he found studies in Germany more congenial, and his mature compositions remain in the Germanic Romantic tradition. It is true that, like Claude Debussy in *Pelléas et Mélisande,* MacDowell wanted to evoke in musical terms the supernatural aura of mysterious nature, but he was more attuned to the murmurs of the Schwarzwald of Wagner's Germany than to either the less forbidding Forest of Fontainebleau in France or the austere Petrified Forest of the western United States.

Interested as he was in the development of an American musical identity, MacDowell seemed to vacillate in his attitude toward the inclusion of African American music as a part of the mix. Initially he opposed Burleigh in his plans to arrange spirituals in art-song settings, but later he endorsed the project. On the other hand, as Dvořák was making use of spirituals and Foster songs for inspiration, arranging Foster's *The Old Folks at Home* for soloists, chorus, and orchestra after hearing Burleigh sing it, MacDowell incorporated American Indian themes in one of his masterpieces, *Indian Suite* (Orchestral Suite No. 2, Opus 48, 1895). While this was MacDowell's major work in this vein, several of his lighter-weight pieces for piano solo are also based on Native American music. Ethnomusicologist Theodore Baker had recently published *Music of the North American Wilderness,* a compendium of fragments he had heard chanted by the Iroquois, Iowa, Chippewa, and other North American tribes. With this material as background Mac-Dowell created his dazzling orchestral tone poem and such piano "album leaves" as *From an Indian Lodge,* the fourth of the ten *Woodland Sketches.*

Woodland Sketches, composed in 1896, begins with one of MacDowell's most familiar pieces, *To A Wild Rose.* This poignant miniature illustrates the virtues as well as the limitations of its composer: its lovely melody is both simple and evocative, its harmonic changes extremely effective. The traditional tonic/dominant opening bars—A major and E^7—move to an unexpected F minor and then, three bars later, to C-sharp minor, the progression creating an open-air and vaguely Native American atmosphere. The rhythmic repetition—steady $\frac{2}{4}$ with one chord per bar in all but a few measures—seems well suited to the harmonic and melodic material, though it would prove tedious in a longer work.

In a lighter moment MacDowell gives us a touch of cakewalk-type syncopation via *From Uncle Remus,* the seventh of the *Woodland Sketches.* This was one of MacDowell's rare uses of African American material. As we discussed in the previous chapter, the cakewalk, although probably not this particular example of its perky rhythmic scheme, was among the earliest aspects of American music to attract French attention. *From Uncle Remus* has all sorts of minstrel show references, but true to MacDowell's theories, it makes no attempt to tell an Uncle Remus story. MacDowell often said that his titles, and even the poems and epigrams he often included in his printed scores, while important to him as inspiration, were intended only to convey the mood of the composer when he sat down to write the piece in question. There was no specific story-telling intent.

The ten miniatures of *Woodland Sketches* project many different moods. *To a Water Lily* (no. 6) is similar in its gentle sweetness to *To a Wild Rose; From an Indian Lodge* (no. 5) is strong and virile; *A Deserted Farm* (no. 8) depicts loneliness and nostalgia; *Will o' the Wisp* (no. 2) is in the "scampering elves" tradition. It is interesting to compare this last named to Debussy's third piano piece from book 1 of his *Préludes, Le vent dans la plaine* (The wind on the plain): both rely on sixteenth-note seconds for a dissonant depiction of the blustering wind, but unlike the Debussy, which avoids tonic definition throughout, the MacDowell is very solidly grounded in its home key of A major. What these ten pieces have in common is sentiment that rings true while avoiding the sentimentality of so many salon-type piano pieces of the time. While forging no genuinely new paths, their composer retains an originality and forthrightness that seems typically American.

In 1896 MacDowell was hired by Columbia University to head its newly established Department of Music. This ensured him a place in the center of the New York music scene. He had already been a major factor in the so-called Boston School, a loosely knit group whose most prominent members included John Knowles Paine (1839–1906), Arthur Foote (1853–1937), George Chadwick (1854–1931), and Amy Beach (1867–1944), America's first—and, for many years, only—woman composer of note. There was also an important literary coterie in Boston at the time, the first such representative group of writers in the United States. Preeminent among them were James Russell Lowell, Henry Wadsworth Longfellow, Nathaniel Hawthorne, and Ralph Waldo Emerson, none of whom was known primarily for the type of lyric poetry that would lend itself easily to art song settings. For this reason, in contrast to the parallel situation in France, the proximity of two such remarkable cultural cliques did not prove to be a major factor in the formation of an American national style. *Art Song in the United States,* a comprehensive listing of 1,892 songs composed in America from 1801 to 1987,[16] lists six settings of Longfellow poems, two Lowell texts, and none by Emerson or Hawthorne, while noting over twenty song texts each by modernist poets e. e. cummings and Wallace Stevens.

Boston, sometimes called the Athens of America, had beaten New York to the punch in most things cultural, boasting the nation's first church organ (1711), its first known public concert (1731), and its first independent school of music, the New England Conservatory (1867). Even before the NEC and the Boston Conservatory—also founded in 1867—opened their doors, Harvard University had been allowing courses of music into its curriculum (1862), and a few years later the Boston Symphony Orchestra played its first season (1882). Despite this remarkable record, Boston was a conservative place, and it is not surprising that the members of the Boston School were, by and large, a conservative bunch. Their close adherence to the German Romantic tradition made their individual contributions to the musical repertoire, with some noteworthy exceptions, more a continuation of the status quo than a means of advancement in the development of an American idiom. In a way they may be compared to Camille Saint-Saëns or Vincent d'Indy in France, composers of real talent and technical ability, but lacking in innovative spirit.

The oldest member of the Boston group was John Knowles Paine. Like MacDowell and so many other Americans, Paine went to Germany, Berlin to be precise, for his advanced musical studies, and it was there that his Mass in D, an ambitious choral work, was first produced. Paine was an important teacher, and it was under his tenure at Harvard, where he became the first holder of a Chair of Music in the United States, that music was at last deemed serious enough to be an area of concentration (1870–71). Paine must be credited with two further accomplishments: since his works were highly regarded in Germany, he at least partially disproved Europe's general opinion of Americans as hopelessly uncultivated, and he was the teacher of the most prolific and most successful member of the Boston group: Arthur Foote. Under Paine's tutelage at Harvard, Foote was the recipient of the first Master of Music degree ever awarded in the United States in 1874.[17]

Foote lived well into the twentieth century, but most of his important compositions were completed before World War I. He wrote reams of organ music (a devout Unitarian, he was for most of his life a church organist), many piano pieces, quartets, quintets, orchestral works, duo-sonatas, chorales, hymn settings, and art songs. Unfortunately much of his oeuvre seems outdated and was deemed so long before his death. His most successful composition comes in two forms, the original piano solo version (Opus 41) and an orchestration thereof which he made himself, the *Four Characteristic Pieces* after Omar Khayyám (Opus 48, 1905). Quite a racy subject for Boston, the city famous for banning books with explicitly sexual passages (hence the familiar phrase "banned in Boston"), this work, once very popular, has dropped from the repertoire in both its incarnations.

Despite the generally European orientation of the majority of his compositions, Foote did make one small step toward the formation of an American style: in his first Piano Trio (1884) he incorporated a bit of American hymnody. Whether or not this perhaps inadvertent musical gesture had any influence on Ives is hard to say, for, as we shall see, that iconoclastic New Englander resolutely marched to his own drummer. At the end of his compositional career Foote began to use some of the harmonies he had heard in Debussy's works; these pieces—*At Dusk* for flute, cello, and harp, and the exotic *Night Piece* for flute and strings—are occasionally encountered in concert today.

Foote's contemporary George Chadwick (1854–1931) was an equally close adherent to the German Romantic tradition, but at the same time he often showed a more fun-loving populist bent than was characteristic of the sober church organist. His *Jubilee* and *A Vagrom Ballad* ("vagrom" is a variant of "vagrant" or "hobo," used by Shakespeare in *Much Ado about Nothing*), both from his *Symphonic Sketches,* are bright, raucous, and somewhat rude. Brass instruments and bassoon seem inspired by the Bronx cheer, and touches of Latin rhythms make one head for the dance floor. Military calls are jauntily mocked, and it is clear that one is not to take the work too seriously (Jacques Ibert's *Divertissement* comes to mind). In this same vein is Chadwick's *Tabasco* (1894), a burlesque operetta that enjoyed great success in its day. (Chadwick was a friend of operetta king Victor Herbert, who came to the United States from Germany in 1886.) Perhaps this insouciance is a characteristic American trait, and if so, these works of Chadwick exemplify it well. Of course, Chadwick wrote many serious classical compositions, including choral works, songs, cantatas, orchestral suites, and chamber music "of clarity and dignity."[18] Like Foote he was enormously prolific and, again like Foote, is now largely forgotten.

As the only female member of the Boston group, and indeed the only American woman whose large-scale music achieved any degree of recognition at the time, Amy Beach—or Mrs. H. H. A. Beach, as she signed her works—was a phenomenon. In their search for worthy women composers of the past, feminists have taken up the cause of Beach's music, and many of her over three hundred published pieces are quite worthy of this present-day attention. Like her slightly older Boston colleagues, Beach was steeped in the German Romantic tradition, but unlike the others she was strictly American-trained—the first successful American concert performer who didn't go abroad for polishing.

Inevitably, given the music with which she was surrounded, Beach's chamber music and orchestral works evince a strong Brahmsian flavor. Nevertheless, the vigor of her rhythms, charm of her melodies, intensity of her emotions, and skill exhibited in structuring large-scale works make listening to her most successful pieces more than just pleasant. When comparing her Sonata for Violin and Piano of 1896 (Opus 34) to that of Arthur Foote, for example, one finds far more energy and individuality in Beach's effort, especially in the rugged strength of her melodic lines. Her sonata lacks the sheer weightiness of the Brahms D-minor sonata, for example, but equals it in passionate involvement in her material. Her harmonies, while remaining traditional, are flexible and often unexpected. In spite of being forced to learn the finer points of harmony and counterpoint on her own, she clearly knew what she wanted to say and how to say it. Among her smaller occasional pieces is *Fireflies,* a charming exercise in delicate, fleeting effects, and smoothly flowing double thirds, which became her signature encore.

At about this time the slowly emerging American style of music got a boost from an unexpected quarter—the marches of John Philip Sousa (1854–1932). Sousa's impact on concert-hall music involves far more than just the rousing rendition of his *Stars and Stripes Forever* so frequently used as an encore by Vladimir Horowitz, in his own inimitable arrangement. As a military-band march it is superb, with its brilliant use of brass and percussion and its unforgettable tune. Leonard Bernstein is said to have remarked that he regretted not having composed it himself! In a way, it epitomizes the American spirit, as does its composer.

Sousa was the son of Spanish and German immigrants. He studied both piano and violin and wrote quite a bit of "serious" music. He was a member of the orchestra recruited to play under the baton of Jacques Offenbach when that prolific French operetta composer was in the United States (1876–77), and his own forays into opera and operetta were big hits here and abroad (*The Charlatan* [1897], for example, saw a very successful run in London). For many years Sousa was the leader of the United States Marine Band, for which he wrote many of his 136 marches. He later (1892) formed a commercial band, which toured Europe four times between 1900 and 1905.[19] The music he transported to the other side of the Atlantic had considerable impact on French composers, as we shall explore in due course.

For Sousa a march had an ethical raison d'être: it represented upright men walking with disciplined step, unlike ragtime swingers and cakewalking strutters. Since he wanted above all to please the audience, he did include some syncopation in his compositions, dressing the harlot up in respectable garb. This injection of moral considerations into what even Sousa regarded as entertainment is probably uniquely American.

A Sousa march is no simple affair. Often in three or more sections, each with its own characteristic melody, his marches and arrangements often feature complex counterpoint. His commercial band started with forty-six players—reeds, brass, and percussion—but at its height it employed seventy fully professional, full-time members. For these impressive ensembles Sousa wrote impressive music, either totally new or highly original arrangements of classical overtures and symphonic movements. An inspired showman, Sousa sprinkled short encore-type pieces throughout his programs, keeping both audience and players on their musical toes (the band didn't know in advance which encores Sousa would choose). Like just about everyone else, Sousa set at least one Foster song for his band.

Sousa's popularity was astounding. His band was often the biggest drawing card at fairs and festivals, and it is said that its presence saved many a project from financial disaster. He was certainly not the only successful bandleader in America, but he was the acknowledged king of the genre.

Sousa marches were not the only "vernacular" music to infiltrate both American and French classical music while both were in their formative stages. Minstrel shows, for all their negative aspects, had a positive role in introducing so-called "Ethiopian"—that is, African—tunes and rhythms, as well as the sound of the banjo, an instrument with African roots.[20] With the efforts of Foster, Dvořák, and these minstrel shows, which also toured successfully in France and elsewhere in Europe, the sound of African American music was firmly established as a vital part of the American musical idiom.

Here one must also mention a brilliant black performer and composer, Scott Joplin (1868–1917), whose influence on popular, and to a lesser extent concert-hall, music was truly astonishing. Joplin brought the style of piano playing known as ragtime to its peak. Ragtime is characterized by a steady $\frac{2}{4}$ or $\frac{4}{4}$ bass consisting of a low single note or octave on the first beat and a chord based on that tone (tonic, dominant, or subdominant are the norms) on the second beat. Because the root note and the chord are usually at least an octave apart, the player needs an unerring physical sense of where things are on the keyboard. This striding bass forms the underpinning for a highly syncopated melodic line in the treble. The idea of syncopation—placing an accent on what is usually a weak beat or anticipating or delaying the beat itself—is as old as the art of music. What was new in ragtime was the unrelenting persistence of the rhythmic device: every measure of a rag's melody has "misplaced" accents, anticipations, and delays. The marchlike steadiness of the bass makes the syncopations absolutely clear and allows the player's right hand to indulge in any rhythmic caprice it can muster without disturbing the basic beat.

Like Sousa, Joplin made occasional attempts at composing for the stage. *Treemonisha*, virtually ignored until two years before his death when it received a single, and not terribly successful, unstaged reading, was the second of his two operas and is occasionally revived today. However, his *Maple Leaf Rag* sold over a million copies when it first appeared in 1899 and remains a perennial favorite, and his rag *The Entertainer* is at least as well known. When the Paul Newman–Robert Redford movie *The Sting*, whose soundtrack featured *The Entertainer* and other Joplin rags, was first released in 1973, arrangements of that catchy rag became available in every degree of difficulty so as to accommodate even the most unskilled piano student.

Because of its emphasis on syncopation, ragtime is considered one of the most important and immediate predecessors of jazz. The principal reason it is not considered to actually belong to that quintessentially American genre is that rags are written down and played much as the composer intended, whereas real jazz is basically improvised. Jazz per se—along with theater songs the two most undeniably American contributions to music—is the subject of the next chapter. Ragtime, its immediate ancestor, illustrates how American music went from being a generally scorned European derivative to a worldwide, easily identifiable, much loved, and much imitated uniquely American statement. That this occurred in a relatively brief period of time is as remarkable as the music itself.

A Brief History of Jazz in America

s befits a type of music as iconoclastic as jazz, just about every-thing one can say about it—from its origins to its very definition—is a subject of controversy. To some, jazz and improvisation are synonymous and you can't have one without the other, while to those who disagree, the written arrangements of Duke Ellington or Fletcher Henderson—to name but two outstanding practitioners—are perfectly valid examples of the genre. Claims are made in some quarters that the basic rhythms and stylistic innovations of jazz are traceable to Africa, while in other corners of scholarship these elements are said to have developed exclusively on American soil as much from European compositional traditions as from those of Africa. While it would be presumptuous to support one side or another, it is illuminating to examine some of the theories.

There is no better place to find these various hypotheses espoused than the highly respected *Oxford Companion to Jazz,* in which different authorities are granted space to present their views. Bill Kirchner, the editor of this 852-page tome, prefaces his introduction with two tantalizing quotes, the first from saxophonist and composer Wayne Shorter, the second from Bill Evans, pianist and composer: "The word 'jazz' means to me 'no category,'" and "Jazz is not a 'what,' it is a 'how,' and if you do things according to the 'how' of jazz, it's jazz." (The latter sounds like the flip side of "It don't mean a thing if it ain't got that swing!") These all-embracing definitions and others found in Kirchner's introduction ("a music of healthy defiance"; "a melting pot of influences and techniques")[1] seem to negate the necessity for improvisation—or anything else, for that matter—as a criterion for inclusion in the jazz canon; they may, in fact, make the very idea of a jazz canon meaningless. Nevertheless, there are great jazz players and great jazz compositions, and a general agreement on who and what they are.

One point on which all scholars seem to agree is that the earliest center of jazz activity was New Orleans, that most cosmopolitan and musical of American cities. In the late nineteenth century New Orleans boasted three opera houses and two symphony orchestras, a plethora of marching bands, innumerable church choirs, and countless individual street musicians.

Until 1803, when President Jefferson negotiated the controversial Louisiana Purchase, giving an overextended Napoleon I $15,000,000 in exchange for the first and biggest single tract of land ever bought by the rapidly expanding United States, the enormous Louisiana territory had belonged to France. Before the French took over, Spain ruled the area, and throughout its history there had been immigration from the Caribbean as well as Europe. Whites of European origin mingled with native blacks far more in New Orleans than in other Southern American cities, so the area's population contained a wide assortment of groups, from the poorest slaves and newly freed blacks to upper-middle-class black Creoles, from aristocratic plantation owners to poor white sharecroppers. The class and color fluidity resulting from the relative—and it was only relative—absence of racial rigidity make it difficult to sort out the origins of anything native to New Orleans, most particularly its jazz. Most often debated is the extent to which the earliest New Orleans jazz musicians, who were mostly—but not exclusively—black, were influenced by African traditions.

To support the Eurocentric arguments, ethnomusicologists cite the undeniable fact that early jazz was invariably tonal, that is, reliant on the Western European tonic-dominant harmonic system. Furthermore, as the French Impressionist composers made the augmented chord and the whole-tone scale vital components of Western classical music, jazz musicians followed suit. In addition, the Classical format of two-bar phrases "answered" by other two-bar phrases was also the norm in jazz. This was exploited so successfully by Haydn, Mozart, and the other Viennese masters that deviations from it were used for special effects and recognized as out of the ordinary. In sum, says William Youngren, author of the article in *The Oxford Companion to Jazz* entitled "European Roots of Jazz," "The various interrelated elements of early jazz—harmony, melody, rhythm and form—are very similar to that of late 18th century music and are in fact derived more or less directly from them by way of the American popular song literature."[2] Youngren also notes that music of ethnic groups like the Klezmers, who were part of the huge migration to the United States from Eastern Europe, "sound[s] remarkably like jazz."[3] His implication is that the Klezmers' highly improvisatory style, with its reliance on individual solos within the larger group and its characteristic instrumentation often featuring the clarinet, might have influenced early American jazz players. Interestingly enough, Klezmer music did not seem to have much effect on nonjazz American popular music, which, again according to Youngren, was virtually unchanging from the Civil War until the turn of the century.

In direct contrast to Youngren's argument, Samuel A. Floyd, Jr., writer of the *Oxford Companion*'s chapter on "African Origins of Jazz," traces every element of New Orleans's particular variety of jazz back to one African tradition or another:

> In short, the shuffling, angular, off-beat, additive, repetitive, and intensive, un-flagging rhythm of jazz comes from African vocal and instrumental procedures: . . . calls, cries, and hollers, call-and-response devices . . . pendular thirds [back-and-forth movement between notes two steps apart], blue notes, bent notes, and elisions, moans, grunts, vocables.

All are to be found in African dance and song. Hence the music of that enormous continent is directly responsible for the

> off-beat melodic phrasings and parallel intervals and chords, constant repetition of rhythmic and melodic figures and phrases, timbral distortions . . .; musical individuality within collectivity . . . and the metronomic pulse that underlies all African-American music.[4]

The only possible exception Floyd allows is the use of tonic-dominant harmony, which is generally thought not to have existed in Africa until it was introduced by Western musicians, but even here he suggests a loophole when speaking of the "tonal mosaic" and "heterogeneous mixture" that define African music.[5]

Compounding the difficulty of resolving such a debate is the fact that the earliest examples of what is acknowledged as actual jazz, in contradistinction to ragtime or popular music, were never recorded or notated, so no one knows exactly what they sounded like. On the other hand, the nature of this intrinsically oral tradition, whereby the younger players learned at their elders' elbows, so to speak, makes it likely that the earliest recordings by such groups as the Original Dixieland Jass [*sic*] Band in 1917 sounded pretty much like the combos that preceded them. It is ironic that these first known jazz recordings were made by the all-white ODJB, whereas most of the originators of the genre were black. The name of the group brings up the question of the definition of "Dixieland": while once again a conclusive answer is elusive, it seems as though that title came to refer to the New Orleans or Southern style of jazz in which collective improvisation was the principal element, to distinguish it from styles developing in Chicago and then New York. In these two cities individual soloists (including Louis Armstrong, Sidney Bechet, and others) and the still later "smooth" sound of the big band arrangements became paramount.

New Orleans or Dixieland usually features marching-band instruments. The street band was everywhere in New Orleans, called upon to accompany every type of festivity from birthdays to funerals. The instruments used included the trumpet or cornet (the terms were used virtually synonymously, although the cornet produced a sweeter sound, while the trumpet had more volume and bite), the clarinet and the trombone for melody, and drums—occasionally backed by banjos, mandolins, or guitars—for rhythm. The trumpet played lead, while the clarinet and trombone improvised behind and around it. Since the players had to begin and end more or less together and at least occasionally form satisfying harmonies, they did not have absolute freedom; nevertheless the loosely organized improvisations, centering around a given tune, were often more chaotically polytonal than deliberately contrapuntal.

The all-important rhythmic support for this free-wheeling melismatic variation was based on a combination of steady $\frac{4}{4}$ march time and highly syncopated ragtime. The piano, the principal instrument in early ragtime (Scott Joplin was a virtuoso keyboard artist), did not loom large in marching bands and so was not a significant part of the earliest New Orleans jazz sound. Superb pianists like Jelly Roll Morton and Art Tatum soon changed all that, but the first jazz combos made do without keyboards. What New Orleans musicians did learn from Joplin and other ragtime pianists, who undoubtedly heard an inchoate version of it from "coon" songs in black-face minstrel shows and in cakewalk dances,[6] was to syncopate any tune—to make it swing as well as sing. They transformed all kinds of compositions—traditional working songs as well as spirituals. Sidney Bechet's *Joshua Fit the Battle of Jericho* as rereleased on Blue Note Records (*Runnin' Wild*, 1998) is a classic example of a "hot" spiritual, and he and just about everyone else had a go at making *When the Saints Come Marching In* part of the jazz canon.

No New Orleans resident could have been completely unfamiliar with the enthusiasm bordering on frenzy of some of the communal singing in black churches. This music was almost "hot" enough to pass as jazz without much alteration! The fervent prayer-singing could trace its pedigree to slave songs. *Slave Songs of America*, the first of many such compilations, was published in New York in 1867. There were dozens of slave songs, and such published versions show the widespread interest in them.[7] The slave songs and much of the church singing made use of "call and response," "shouts," and "signifying," all common devices in African music. "Signifying" was a form of homage to fellow musicians, as the performer made his spontaneous musical and sometimes verbal "comments" on other composers' works.[8] Interestingly, we might note that the trouvères and troubadours of eleventh- and twelfth-century Provence constructed their lays and aubades in much the same way.

Popular and theater songs were grist for the jazz mill, and even an occasional operatic aria was given the treatment. Opera was a big influence on New Orleans jazz composers like Louis Armstrong,[9] who based many of his high-flying cadenzas on flourishes given to or taken by divas and leading tenors. Jelly Roll Morton included various versions—from straight to swinging—of the *Miserere* from Verdi's *Il trovatore* (at one point Morton throws in a bit of the "anvil" chorus for good measure) in some remarkable excerpts included on volume 1 of the 1938 Library of Congress recordings, released on Rounder CD 1091 in 1993. Most New Orleans citizens, blacks and whites alike, were at home in the world of opera, which is not surprising since the city supported three opera houses. In fact, the general interest in opera in the United States at this time was very keen, as may be attested to by the fact that the best-selling artists on early recordings were the legendary tenor Enrico Caruso and composer John Philip Sousa, who wrote some successful stage works.

To make a tune "hot," jazzmen played principal notes before or after the main beats, slid in and out of notes and measures, recomposed the tunes by changing their rhythmic structures, distilled melodies into their rhythmic outlines, and played only those essential notes. Their treatment of existing music or original compositions was a new and daring version of the ancient theme-and-variation format. What was different was that this was all done collectively and spontaneously, which was part of the challenge and part of the fun. It gave New Orleans jazz a funky, often downright funny character, especially when the trumpet wah-wahed or growled, the clarinet wailed or bleated, and the trombone skated from note to note.

As a precursor and continuing component of jazz, the more reflective *blues* were an equally important counterpart to the generally upbeat but relaxed ragtime. The blues told a story, and the story was almost always one of loss and deprivation, either personal or political. The lyrics of *Joe Turner Blues*, often called the first authentic example of the genre, deal with the notorious eponymous overseer who was responsible for delivering black criminals from Memphis to the penitentiary in Nashville, Tennessee; evidently his method of shackling the men's handcuffs to a metal chain was quite innovative.[10]

Like so much else in jazz, the blues can be traced to the earliest days of slavery. Evidently silence was looked upon as dangerous or at least disrespectful, and masters or overseers would demand that the slaves "make a noise."[11] The music couldn't be too lugubrious, since that would slow the workers' tempo, but the words—often poorly understood by the whites in charge—could be as sorrowful as the singers desired. (This was, surprisingly enough, much the same in many concentration camps during the Holocaust, when Nazi guards would require song from their victims.)[12]

Singers played but a small role in early Dixieland, where the rhythm always took precedence over the melody, but they were vital to the blues. They often imitated instrumental growls and wails, but their emphasis was always on the words. Great blues singers like Ethel Waters and Bessie Smith put their private anguish into every song, and the listeners responded. You needn't have suffered the same losses they had, but if you were human, you had suffered plenty of your own. Here "sharing your pain" was no idle cliché, it was the soul of the performance.

Along with gut-wrenching emotion, the blues gave to jazz a definite structure: typically a twelve-bar chorus in which the lyrics and music are in AAB format. Since the words rarely filled the allotted measures, the backup instrumentalists had time for riffs, which were most often improvised. Melodically the blues was characterized by flatted thirds and sevenths as well as so-called "bent" notes (playing or singing "between the cracks"); harmonically it relied on tonic, dominant, and subdominant-seventh chords. Blues also served as a conduit for the introduction of Latin American styles, primarily from the Caribbean community in New Orleans.

Of all forms of jazz, the blues may be most closely tied to its African ancestry. Analysis has shown that the traditional songs brought over by the imported slaves are similar in melodic content and feel to those created by the next generation of black composers of blues,[13] and the instrumentation—primarily banjo and guitar—was the same. The guitar was especially effective in accompanying the blues, for rubbing a knife or some other implement over its strings produced the plaintive sound favored by the vocalists. Whites as well as free blacks were able to hear this authentic music because in nineteenth-century New Orleans, which was never as racially segregated as so many of its Southern sister cities, the slave population was officially permitted to perform native songs and dances in Congo Square. A large audience, black and white, was always on hand to listen and watch. In this way second-generation performers and composers had immediate contact with their musical roots.[14]

Many jazz musicians attribute the first successful combining of the characteristic sound and structure of the blues with the popular song idiom to bandleader Buddy Bolden (1877–1931), whose group unfortunately stopped performing before it could be captured on records. The reputation of the legendary and mysterious Bolden has assumed mythical proportions among jazz aficionados. Whatever the case for Bolden's seminal role in the formation of the blues, it is indisputable that the first composer to bring the form/style to popularity was William Christopher (W. C.) Handy (1873–1958).[15] Boldly entitling his autobiography *Father of the Blues*, Handy may not have been overstating the case, for his *Memphis Blues, St. Louis Blues, Yellow Dog Blues*, and *Beale Street Blues*—to name but a few of the most famous of his dozens of compositions, all written and published in the first two decades of the twentieth century—form a large segment of the core repertoire of this particular type of jazz.

The third major component of early jazz was the popular music heard in the ubiquitous minstrel shows. These touring theatrical entertainments featured both white and black performers, the blacks often further darkened by grotesque makeup. The fact that the songs and dances of this essentially vaudeville genre often caricatured African Americans in most unflattering—one might say insulting—ways does not diminish their importance in spreading the music composed for them and the fame of many of the performers.

The heyday of the minstrel show was from 1898 to 1908, the same decade that saw the rise of ragtime, but examples may be traced to the pre–Civil War era. *Clorindy, or the Origin of the Cakewalk,* productions by Sam T. Jack's *Creole Burlesque* and John Isham's *Octoroons* troops, and *A Trip to Coontown* were among the many shows on the boards by the turn of the century. They made such dancers as the cakewalking team of Ben Williams and George Walker famous and relatively prosperous, although the almost exclusively white managers and producers raked in most of the profits. The most polished of these productions, and the one with the most coherent book, was *In Dahomy,* a bona fide musical comedy rather than a series of vaudeville acts. Since, as we shall see, many of these shows toured France and England, they are important to our story.

Seminal in the field of black theater was William Marion Cook (1869–1944), whose ability to combine the syncopation of ragtime and the feel of the blues with the smoother orchestral sound of European-derived music appealed to the black and white theater-going publics. Cook's particular blend of idioms was too conservative for later creators and lovers of jazz, as may be seen in Duke Ellington's somewhat left-handed tribute to the man he called "the King of Consonance."[16] Cook was a typical New York figure, more than a bit removed from the funky New Orleans style, and his influence on James Reese Europe and other jazz innovators was immense.

Louis Armstrong is often quoted as saying, "There are only two kinds of music, good and bad, and if you can tap your toes to it, it's good." While toe-tapping doesn't seem a good criterion for the slow movement of Bach's Concerto for Oboe and Violin or Desdemona's *Willow Song* in Verdi's *Otello,* to name a couple of exceptions the musically sophisticated Armstrong would undoubtedly have endorsed, it isn't a bad index for jazz. You might want to hold your breath so as not to break the spell of Verdi's great musical prayer, but it's natural to want to move to jazz, as the history of jazz dancing illustrates.

In the closing decade of the nineteenth century, ragtime brought the first of the many dances associated with jazz, the cakewalk, a jaunty cross between a strut and a saunter. Performed alone or by couples, the cakewalk worked well with the street bands of New Orleans, where following the musicians and keeping in step with their rhythms was a normal activity. Even when done in twos, the cakewalk involved much less body contact than the waltz, for example, for the dancers simply linked elbows and strutted side by side. The two theories espoused as to the origin of the name seem equally plausible—one that the participant bringing up the rear of a brass band–led funeral procession bore the cake for the festive send-off following the burial, the other that the prize for the best strutters in the ubiquitous dance contests was a cake. Part native exuberance and part parody of upper-class pomposity, the cakewalk mirrored and mocked the cotillion dances seen at plantation celebrations. This aspect of the dance fit right in with the parodistic, or at least ironic, mode of much of New Orleans instrumental jazz.

Fads in dances came and went, but one of the most enduring was the foxtrot, introduced by the elegant white husband-and-wife team Irene and Vernon Castle and the black orchestra leader they most relied on, James Reese Europe. This public biracial collaboration (there were, of course, many such collaborations behind the scenes) was unusual, to say the least, in an era when the lighter-skinned players in Duke Ellington's orchestra were forced to blacken their faces with makeup to avoid accusations of integration when they were engaged to appear in a Hollywood film.

James Reese Europe (1881–1919) was one of the more interesting musical figures of the early twentieth century. Born to a middle-class family in Washington, D.C., he had a thoroughly traditional musical education, learning piano and violin. When his father died, in 1899, Europe went to work, joining his pianist brother's New York–based band. He soon led a band of his own, and, along with William Marion Cook, he popularized the syncopated music of ragtime, composing songs and instrumentals in that idiom. His Clef Club, begun in 1910, became a booking agency and hangout for New York black musicians, classical as well as popular; and in 1912, nimbly leaping the color divide, he organized two Carnegie Hall concerts featuring only African American musicians.

Europe's style was generally up-tempo and danceable; despite being written out and rehearsed, his characteristic syncopations had "a wildly ragged and intense quality of abandon."[17] His large dance band was the first choice for most New York white society functions, for he could and did play waltzes, polkas, and other tamer social dances as well as the newer music. With the Castles, who adumbrated such teams as Fred Astaire and Ginger Rogers, his polished versions of farm-animal down-home cavorting— the Turkey Trot, the Bunny Hug, and finally the foxtrot, captivated the younger set.

None of Europe's wonderful dance music was, strictly speaking, authentic jazz, but it is of vital importance to our story. In 1916 British-born Vernon Castle left America and enlisted in the British air force. Inspired by this patriotic decision, Europe enlisted in a fighting unit of the American army. He was almost immediately recruited to form an all-black brass band to attract African Americans into military service. This was no problem for Europe, who had grown up listening to Sousa's marches, and his recruitment efforts ultimately resulted in the renowned 15th Regiment. The story of the Harlem Hellfighters, as the regiment came to be called, is told in the chapter on the 1920s, the period of the greatest influence of black musicians in France, but Europe's personal tale is a brief one. Conducting his band throughout France, Europe led the Hellfighters at the head of the great Armistice parade in France, and received a ticker-tape welcome back home in New York. Europe had survived months of actual combat duty overseas, yet soon after his return to America he was murdered by one of his own disgruntled band members, who was upset over what he saw as unfair treatment.

Meanwhile there were far wilder dance crazes back home, including the athletic Jitterbug. Was the name "Jitterbug" derived from the little bugs that jitter across stagnant ponds or from the mugs of whiskey, sometimes called "jitter," common at the time? Or was it an obscure sexual allusion? The later "Lindy Hop" was certifiably so dubbed in honor of Charles Lindbergh's nonstop trans-Atlantic flight of 1927, but the "Jitterbug" has no such clear connection. Whatever the name may imply, the more acrobatic tossing about of the female partner seems to have been a benign but exaggerated version of the "Apache" dancing that originated in France.

Street gangs that terrorized Paris around the turn of the century had adopted the name of the ferocious American Indian tribe. The dingy clothing and even some techniques used by these gangs to rough up one another or their higher-class victims were stylized into "Apache" dances. (Richard Rodgers's *Slaughter on 10th Avenue* is an American version of the costumes and choreography; the Apache dances were toned down by the upper classes into something akin to the tango.) The influences thus shifted back and forth across the Atlantic: an American Indian tribe lent its name to a French style of gangster whose urban street gang maneuvers were then put into a dance form that influenced American dancers for generations.

The French have a saying—*plus ça change, plus c'est la même chose,* the more things change, the more they are the same—that neatly describes what happened to early jazz music and dance. As so many of its practitioners moved north to Chicago and New York, where musical theater thrived, the recording industry was trying its wings, and sheet-music publishers were flourishing, New Orleans–style jazz changed. It became "smoother," less cacophonous, less spontaneous, and more centered on individual players. Nevertheless, in a way Dixieland remained the same for many players, especially those who stayed in the New Orleans area. Sidney Bechet is one such player; although he traveled widely and heard everyone, his last recording sessions from the 1940s and 1950s have all the characteristics—the freely improvised riffs, the emotional intensity, the rhythmic security, and, above all, that inimitable vibrato—of the earlier sessions of the 1920s. Gradually popular tastes veered more to the elegant and formal big bands, where almost everything was written out, rehearsed, and played as notated, but there was always at least a small audience for the more raucous, rambunctious earlier sound. Since revivals of interest in "genuine" Dixieland occurred, and indeed still occur periodically, "the real thing" can be found if one looks hard enough. It was this earlier form of jazz, brought to their shores first by the Harlem Hellfighters and then by African American expatriates right after World War I, that most influenced French popular and classical music.

5

American Composers in the 1920s, Part I
Charles Ives, Aaron Copland, Virgil Thomson

he four most important events of the early 1920s in the United States in the development of classical music on these shores centered around compositions of Charles Ives, Igor Stravinsky, George Gershwin, and Aaron Copland. The year 1921 brought the long-delayed publication of Ives's monumental Piano Sonata No. 2, *Concord*. His most important work for solo piano, the sonata was written between 1908 and 1915, but was virtually unknown until its composer decided to have it published at his own expense (today, the piece is still hardly a staple of the recital stage). Equally long overdue was the American premiere of Stravinsky's *Rite of Spring* in 1922, nine years after its premiere in Paris. George Gershwin's *Rhapsody in Blue* was featured in Paul Whiteman's eclectic Carnegie Hall concert in 1924. Finally, Aaron Copland returned from his Paris-based studies with Nadia Boulanger bearing, at his teacher's request, an organ concerto for her to perform with American orchestras.

But were these avant-garde works the music most American concert-goers were hearing? A glance at the microfilmed programs of the New York Philharmonic during those years gives us the answer, and with the exception of the instantly popular Gershwin piece, the answer is a resounding no. Program after program for concerts in the 1920s lists the usual repertoire—Beethoven, Brahms, Liszt, Schubert, Schumann, and Wagner for the main course, with a smattering of Grieg, Dvořák, Smetena, and others for ethnic flavor. Russian composers are well represented, especially Tchaikovsky, Rachmaninoff, and Rimsky-Korsakov, and the French are not ignored. Debussy's *L'après-midi d'un faune* and *Nocturnes* for orchestra appear from time to time, as do works by Ravel, d'Indy, Franck, Saint-Saëns, and Berlioz; and Chabrier's *España* seems to have been a special favorite. (Oddly enough, the Andante from Debussy's String Quartet, one assumes in an orchestrated version, shows up on a program or two.) Once in a great while an American work is featured—MacDowell's *Second Orchestral Suite*, loosely based on American Indian themes, for example.

One encounters a few unfamiliar names—Zdeněk Fibich (1850–1900), a now virtually forgotten Czech composer, his compatriot Vitězslav Novák (1870–1949), and Bohemian-born Josef Stransky (1872–1936), yet another composer/conductor who followed Dvořák to America. As part-time conductor of the New York Philharmonic, Stransky scheduled many of his own compositions, even, on more than one occasion, leading a complete program of his own works. In addition to MacDowell, among the few American composers we find George Chadwick (1854–1931) of the Boston School, and we know that Amy Beach was a welcome guest performer of her own Piano Concerto at many orchestral concerts. Toward the end of the decade, under German-born conductor Walter Damrosch's baton, Gershwin's *Concerto in F* and *American in Paris* were both heard, and by that time performances of his initial success, *Rhapsody In Blue,* had become standard.

In short, today's concertgoer would find very little difference between the music on their subscription series and what their great-grandparents were willing to pay good money to hear. In fact, the only really startling change is the price of tickets, which in 1921 ranged from fifty cents to two dollars. Yet the European tradition, with an emphasis on the Germanic style, still dominated American classical music. Chadwick, Beach, and even the slightly more "Americanized" MacDowell, had not in any significant way broken with it. But in no way does this change the fact that many new ideas were brewing behind the scenes. Most salient is the case of Charles Ives (1874–1954). In the opinion of many, an opinion with which I concur, Ives was the most innovative American composer of his day, perhaps of any day, exemplifying the American traits of independence and individuality.

Of course, Ives admired Beethoven—he quotes the four-note theme from the Fifth Symphony in three of the four movements of the *Concord Sonata*—but after listening to an entire program of the master's music, Ives found that he longed for something other than the major-minor tonic-dominant formulas.[1] Consequently there are few references to these time-honored systems in the sonata. But neither do we hear a Schoenbergian twelve-tone framework. Instead we have a compendium—a layering, if you will—of hymn tunes, patriotic songs, popular music, and classical quotations in a highly original matrix of Ives's own invention.

Although Ives labels the *Concord Sonata* a sonata—the full title is *Sonata No. 2 for Piano, Concord, Mass., 1840–60*—there is no attempt at sonata form in any of its four movements. Ives preferred what he called "cumulative form," in which the effect of the disparate themes, which appear, disappear, and reappear, builds of its own momentum. He was quite articulate about his aims and methods, publishing verbal explanations along with the scores. Of the piece he said,

> The sonata is an attempt to present [one person's] impression of the spirit
> of transcendentalism that is associated in the minds of many with Concord,

Massachusetts, of over a half century ago. This is undertaken in impressions of Emerson and, Thoreau, a sketch of the Alcotts, and a scherzo supposed to reflect a lighter duality which is often found in the fantastic side of Hawthorne.[2]

Despite this verbal guide, one cannot mistake the *Concord Sonata* for program music. Unlike a tone poem by Liszt or Richard Strauss, it tells no story and needs none (it is fun to follow Till Eulenspiegel to the gallows after all his merry pranks, but Ives had no comparable program in mind). In fact, only in the final section, *Thoreau,* does the music fit the general impression that has been passed down of the rather somber, high-minded transcendentalists, whose serious essays and moralistic fiction seem far removed from the rambunctious, virtuosic, flamboyant, and sometimes funny music created by Ives. There is only one programmatic moment, and that occurs at the end of *Thoreau,* when a flute is introduced for a few measures in reference to Thoreau's playing of that instrument.

Emerson, the first movement, opens with "a burst of sounds that were unavailable to Beethoven."[3] Its texture is dense and amorphous, with plenty of rhythmic pizzazz, including some mighty jazzy sequences, but no discernible rhythmic pattern. It is by turns gentle, raucous, noisy, and peaceful. A theme that resembles the popular song *Autumn in New York,* which was written in 1934 by Vernon Duke (the pseudonym used by the Russian-born Vladimir Dukelsky for his popular compositions)—coincidence, or borrowing on "Mr. Duke's" part?—comes and goes, harmonized in various ways. The four-note theme of Beethoven's Fifth Symphony is introduced but not stressed—in fact, unless you know it is there, you might miss this first reference to it. Toward the end the Beethoven theme becomes more obvious, and the section concludes with the theme deep in the bass.

The second movement, *Hawthorne,* has a jazzlike opening. It is playful throughout in a way that readers of *The Scarlet Letter* or *The Birthmark* might never associate with this usually dour author. Despite its enormous rhythmic and harmonic complexity, it often feels like popular music. A hymn tune appears, is interrupted by furious chaos, and then returns. Syncopations and bits from *Columbia the Gem of the Ocean* follow. The whole movement is full of wit and surprises.

The Alcotts, the third movement, has a quiet, simply harmonized hymnlike opening. Suddenly Beethoven's Fifth comes through loud and clear. Its famous four notes are developed and varied before morphing into a New England hymn. Another long section devoted to the Beethoven theme gradually begins to resemble Stephen Foster's *My Old Kentucky Home.* The final section, *Thoreau,* sees the return of many of the themes already heard. It is the most contemplative of the four, and the most easily associated with its namesake.

It has been said that the composition's "layering," the superimposing of one musical phrase on top of another, makes what is heard more or less up to the individual, each listener in a way creating his own *Concord Sonata.* The performer can control this to some extent by stressing one layer over another, just as the performer of a Bach fugue determines whether to bring out the principal theme or stress the inner voices (although on the harpsichord, of course, such emphasis was usually not possible). In the Ives, however, the sheer density of the texture makes it difficult to bring inner voices to the fore. In any case, with so much to listen for, repeated hearings will result in varied impressions.

One has only to listen to this fascinating and entertaining work, which lasts a little under an hour, to hear how avant-garde it was, not only when first composed, but when first performed, decades later, during the 1938–39 season. It still sounds fresh and new almost a full century after Ives first began to work on it. To be fair, one must note that Ives continually revised this and all his other major works for many years—on some occasions apparently changing the dates on his manuscripts to make his compositions look even more forward looking. Pianist John Kirkpatrick, the first to perform and record the entire piece, sought Ives's guidance in preparation for this daunting feat. Evidently every time he asked the composer a question about the score, Ives rewrote the passage under discussion, virtually creating a new piece as they went along. Yet even in its final version, the *Concord Sonata* was well ahead of its time.

Having acknowledged its importance historically, the question remains: Is the *Concord Sonata* a seminal work? Can a composition be considered seminal if its seeds are planted where their fruits are unlikely to be seen, or in this case heard, for so many years? The performance history of the *Concord Sonata* is a case in point. The second of its four movements, *Hawthorne,* was introduced at its first complete performance by John Kirkpatrick, who won great reviews for his laudable venture, at the work's first complete public performance on November 28, 1938. *The Alcotts,* the first movement played in public, was given in a recital in 1921; *Emerson* and *Thoreau* were first publicly performed in 1928. It was not until the late 1930s or early 1940s that musicians began to reckon with the *Concord Sonata*'s import, by which time some of its most innovative characteristics had been independently introduced by other composers. Unfortunately, undoubtedly because of its length and difficulty, to this day it has been performed too infrequently to make much of an impression on the general concert going public. Direct influence on other composers, American or French, is hard to trace, but many of Ives's innovations have become commonplace: quotations from other composers, layering, the inclusion of vernacular styles and materials, cumulative effect rather than formal structure, rhythmic incisiveness without definable rhythmic patterns—these are all part of the musical vocabulary of today.

Perhaps one reason for the timeless effectiveness of the *Concord Sonata* is Ives's personal view of the underlying principle of composition. Unlike his contemporaries such as American composers Edgar Varèse or George Antheil and to a lesser extent the Russian Sergei Prokofiev, who thought that twentieth-century music must reflect the percussive noise of the impersonal machine-age world, Ives felt that music should be the expression of the composer's inner emotional experience. This was no different from the Romantic aesthetic; what was completely different was Ives's way of expressing this inner emotional life. Many composers who followed Ives, having gone the impersonal, machine-driven route, have returned to the difficult task of expressing their own emotional lives in ways compatible with the modern world. This is perhaps the most "seminal" aspect of Ives's work.

The *Concord Sonata* is extremely difficult to master, and there are not many opportunities to perform it. For these reasons few pianists are likely to include it in their repertoires. Ives's Second Sonata for Violin and Piano, with its jaunty *Turkey in the Straw* movement, is one possible entry vehicle, but for most keyboard artists the best way to immerse oneself in the remarkable world of Charles Ives is through his 114 songs. These delightful works span his creative life; like the *Concord Sonata* they were first published in 1922. Technical challenges abound, but, of course, the songs are much shorter and hence easier to program. Because of Ives's choice of texts, they are also more obvious in their concentration on Americana, although it is pretty hard to miss all the references to American vernacular and religious music in the composer's instrumental output.

A typical Ives song is *General William Booth Enters Heaven* (text by Vachel Lindsay). In this song Ives fuses hymn melodies ("Are you washed in the blood of the lamb" is the refrain), clusters of chords in unrelated keys, banjo music (*Polly Wolly Doodle*), a bugle call, a folk song, and snatches of other well-known tunes. Much of this potpourri is, of course, found primarily in the accompaniment. Tonality seems to phase in and out, and the final chord implies no tonal center. The overall mood is jaunty and appropriately mock-serious, for Booth was a Salvation Army general.

The Circus Band and *The Side Show* are as amusing as Ives's portrayal of General Booth. Both have music-hall style accompaniments replete with the clichés of the pop piano players of the early 1900s. (Had Ives heard Debussy's *Minstrels* from the first book of *Préludes*?) The words, in this case by the composer himself—"Cleopatra's on her throne/That golden hair is all her own" from *Circus Band*—are amusing too. In *Side Show* the singer gets just a bit out of phase with the accompanist, a comic effect harder to achieve than the listener might imagine.

Some of the songs reflect the more serious side of the composer. *Tom Sails Away,* for example, is an impressionistic song of parting. It quotes a few bars of George M. Cohan's *Over There*, a patriotic pop song of World

War I. In *In Flanders Fields,* a grim memorial to the thousands who died in
that first Great War, Ives quotes *Columbia the Gem of the Ocean.*

In all of these songs, ranging so widely in mood and purpose, one hears
Ives's love for small-town America—its country fairs, Fourth of July celebrations, simple church services, marching bands, circuses, and cowboys.
In a way he was the most American of all American composers. In looking
for transatlantic influences, it seems that Ives might have been at least
aware of the music-hall flavor and clichés of popular music heard in a few
of Debussy's lighter *préludes.* Whatever he might have borrowed from the
French, if indeed he did, he made it his own, and hence American.

Charles Ives was unique in many aspects of his professional life; he was
a successful executive in the insurance industry for all the years he was
composing. Virtually every American felt it necessary to go to Europe for
a complete musical education, yet in this regard Ives again was unusual.
For his musical studies, he never went any further than Yale University in
New Haven, Connecticut.

Before World War I the country of choice for overseas study was almost
inevitably Germany; after that cataclysmic event, when Germany had
become the devastated victim of its own aggression, France seemed more
welcoming. The Paris Conservatoire, however, had not changed its mind
about welcoming American students, whom they regarded as too recently
descended from the apes. Therefore, many aspiring Americans wound
up at the less condescending École Normale de Musique (Preparatory
School of Music), and also at the newly established American Conservatory
at Fontainebleau, which held its sessions during the summer recess of
L'École Normale. At both of these institutions, they found a young woman
who soon became the most renowned composition teacher of her generation, Nadia Boulanger (1887–1979).

Boulanger, or "Mademoiselle," as she was later called, was one of the
most remarkable musicians in all of Europe. Gifted with an impeccable
musical ear, which was honed from her earliest childhood first by her parents and then by the strenuous training common in French schools, she
could "hear" any score, no matter how complex, from the printed page.
Unflagging through her eighties and unaffected by vision so severely limited as to be almost blindness, her energy was legendary, as was her rever-
ence for the art of music. Before allowing her American students to work
on their own compositions, she insisted on bringing their listening and
analytic skills to the highest level they could achieve, an exercise few had
encountered at home.

Aaron Copland (1900–1990) was the first American to study with
Boulanger and the first to register at the newly formed American Conserva-
tory.[4] Arriving early in the summer of 1921, he spent only a short time in
Paris before heading for Fontainebleau, but he made the most of his brief

introduction to the city. On his first night there, he attended a performance of the Ballets Suédois, a company formed by art collector Rolf de Maré to rival Diaghilev's Ballets Russes. There he saw Milhaud's sensuous *L'homme et son désir* (Man and his desire) and *Les mariés de la Tour Eiffel* (The newlyweds of the Eiffel Tower), a surrealist performance piece concocted by Jean Cocteau and five of the composer-members of Les Six.[5] It wouldn't have made much difference if the newcomer's French were weak—Cocteau's libretto is deliberately nonsensical. Stravinsky was joined by Satie, Milhaud, and even Cole Porter in this Parisian trend of ballet composition, and Copland soon followed their lead with the grotesque, macabre *Grohg,* parts of which eventually found their way into his *Dance Symphony.*

Before leaving America Copland had never heard of the young Boulanger and, originally intending to study with well-known composer Paul Vidal, stumbled upon her more or less by chance.[6] After only a few lessons he knew he had found the right teacher and enrolled in her classes at L'École Normale for the winter session. He stayed under her tutelage for over three years.

Copland had composed several works—now considered his juvenilia and unpublished—while still in the United States. Among his early efforts, written when he was eighteen, was the charming *Scherzo humoristique* (Humorous scherzo) for piano solo subtitled *Cat and Mouse.* In this four-minute piece he uses Debussian augmented chords without sounding as though he is imitating the French master, proof of the young Copland's skill and originality. *Cat and Mouse*'s scampering figures and long glissando are delightful representations of a chase, and the limping, mock tragic close makes one infer a sad ending for the mouse. Debussy's publisher, Durand et Cie., heard the brief work at a recital and bought it from the flattered young composer for twenty-five dollars. It was his first published work.

Cat and Mouse is far from the only example of Copland's interest in French music: the second of his twelve songs to texts of Emily Dickinson, *There Came a Wind like a Bugle,* for instance, uses minor seconds to create much the same blustery effect found in Debussy's third prelude from Book 1, *Le vent dans la plaine* (The wind in the plain). (As pointed out earlier, Edward MacDowell also seemed to refer to this piece.)

Copland's first important composition for piano solo, his *Passacaglia,* was published only one year after his arrival in France and marks an enormous leap in his development. Perhaps Boulanger's subtle influence may be seen in Copland's choice of form, one which had been much utilized by seventeenth-century composers. It was Boulanger who introduced her students to the compositions of such early masters as Claudio Monteverdi (1567–1643), recording many of Monteverdi's madrigals, and thus making them known to a larger public. The piece begins with an eight-bar theme, baldly stated in octaves. This theme is rhythmically square: two four-bar segments divided by a held note in the middle. True to standard traditional passacaglia form, the eight-bar opening statement underlies the entire piece, retaining its rhythmic stolidity throughout. Melodically the most interesting aspect of the theme is the half-step interval between its last two notes: having begun a descending diatonic scale fragment in the sixth measure, Copland creates the expectation of a whole tone at the end, but the satisfying mi-re-do doesn't happen. While dissonances abound in the piece, there are many moments of soothing harmony, and its basic tonality is never obscured. The ending is a resounding G-sharp minor tonic chord.

The *Passacaglia* is a wonderful piece—well-crafted and exciting in its virtuosic demands on the performer. It is the first of Copland's three major abstract works for solo piano, followed by the Piano Variations (1930) and then the Sonata (1939–41). Four *Piano Blues,* the *Children's Pieces,* and a few other short works complete Copland's output for solo keyboard. Yet his Piano Concerto, the piano accompaniments to his songs—especially *12 Poems of Emily Dickinson*—and the keyboard part in his *Vitebsk Trio* for violin, cello, and piano are equally fascinating.

Most difficult of these compositions for performer and listener alike are the Piano Variations in which Copland—atypically—incorporates serial techniques without quite using a complete twelve-tone row, and yet without completely abandoning tonality. Boulanger, perhaps because of her friendship with and high regard for Stravinsky, discouraged her students from using the Schoenberg twelve-tone row as a compositional device, but by 1930 Copland obviously felt free to experiment any way he liked. The piece is a curious mixture of extreme austerity—the opening statement consists of percussive unaccompanied and disjointed tones—and jazz. Even the rhythmically exciting jazz-derived passages, however, are somehow robbed of their usual entertaining insouciance. All the elements are there, but they don't "swing." Only reluctantly did critics accept this as a significant and potentially effective piece, and many audiences still bridle at it.

Of the three major piano pieces, the Sonata is the most easily identified as "American," particularly in its middle movement. The first movement, in sonata form, is often polytonal, with many of its chords analyzable in two or more keys. There is a key signature—five flats—but whether this indicates D-flat major or B-flat minor is never absolutely clear (the final B-flat minor chord is colored by a G flat in the treble.) Unlike the *Passacaglia,* the Sonata's rhythms are complex and ever changing, with measures of two, three, four, or five beats freely juxtaposed. The presence of a steady quarter note, however, is a unifying factor and lends rhythmic coherence.

The middle movement of the Sonata points to a paradox found in so much of Copland's oeuvre: having grown up in noisy, bustling Brooklyn and having cut his musical teeth on urban Tin Pan Alley tunes, Copland nevertheless captured the sound and feel of the wide open spaces of the American West better than any other composer. Interestingly, Virgil Thomson, another Boulanger student who will be discussed more fully below, always claimed to have pointed the way to this American-prairie sound, and perhaps to some degree he did. Copland creates this distinctive effect in the Sonata's central section by beginning with an unaccompanied theme punctuated by long held notes which seem to imply silence. Gradually increasing the pace of his angular theme, which consists of eighth notes in $\frac{5}{8}$ or $\frac{7}{8}$ meter, he conveys—at least to this listener—the aura of a prairie awakening to the morning sun (this is not meant to imply a "program" for the Sonata). It has been said that Copland achieved an American sound primarily through the use of folk tunes, and the examples usually given are his ballet scores *Appalachian Spring, Rodeo,* and *Billy the Kid.* These ever-popular works do indeed evoke the American myth through folk music, but the middle movement of the Sonata does so through strictly abstract means.

In the Sonata's third and final movement Copland finds another way to imply space and silence, with long sequences of very slow, widely spaced (as much as four-and-a-half octaves apart) intervals. These increasingly *meno mosso* and *più piano* measures bring the long work to a quiet, ethereal close.

Despite Boulanger's emphasis on the achievements of Stravinsky, Copland's works bear little resemblance to those of the Russian expatriate. Like Stravinsky (until his later years), Copland chose tonality over twelve-tone technique, and like him, he used Baroque or Classical forms; but with his instinct for things American and, for that matter, Central American, he created his own content to fill those forms. It was one of the defining characteristics of Boulanger's teaching methods and aims to allow each composer to develop in his or her own way, and to give each the tools necessary to express what he or she wanted to say. Indeed, this is what drew so many young American hopefuls to her studios in Fontainebleau and Paris.

F. Scott Fitzgerald always took credit for giving a name to these years with his *Tales of the Jazz Age,* published in May 1922. This collection of short stories chronicled the era, with its "flappers" jauntily portrayed by cartoonist John Held, its Prohibition-driven crime and bad booze (the Volstead Act of January 1920 made it illegal to sell or transport any liquor with more than ½ percent alcohol content), and its newly enfranchised, cigarette-smoking, bobbed-haired women (the Nineteenth Amendment to the Constitution gave American women the right to vote in August 1920). It is no wonder that his descriptions of the era rang so true, for Fitzgerald and his wife, Zelda, lived it to the fullest.

The period of Copland's studies in Paris—1921–25—was a rich one for the development of jazz in both the United States and in France. Just as the 1913 Paris premiere of Stravinsky's *Le sacre du printemps* (The rite of spring) seems the definitive beginning of modern classical music, so the arrival in 1922 of Louis Armstrong in Chicago, where he joined King Oliver's brilliant Creole Jazz Band, marks for many the real beginning of the jazz age.[7] With not one but two virtuoso cornet players now on board, Oliver's group could present endlessly imaginative melodic lines as the leader and the newcomer, who had been his student, inspired each other in magical riffs. The earliest recordings of jazz, by the Original Dixieland Jass Band in 1917, were in wide circulation, and jazz elements had already begun to infiltrate Tin Pan Alley and Broadway shows.

At the same time Paris was welcoming the expatriate community of black jazz musicians who went there right after World War I to find a life free—or relatively free—from discrimination. (This community and its contribution to classical and vernacular music in Europe will be discussed in chapter 7.) Never one to isolate himself from popular culture, Copland was well aware of the new trends in music and incorporated many of them in his "serious" works.

Over the years Copland's attitude toward jazz changed. His first published piece, *Cat and Mouse,* has the syncopated rhythms characteristic of jazz, and his *Piano Blues* are obviously based on that particular expression of the black experience in America. Of the three major works for solo piano discussed above, the first and third are not particularly evocative of this new music, while the second, the Piano Variations, gives a most austere version of the idiom. The Piano Concerto (1926), however, is definitely jazz-based. Oddly enough, the Concerto shares a familiar blues theme with George Gershwin's *Second Piano Prelude;* since both were published the same year, neither composer can be accused of having copied from the other. In any case Copland's Concerto is a far more austere work than anything Gershwin ever composed.

Copland's Organ Concerto (also known as his First Symphony; 1924–25), written at Boulanger's request as a vehicle for her American début as organist and conductor, includes the jazz timbre of an alto sax and lots of jazz rhythms. Apparently Boulanger enjoyed playing the work, for she scheduled it on many occasions. Boulanger was also especially fond of the madrigals of Monteverdi, recording and featuring them in many concerts. She must have been open-minded about reinterpretations of these a cappella part-song settings of pastoral poems, for her student Copland dubbed his early choral work *Immorality* "a hot jazz madrigal."[8]

For a while Copland continued to fuse jazz and contemporary classical composition in what was later called "Third Stream" fashion; during this stage of his career he wrote several short pieces, the popular *Music for the Theatre* (1925), and the Piano Concerto. In "Jazz Structure and Influence," his 1927 article for *Modern Music,* he said, "The characteristic rhythmic elements of jazz . . . being independent of mood yet purely indigenous, will undoubtedly continue to be used in serious native music."

Gradually Copland became less convinced that jazz was a fruitful source of inspiration for a new style of classical composition, and he drew away from it. The Piano Concerto, Copland's only exercise in the genre, was the last major work in which he deliberately emphasized jazz elements until the Clarinet Concerto of 1948. The fact that this piece was composed for Benny Goodman as well as the sound of the featured instrument itself undoubtedly inspired this return to the jazz idiom.

As a new source of inspiration for a truly American, truly accessible style, Copland turned to folk music. His most popular works were the result: the ballets *Appalachian Spring, Rodeo,* and *Billy the Kid.* Other works specifically designed for popular appeal, like *The Lincoln Portrait* and *Fanfare for the Common Man,* are also favorites, especially on patriotic occasions. Copland's interest in Americana included the music of Latin America, as his catchy *El salón México* attests. He wanted classical music—or at least his classical music—to have as broad an audience as possible, and he worked toward that goal with great success. None of these major populist pieces was written for piano solo.

Copland never lost his respect and admiration for Boulanger. He encouraged other American composers to follow him to France, and many did. In the first wave of American Boulanger students we find Virgil Thomson, Elliott Carter, Walter Piston, Roy Harris, Douglas Moore, Roger Sessions, and Marc Blitzstein, along with a few whose names are now unfamiliar to music lovers. In 1926 Boulanger organized a concert to showcase the works of her pupils from across the sea. Copland, Thomson, Antheil, Piston, and two lesser knowns—Herbert Elwell and Theodore Chanler—were featured. Three years later she promoted a second such concert, this one financed by a New York patron interested in Copland.[9] This time the composers favored were Copland, Thomson, Harris, Israel Citkowitz, and the Mexican Carlos Chávez. Through this kind of exposure Copland and the others met everyone important in the musical world of Paris.

No two of these Americans composed in the same style or followed the same path. Elliott Carter developed the thorniest, most abstruse ways of expressing himself. In one of his string quartets, for example, the rhythms are so complex and the texture so dense that the four players must wear click-tapes—individual metronomes in ear phones—to keep track of what they are doing. Marc Blitzstein's music went in the opposite direction: with his social and political beliefs paramount, he used a populist style and simplistic texts. His best-known work is perhaps the musical play *The Cradle Will Rock,* a deliberately agit-prop piece whose professional production was thwarted in the 1930s because of its subversive nature. Roy Harris is perhaps best known for his symphonies. Unwilling to break with the past, Harris devised his own way of incorporating Renaissance and Baroque polyphony with the Classical ideals of thematic development without sacrificing freshness, individuality, and a distinctly American sound. Theodore Chanler became a distinguished music critic, and Walter Piston was a renowned teacher at Harvard whose books on harmony and counterpoint became classics. Roger Sessions was also very active as a teacher, and much of his time was devoted to the promotion of the music of young composers. The relatively few works he did write were well received and often performed at the time. He and Copland began the Copland-Sessions concert series specifically to provide opportunities for the growing number of American talents to be heard.

Almost all of these Boulanger students have an early piano sonata listed in their catalog of composition, which was perhaps an assignment from Mademoiselle. Yet aside from Copland, the only one of her first wave of American students to make a large contribution to the piano literature was Virgil Thomson. (Carlos Chávez wrote a great deal of music for keyboard, but since he was Mexican and often emphasized the folk music of his native land, he falls outside the scope of this study.)

Virgil Thomson was as caught up in Parisian musical, artistic, and social life as any of the other Americans, and greatly admired the oh-so-French insouciance of Erik Satie. It is somewhat paradoxical, then that he should have produced such obviously and insistently American music. According to composer and author Ned Rorem, who was his student and knew him well, Thomson did not rely on interesting musical ideas "but on the uses to which dull ideas could be put. Displacing the ordinary, he renders it extraordinary."[10]

As noted earlier, Rorem has said that the difference between French and German music was that the French was profoundly superficial while the German was superficially profound. Like all memorable bons mots this one bears a seed of truth, especially when applied to Satie and his devoted French disciples, the group Les Six. (John Cage, who made a detailed study of the complete oeuvre of Thomson, was himself among Satie's most fervent American admirers.) Thomson, to whom humor was essential in even the most serious literary and musical creation and who detested pretension of any kind, would certainly be included in the French camp when dividing the profoundly superficial from the superficially profound.

The French penchant for humor with serious underpinnings, which is one possible interpretation of "profoundly superficial," coupled with the political disillusionment and cynicism that began to form in Europe during World War I, gave birth to the Dadaist and Surrealist movements. The painters, writers, and composers who promulgated Dadaist and Surrealist ideals—some of the most creative minds of their time—deliberately chose to jettison establishment values in literature and art. Their goal was "the attainment through art of the infinitely irrational."[11] Satie was certainly a Surrealist in many of his works—*Parade,* for example—and Thomson was at least a fellow traveler. Most Americans were shocked and dismayed when they first encountered the paintings of Marcel Duchamp, one of the leaders of the movement, and his disciples, and were unlikely to be subjected to the nonsense poems of Romanian-born Parisian Tristan Tzara, which were written in French. Perhaps because abstract music makes its points more indirectly than either painting or literature, or perhaps because of its references to popular favorites, its apparent simplicity, its brevity and wit, and its accessibility, the music of Thomson and Satie was accepted and admired.

Thomson arrived in France to study with Boulanger only a few months after Copland, too late for the Fontainebleau session, but in time for the 1921–22 season at L'École Normale. This Missouri-born, Harvard-educated Midwesterner, finding himself completely at home in Paris, stayed in France much longer than Copland, returning to the United States for a brief period of study after his time with Boulanger and occasional visits but basically living abroad until Hitler came to power in Germany. Despite this self-imposed exile, or perhaps because of it, Thomson incorporated American vernacular music in most of his works. Indeed, in the words of musicologist Wilfrid Mellers, his compositions presented "a *bric-a-brac* of [American] hymn tunes, band music, rags, and parlor pieces."[12]

Unlike Charles Ives, who also used this sort of material, Thomson did not seek to create impressive aural edifices by means of layering or cumulative structure. Ives could be disingenuous, but one always senses the larger aims of a powerful musical mind controlling disparate elements in his major works. Thomson, equally intellectual, analytic, and technically knowledgeable in his perceptions of music, as his many essays and critiques prove, preferred to present a deceptive naïveté in his compositions.

One of Thomson's principal compositional devices is the fusion of Baroque-style polyphony with twentieth-century dissonance. This may in part be attributed to Boulanger's dual stress on Bach and Stravinsky, but to the listener it certainly seems natural to Thomson. Many of Thomson's 150-plus *Portraits,* brief musical sketches for which the subjects "sat" as though for actual physical likenesses, are in this charming and distinctive style—*Philip Claftin dans les temps très noceur* (Philip Claftin in very licentious times) of 1935, for example. The *Portrait* entitled *Dora Maar in the Presence of Picasso* of 1939 is like a Bach Two-Part Invention with lots of wrong notes; its skittery figuration, first in the right hand and then in the left, dances around a simple tune, but it's anyone's guess which voice is Dora's and which Pablo's.

Most of the *Portraits* are very short—some under a minute—but Thomson evidently took them seriously, as he revised a good number of them in the 1950s and later. They were not all contrapuntal, some being waltzes, tangos, and combinations of pop and jazz. By and large they are delightful, but listening to too many of them at a time is like eating too many sweets—they begin to cloy. The same may be said of his many other short works for piano solo—individually effective, but not substantial enough in the agglomerate. Many of them would make ideal encores.

Thomson had what John Cage has characterized as "a life-long friendship with the waltz."[13] This may seem contradictory in someone so influenced by jazz, which is almost invariably in $\frac{2}{4}$ or $\frac{4}{4}$, but Thomson's broad streak of nostalgia probably explains it. His *Synthetic Waltzes* for piano four-hands is worth looking into for four-hand teams. In a slightly more extended work, the Piano Sonata No. 2 of 1929, we find his familiar two-part polyphony in the first movement, marked *Cantabile*. At first the two voices are as abstract as Bach would have wished, but gradually hints of folk tunes—still in two contrapuntal voices—develop. The second movement, marked *Sostenuto,* continues in the style of the first, but is melodically less interesting. In the third, *Leggiero brilliante,* Bach meets Czerny. In total the sonata lasts a little over seven minutes—no *Hammerklavier* here.

Undoubtedly the most important event in Thomson's Paris sojourn was his 1926 meeting with Gertrude Stein, the American expatriate writer who lived in France most of her adult life. (The Jewish Stein was unwilling to leave her adopted home even in the face of Hitler's extermination squads, and she survived World War II living in the French countryside.) Thomson was introduced to Stein through his friend and countryman George Antheil. (Antheil made much more of an impact in France than he did back home, and so will be discussed in the section on French music). Evidently too timid to meet the formidable Stein by himself but reluctant to turn down an invitation to the art-filled Parisian apartment she shared with Alice B. Toklas, Antheil invited Thomson to come along. The rest, as they say, is history.

Stein's idiosyncratic use of the English language intrigued Thomson, who, with her permission, began to set some of her short works to music. He knew that it would be crucial not to obscure her texts with overly elaborate settings, for it was difficult enough to decipher her prose even when every word was clear. In *Susie Asado, Preciosilla,* and *Capital, Capitals,* three of his Stein songs, he keeps the accompaniment discreetly in the background so the listener can concentrate on the words. Unlike so many settings by Schumann, Fauré, or Debussy, these accompaniments do not make interesting piano pieces in their own right. In light of the extreme modernism of Stein's writing, Thomson's use of Baroque-style polyphony seems, in Cage's words, "outlandishly behind-the-times."[14] Yet this temporal disjunction between text and music is clearly deliberate.

Capital, Capitals is the most extended of the Stein-Thomson songs—some thirty-four pages of music—and may be regarded as preparation for the opera that followed, *Four Saints in Three Acts* (mostly composed in the late 1920s, it premiered in 1934). This opera, and its much later successor *The Mother of Us All* (1947), are undoubtedly Thomson's most famous works. No matter how bizarre Stein's texts—and bizarre they were—Thomson stuck to his simple, semivernacular style, with hymn tunes, street music, patter songs, foxtrots, waltzes, and—of course—Baroque polyphony all taking their turns. Using plagal cadences (iv–I) and *parlando* passages, he rarely veered from diatonic harmonic progressions, leaving advanced chromaticism and serial techniques to others. Like Satie or Poulenc setting Cocteau, Thomson found that simplicity and pastiche/parody were most effective for "difficult" texts.

It has been said that Aaron Copland and Virgil Thomson are the two fathers of American music. Anthony Tommasini credits Copland, Thomson, Paul Bowles, and a few others with the invention of "the distinctive American sound of mid-twentieth-century American music—a Coplandesque tableau of widely spaced harmonies and melancholic tunes run through with elements of elegiac folk music and spiked with perky American rhythms."[15] Although he credits several composers with helping to create this style, Tommasini's use of the term "Coplandesque" acknowledges that composer's central role. Nevertheless, the music of Thomson, while not heard today as often as that of Copland, is in its own way inimitable and indispensable.

6

American Composers in the 1920s, Part II

Charles Tomlinson Griffes, Henry Cowell, Ruth Crawford, George Gershwin

harles Tomlinson Griffes lived and worked just at the cusp of our study, from 1884 to 1920. Despite his quiet life as a teacher at Hackley, a private boys' preparatory school, and his tragically premature death at the age of thirty-five, this New York–born composer had begun to make a serious impression on America's musical world, especially with his major orchestral work, *The Pleasure-Dome of Kubla Khan* (1920).

Griffes pursued his obligatory European studies in Berlin, but in his piano works, which are worthy of much more attention than they get in today's concert halls, the influence of the French Impressionist composers is at least as obvious as that of the German post-Romantics. Most intriguing of all is his last work for solo piano, the Sonata of 1919, in which he seems to have found a truly unique personal voice, at once austere, virtuosic, and dramatic. In this late work the astringency of Stravinsky and the propulsive percussiveness of Prokofiev are mixed with an ecstatic outpouring that is Griffes's own and that makes one mourn for a future that never came.

With the Sonata, which was his first extended work for piano and which Virgil Thomson called "shockingly original," Griffes seems to have sublimated foreign influences into something genuinely new. Ruled by sound and rhythm, the piece—unlike most of Griffes's previous works—suggests no imagery, no extra-musical references. Its virtuosic demands are a formidable challenge to the performer as is its uncompromising modernity to the listener.

The Sonata's three sections, quasi movements, are in the usual fast-slow-fast format, sections one and two played without a pause and section three coming after a brief, notated (that is, timed) break. The first movement opens with a section marked *Feroce*, an almost barbaric, intensely dramatic explosion of sound. The *Andante tranquillo* section which follows allows for quiet lyricism, but the final *Allegro vivace* returns to the motoric propulsiveness of the beginning. This section features an insistent repeated-note theme and extreme dynamic range.

Rather than adopt Schoenberg's twelve-tone scale, Griffes invented one of his own for the Sonata: D, E-flat, F, G-sharp, A, B-flat, C-sharp, D, or half-step, whole-step, step-and-a-half, half, half, step-and-a-half, and a final half step. The interval of one and a half steps occurs only in the so-called harmonic minor, a scale dear to Liszt in his *Hungarian Rhapsodies* and common in all minor-mode music (the raised seventh in the minor scale, which creates the wider interval, is necessary both for the dominant triad and for a sense of arrival at the tonic tone), but the occurrence of two such intervals in one scale is quite original and distinctive. The concomitant three half-step intervals—there are ordinarily only two in either major or minor scales—makes for extreme chromaticism, which is indeed a characteristic of the Sonata.

Griffes's best-known piano solo, although even it is rarely heard today, is *The White Peacock*, the first of his four *Roman Sketches* (Opus 7, 1915–1916). Like almost all of Griffes's works until the Sonata, it is descriptive: as it opens, the listener, without stretching too much, can imagine a proud white peacock slowly spreading its glorious plumage. The piece's asymmetrical rhythms, unusual chords, and highly developed sense of pianistic coloration mark it as far outside the genre of salon music; its abrupt ending without hint of a final cadence is a startling ploy used by the composer in several works. The three other sketches in the group, *Nightfall*, *The Fountain of the Acqua Paola*, and *Clouds*, are equally distinctive: *Nightfall* has very modern harmonic overlappings; *Fountain of the Acqua Paola* is reminiscent of Ravel's *Jeux d'eau* and Liszt's *Fountains at Villa d'Este*, with cascading but often dissonant arpeggiated figures to connote shimmering, glistening water; and *Clouds* floats some beautiful modulations in relative quiet.

It is interesting to trace Griffes's development from his earliest juvenilia to the Sonata. One might begin with the very Chopinesque but very sweet Prelude in B Minor or the equally charming arrangement of the *Barcarolle* from Offenbach's *Tales of Hoffmann*, the latter one of three *Fantasy Pieces* composed from 1912 to 1914. Along the way, in addition to the Impressionistic *Roman Sketches* described above, we find *Three Tone-Pictures* (Opus 5, 1910–1915): *The Lake at Evening*, *The Vale of Dreams*, and *The Night Winds* (1910–1915). These three short pieces are in the composer's most Impressionistic style with lush harmonies. Debussy's prelude from Book 1, *Voiles*, or his song *L'extase* come to mind when listening to *The Vale of Dreams*, and Debussy's third prelude in Book 1, *Le vent dans la plaine*, surely influenced *The Night Winds*. Griffes considered his *De profundis* of 1915 his tribute to Wagner, and in *Winter Landscape* (1912) one can hear the nobility and drama of Wagner and late Liszt.

What is truly remarkable about this trajectory is the rapidity of his development. Considered by many at the time to be America's most promising young composer, Griffes moved from the influence of his training in Germany, where he studied with *Hänsel und Gretel* composer Engelbert

Humperdinck, through the French Impressionism he heard and loved, to a distinctive and personal style in the Sonata. His entire life as a mature composer spanned barely a decade, but the music he wrote in that brief period of time is a unique and valuable contribution to the development of American music.

High on anyone's list of truly original musical creators would certainly be Henry Cowell (1897–1965). Cowell's birth in California may account for his eclectic aural experience, encompassing a wide variety of Asian traditional music, which he added to the Irish folk music he heard through his father and the Midwestern tunes he learned from his mother. From his parents, both of whom were philosophical anarchists, he also learned independence of thought and freedom from preconceived restraints.

Absorbing and appreciating all the disparate forms of musical expression he had heard, Cowell was among the first serious composers to become interested in what is now known as world music, studying the gamelan and other exotic forms of sound production (though Debussy had also been influenced by gamelan music, which he heard at a World's Fair in Paris). Never having felt himself limited to European instrumentation, Cowell sought more effective ways of producing the sounds he wanted to hear, whatever their origin, and developing his own where need be.

Another liberating factor in his development was the fact that Cowell began to compose as a teenager, before he had any formal education, musical or otherwise. He eventually acquired the instruction necessary to become a serious composer and deep thinker, beginning music lessons at the age of sixteen, but his early experiments before he was immersed in the usual conventions gave him the self-confidence to go his own way, no matter what.[1]

Despite his determination to keep himself free of European influences, when he was still quite young Cowell embarked on several European tours (in 1923, 1926, 1929, 1931, and 1932) and one excursion to Cuba (in 1930). In 1929 he accepted an invitation to play in the Soviet Union; he was the first American composer to be so honored. The purpose of these trips was to expose the rest of the world to his works, not to study with European masters. Apparently he was taken more seriously abroad than he was at home, and in Russia he was regarded as "the personification of industrialized America." The Russian reviewer of his Leningrad concerts wrote, "I saw clearly the electric floodlights of Broadway filling the room and the New York skyline hovering above the mist." [2]

As soon as Cowell had access to a piano he began to devise unconventional techniques to play it, hitting groups of notes with fist, forearm, or elbow to produce what he called tone clusters, groups of contiguous notes in no particular key. He introduced this startling innovation, which may be heard in many of his works including *Dynamic Motion* of 1916 and *Tides of*

Manaunaun of the following year, at the San Francisco Musical Society in 1914. He was then seventeen years old.

Dynamic Motion, parts of which sound like either a New York subway train or a serious thunderstorm, begins with abrupt isolated chords separated by long silences. Its tone clusters are allowed to reverberate—another Cowell characteristic—and slowly fade away (Poulenc favored this effect as well). Passages of notes, played in normal fashion with the fingers, introduce jazzy rhythms which then alternate with the chordal sections. Although the piece is short, it has an enormous dynamic range. Obviously allowing many neighboring strings to vibrate simultaneously, especially in the lower registers of the piano, creates tremendous volume, as sympathetic vibrations are activated in all the strings if the dampers are held up by the pedal. According to liner notes of the New Music Association recording of many of Cowell's piano works, taken from live performances at Hertz Hall in Berkeley, California, in January and February 1997, a London critic dubbed Cowell "the loudest pianist in the world" and one can believe it! (Since the prodigiously prolific Cowell composed almost a thousand pieces, this disc provides only a small sample of his output.) Fittingly, the concerts and CD were funded by the Aaron Copland Foundation for Recordings, illustrating how Copland's legendary largesse toward his fellow composers continues after his death.[3]

A subsidiary effect connected to the use of tone clusters and exploited by Cowell is that if one strikes bass notes solidly while depressing keys in an upper register slowly enough so that they don't actually sound, when the lower notes are released, the strings of the upper tones, whose dampers are raised, will vibrate in sympathy with the lower tones, creating an eerie, other-worldly sound. This is not a completely new trick, but it remains difficult to achieve, and pianists are even more at the mercy of their instruments than usual when attempting it.

Cowell's second major innovation for the piano—it was in solo piano music that he made his most significant contribution—was to play directly on the strings, brushing them, plucking them, tapping them, making them resonate in as many ways as he could think of. His best-known use of this technique is in *The Aeolian Harp* (1923), a lovely, tightly controlled three-minute evocation of a breeze setting taut strings in motion. In this piece one can clearly hear the way Cowell uses the effects produced by brushing the strings to color the basically diatonic melody notes. Another short piece illustrative of this effect is *The Banshee,* in which eerie glissandos, formed right on the strings, bring to aural life the ghosts of Cowell's Irish ancestors.

One would expect a lot of noise and cinematic sound effects from these methods of playing—or perhaps one should say using—the piano, and indeed there are plenty of squeaks, howls, and other extra-musical sounds throughout Cowell's oeuvre, but there are also surprisingly charming and subtle results as well. For instance, *What's This?* ends with a questioning note in much the same way "The Pleading Child" in Schumann's *Kinderszenen* concludes. (Is there some special relationship between Cowell and Schumann to be discovered?) *Advertisement* is a sort of neurotic and noisy waltz featuring tone clusters and some frenzied scurrying down the keyboard. *The Fairy Answer* has brushed strings echoing keys hit in the normal way, a spooky but nice effect. The group humorously entitled *Nine Ings* (all the titles are "ing" verbs) includes the rather quiet *Floating*, the furious forty-six-second *Seething*, *Whisking* with its scampering little scale fragments, and the waltzlike *Fleeting*. *Wafting*, which exploits the higher registers of the piano, is almost Romantic, with a quiet beginning followed by a lovely little waltz. Here the pianist feels justified in the use of considerable *rubato* and a limited dynamic range. In most of the "ings," tone-clustered or not, tonality is established well enough so that when a note, especially a final note, is not the normal one in that place for that key, the listener is well aware of the deliberate dislocation (Cowell was not, however, an atonal composer).

Least expected from a composer as avant-garde as Cowell are his versions of Irish folk music such as *Slow Jig* and *High Color* (the latter is the second of a set called *Two Movements*). In both of these pieces, the second of which is rather extended for Cowell—over five minutes in length—the original Irish tunes and the tonic-dominant tonality in which they are usually couched are clearly discernable. *High Color* is in theme-and-variation form. Calling for professional-level virtuosity on the part of the performer, it is exhilarating fun in recognizable Cowell style: with tone clusters and rumbling sound effects, it points out the paradox inherent in this combination of the ultra-new and the really old-fashioned.

Cowell's search for new sounds through which to express modern life led him to experiment with an electronic device called the *rhythmicon*, which could play metrical combinations of virtually unlimited complexity.[4] He was certainly not the only composer of his time to be thinking in terms of technological means of expanding compositional possibilities— the idea was in the air—but his efforts were just a bit premature.

In addition to being a composer and performer, Cowell was an educator. He taught at New York's New School for Social Research and Columbia University and at the Peabody Institute in Baltimore. An articulate spokesperson for modern music, he was the editor of, and one of the principal contributors to, the journal *New Music* from 1927 to 1936. Among his most famous students were John Cage and Lou Harrison, and even George Gershwin was influenced by him. A generation later, American composer George Crumb's setting of the García Lorca poem *Ancient Voices of Children* (1970), in which a boy soprano produces ethereal evocations of wind and sea by singing directly at the strings of an open piano, is clearly indebted to Cowell.

Cowell's theories and opinions are forcefully stated in *American Composers on American Music,* a collection of brief biographical and critical sketches by composers about other composers. Cowell organized and edited the book and wrote several essays for it. First published in 1933 and reissued—unchanged save for a new foreword by Cowell—in 1961, the book features articles by Copland, Roy Harris, Charles Seeger, Gershwin, and a half-dozen other lesser-known composers.

In his introductory chapter to the book Cowell divides the then-current crop of composers into those who were traditional, that is, either French or German oriented, versus those who were more American in style, inspiration, substance, and focus. His judgments are often surprising, as when he lists Copland in the former group, quite arbitrarily dismissing him as unoriginal even though Copland had already written his Symphony for Orchestra and Organ, *Music for the Theatre, Vitebsk Trio,* Piano Concerto, and Piano Variations. Cowell asserts that "[Copland makes] no attempt to develop original ideas or materials [and] uses jazz themes and rhythms in music which is otherwise French."[5] Cowell, as one would expect, is far kinder in his essay on Mexican composer Carlos Chávez, although he was certainly not unaware of the latter's limitations. Cowell's comments on Chávez are at least as valuable a clue to his own compositional point of view as they are for the work of his ostensible subject: "He is modern because he uses his composer's gifts for the expression of objective beauty of universal significance rather than as a mere means of self-expression."[6]

Among Cowell's bêtes noires seems to have been George Antheil, to whom he devotes several paragraphs of invective, stating that "Antheil's real talent is in discovering very quickly what the latest trend is, and imitating it immediately, exaggerating it if possible."[7] He agrees with Gershwin that jazz is a viable source for American concert music, but is dubious about Gershwin's use of it. He claims that "George Gershwin is the greatest master of real jazz . . . but puts it into typically European, sentimental style, mixing Liszt, Puccini, Stravinsky and Wagner when he tries to write classical music."[8] Most interesting is Cowell's attitude toward nationalism in music, especially since he was apparently an ardent promoter of the American composer as such:

> Nationalism in music has no purpose as an aim in itself. Music happily transcends political and racial boundaries. . . . [Many believed that] in time one single musical style would develop to represent all of us. . . . I have never believed that any one individual could speak for an entire continent. . . . [I]t seemed to me that to be American was to honor differences, and to welcome the experimental, the fresh and the new.[9]

"Self-conscious nationalism," he went on to say, would be necessary in America only until works worthy of international respect were composed;

then it could wither away. Cowell's crystal ball may have had its cloudy spots, but when one considers the international style of composition that generally prevails today, one must admit he had a rather clear vision of the future.

The only woman to attract Cowell's critical attention in *American Composers on American Music* was Ruth Crawford (1901–1953), or Ruth Crawford Seeger as she chose to call herself after her marriage to pedagogue and folk-song collector/publisher Charles Seeger. In the early 1920s Crawford wrote some very charming keyboard works—*Little Waltz, Little Lullaby, Jumping the Rope, Mr. Crow and Miss Wren Go For a Walk,* among others—for children. Lasting only a minute or two each, these pieces are bright, gay, and, while still completely traditional, early manifestations of a delightful musical personality. Although not without some technical hurdles, they would make wonderful teaching pieces. In 1923 Crawford wrote a sonata, but even in this piece her ambitions were limited: despite its big, spacious opening and a lovely lyric section, the entire sonata lasts but a little under six minutes and never stretches the boundaries of traditional harmony.

Then, apparently all of a sudden, Crawford began to write avant-garde works of strength, passion, and individuality. First, in 1924, came *Five Canons,* probably student exercises in contrapuntal writing, but tremendously effective nevertheless. The *Canons* were followed by a series of piano preludes, first a set of five and then an additional group of four, which appeared from 1924 to 1928. The first prelude is dark, moody, melancholic. The second is livelier and more virtuosic, but not really gay; despite its mere two-minute length, it is full of variety. Like many of the others it is in ABA form. The third prelude has the gentle rocking rhythm of a lullaby (did David Amram have this piece in mind when he wrote the second movement of his own sonata some forty years later?), while the fourth has a *Tristan*-like theme. The last of this set has ambiguous repeated chords in the bass with a constantly moving melodic line far above it.

Preludes six through nine, which were published in 1928 in Cowell's *Musical Quarterly* (the first set remained unpublished until 1993), are equally evocative. Critics have traced the musical influence of Skryabin and the spiritual underpinnings of Chinese philosophy in them, in particular the *Tao te Ching* by Lao-tzu which inspired the ninth. Indeed, this ninth prelude is the most mysterious of them all, with sections of celestial registration for the right hand over *pianissississimo* dyads way down in the bass and a gulf between. The dissonant harmonies, changing meters, and irregular rhythms of these preludes place Crawford at the cutting edge of twentieth-century composition.

Crawford wrote a few other compositions involving piano in the second half of the decade: *The Adventures of Tom Thumb,* which requires a narrator as well as a pianist, appeared in 1925; *We Dance Together,* a forty-two-second charmer, in 1926; and the difficult, three-part *Piano Study in Mixed Accents* in 1930, but with the preludes her major contribution to the keyboard literature ceased. In fact, after composing a string quartet in 1931, Crawford stopped composing in any serious way. She was at the height of her creative powers, and it is not known why she chose to stop at this time. None of her keyboard compositions is very long, and her entire output for piano, including the twelve-minute *Tom Thumb* cycle, can be heard on one CD, a 2001 release by Bis Records (1310-B15) featuring pianist Jenny Lin.

Literature professors are fond of saying, with a rueful smile, that the reason controversies over theories of literary criticism rage so fiercely is that there is so little at stake. Perhaps the same might be said of the battles, which even now refuse to subside, over the music of George Gershwin (1898–1937). Are the pieces he wrote for the concert hall classical? Does the *Rhapsody in Blue* have real blues in it? Are his hundreds of songs in any sense jazz, and if not, why do jazz musicians love to play them? No matter what their quality, are these songs "just" pop?

Richard Crawford, author of *America's Musical Life,* an exhaustive study of music in this country from earliest colonial days to the present time, chooses to divide music into composer-oriented and performer-oriented compositions rather than classical and popular, deliberately implying no value judgments. By "composer music" Crawford means compositions intended to be played note for note as written (differences in interpretation are considered inevitable and usually desirable), while in "performer music" the interpreter is free to change the actual notes to suit his or her tastes and purposes. There are borderline cases, as when vernacular composers or performers "borrow" bits of Rachmaninoff, Chopin, or others to create pop pieces, thus turning composer music into performer music, but this fairly common practice does not—or should not—change the listener's perception of the original works. Although there are several published versions of *Rhapsody in Blue*—for piano and orchestra, piano and band, piano solo, two pianos—it and Gershwin's other concert pieces are generally played as scored. But what about the many songs in which Gershwin very carefully wrote out piano accompaniments with the harmonies and rhythms he thought best suited to his melodies? Jazz and popular singers and instrumentalists have always felt entitled to do with these tunes whatever they wish, even though in some cases Gershwin himself made solo piano concert arrangements.

As far as the dichotomy of classical and popular, Gershwin would have none of it. Even after *Rhapsody in Blue* (1924), *Concerto in F* (1925), the three Piano Preludes (1926), *An American in Paris* (1928), and *Porgy and Bess* (1935) had made him famous—and rich—as a "classical" composer, he continued to write songs for Tin Pan Alley and the Broadway theater.

Much like Schubert, he was first and foremost a melodist, and the melodies kept pouring out.

And, like Schubert, Gershwin was an innovative song composer. Compared to the other Tin Pan Alley and theater songwriters of the day, Gershwin's pieces showed remarkable emotional intensity. His unexpected modulations—he would often leap from one key to another—enriched the tonic-dominant landscape he and the others writers of popular music inhabited. (Debussy, Schoenberg, Bartók, Stravinsky, and others had already gone beyond the confines of the tonic-dominant system, but few vernacular creators ventured so far afield.) His rhythms were obviously innovative, especially but certainly not exclusively in such songs as *I Got Rhythm* and *Fascinating Rhythm*. He could be flexible yet driving, relaxed yet pulsating, complex yet immediately understandable.

The common thread in all Gershwin's compositions is memorable, original, attractive, and singable tunes. Defenders of Gershwin's classical credentials have taken great pains to counter the accusation that the *Rhapsody in Blue*, for instance, is "nothing more" than three or four wonderful Gershwin tunes strung together. Similar canards have been hurled at Schubert's piano sonatas, but in that case, whether the indictment is true or false, no one today would deny their composer an honored place in the roster of serious classical composers. It is easy to forget that in his lifetime many regarded Schubert as a lightweight tunesmith, and no one was interested in performing his major symphonic works.

For every critic who would deny Gershwin's concert pieces the status of "classical," an opposite and equal number would strip him of his jazz license. Many Gershwin songs are punchy marches (*Swanee, Strike Up the Band, Of Thee I Sing*); some of his slower romantic ballads and arias also begin on the downbeat (*Summertime* and *Bess You Is My Woman* from *Porgy and Bess*) as do a fair number of up-tempo "swing" pieces (*Nice Work if You Can Get It; Oh, Lady, Be Good!*). Even these melodies usually have blatant or implied inner syncopations, easily and happily exploited by jazz performers. The melodies most often cited as Gershwin's connection to jazz, however, are those based on a syncopation that begins with the opening statement and continues to characterize the piece or section. In this category are *I Got Rhythm, Fascinating Rhythm, Somebody Loves Me, Embraceable You,* and all but the slow theme, the *Andantino moderato* section, of *Rhapsody in Blue*.

Another characteristic of jazz found in much of Gershwin is the use of a repeated melodic note under which the harmonies change in variable patterns (the bridge section of *Oh, Lady, Be Good!* for example). The repetition of less static melodic phrases is another jazz-based way often chosen by Gershwin to allow harmonic changes under unchanging melodic lines (*'S Wonderful* and the "blues" theme of the slow movement of the *Concerto in F* come to mind). Above all is the rhythmic drive—so full of energy, so American—found everywhere in his music.

And just how "blue" is the *Rhapsody?* In this work, in the second of the *Three Piano Preludes,* in the slow movement of the *Concerto in F,* and in many of his songs, Gershwin features flatted thirds and sevenths within major scales, a typical blues device. He also brilliantly conveys the slow swinging "wail of a down-hearted frail" (to quote a snatch of the lyrics of W. C. Handy's *St. Louis Blues*) in both songs and abstract compositions.

For those who insist on a narrow definition of jazz, only the improvised creations of African Americans can be authentic; the most generous concession they will make is that Gershwin's music *evokes* jazz and the blues. Judging from the nearly universal appreciation of his music—he is undoubtedly the best-known composer America has produced—the public has chosen to ignore the taxonomic nitpicking of the experts. Audiences like to listen to Gershwin's concert music *and* his songs, many of which—after almost three-quarters of a century—are still part of the popular idiom. Beginning his musical career as a promoter of Tin Pan Alley songs—his own as well as those of other composers—Gershwin's primary goal had always been to please the listener. His dependence on and respect for popular taste coupled with his desire to create music of lasting value produced a unique amalgam of the accessible and the thought provoking.

The generally accepted story of the genesis of *Rhapsody in Blue* is only partially true. Yes, Paul Whiteman asked Gershwin to write it for a concert that would show that "the new rhythmically vivacious dance music called jazz . . . was elevated by the symphonic arrangements in which Whiteman's band specialized,"[10] and yes, Gershwin tossed it off in a matter of weeks. It is also true that before the *Rhapsody*, Gershwin's fame was based on his Tin Pan Alley and theater songs, but this wildly successful concert piece was hardly the work of an intuitive but naive beginner. In 1919 Gershwin began to study harmony, counterpoint, orchestration, and musical form with Edward Kilenyi (1884–1968), a minor figure in New York's musical life whose main claim to fame was that Gershwin had been his student. They continued to work together for two years, during which time, perhaps as an assignment from his teacher, Gershwin wrote a *Lullaby* for string quartet. *Lullaby* is occasionally heard today despite its being not entirely successful, and it is interesting as a precursor of his more important works. Gershwin's next excursion into extended musical forms was a one-act, twenty-five minute opera called *Blue Monday*. Gershwin wrote all the music for the *George White Scandals* series from 1920 to 1924, composing *Blue Monday* for the 1924 season. (The opera failed to please, however, and was dropped after one performance.) At least one of his other contributions to the 1924 musical revue—*Somebody Loves Me*—fared much better than the opera and remains in the popular canon. That same year Gershwin wrote the entire score for the show *Lady, Be Good!* with its inimitable hit *Fascinating Rhythm*, and, of course, the *Rhapsody*.

Obviously, between the *George White Scandals* and *Lady, Be Good!* Gershwin was a pretty busy fellow, but when the call came from Paul Whiteman, the most successful white dance-band leader in New York, asking for an extended piece for his upcoming Aeolian Hall concert, the composer immediately accepted. Whiteman—"Pops" to musicians and "the King of Jazz" to the public—was not a jazz musician himself, but he knew the bona fide practitioners of the art and felt free to use their talents. Since segregation in performing groups was the de facto rule of the day, he could not hire African Americans to play in his orchestra, but such jazz composers as Fletcher Henderson often made arrangements for him.[11]

The concert, which took place on February 12, 1924, was billed as "An Experiment in Modern Music." It was not the first time jazz or jazz-based dance music had been presented in a concert-hall setting. James Reese Europe, founder of the Harlem Hellfighters Band and leader of the Clef Club Orchestra, had presented "Concerts of Negro Music" in Carnegie Hall in 1912, 1913, and 1914, and a singer named Eva Gauthier had given a program of operatic arias, art songs, and well-known pop tunes (*Swanee, Alexander's Ragtime Band, I'll Build a Stairway to Paradise*) in Aeolian Hall in November 1923. Gershwin himself accompanied Mme Gauthier in the pop half of the program.[12]

Whiteman's purpose in organizing and presenting the concert was self-serving, to demonstrate how his orchestra and its arrangements "elevated" the new dance music to concert status. The program was, to say the least, eclectic with several of Whiteman's own recorded "jazzed classics" such as *Avalon,* which was based on an aria from Puccini's *Tosca,* and *The Dance of the Hours* ballet from Ponchielli's *La Gioconda,* the two most familiar works of this genre. MacDowell's beloved *To a Wild Rose,* semi-symphonic arrangements of such old jazz standards as *Livery Stable Blues* and *Limehouse Blues,* some Irving Berlin songs, and "novelty" numbers like *Kitten on the Keys* were also cheerfully juxtaposed. Aside from the *Rhapsody,* the most extended work on the program was a *Suite of Serenades,* each in the style of a different country, by operetta composer Victor Herbert.[13]

The *Rhapsody in Blue* was the penultimate of the concert's twenty-four selections, the eleven o'clock number in pop parlance. Its effect, after the hodge-podge that preceded it, was understandably electrifying. The famous clarinet glissando with which the piece begins was only partly created by Gershwin; he had originally written a normal ascending scale for B-flat clarinet, but in rehearsal one day the clarinetist, more or less fooling around, played a glissando instead. Gershwin loved the effect, and so it became standard, leaving the pianists who play the solo version with an impossible task of attempting a glissando on the keyboard by combining black and white notes. Although Gershwin had sketched in his harmonies and rhythms for the orchestra, it was Ferde Grofé, one of Whiteman's regular arrangers and later a popular composer, who completed the orchestral score.

The *Rhapsody* is an effective and entertaining composition with its own niche in the literature. It is not, however, as some would have it, the first composition to combine jazz elements and concert-hall aims. As early as 1919 French composer Darius Milhaud had written several works for jazz band, including *Le tango des Frattellini* and *Le boeuf sur le toit*. These trail-blazing pieces were followed in 1923 by *La création du monde*. Both *Le boeuf* and *La création* were used as ballet scores by Jean Cocteau, and Gershwin most certainly was aware of them. He was also well acquainted with the brilliant orchestral scoring of Maurice Ravel, whose *Shéhérazade* and *Rapsodie espagnole* were composed in 1903 and 1907, respectively. (It is said that Gershwin wanted to study orchestration and composition either with Ravel or with Nadia Boulanger, both of whom evidently felt that with his peculiar gifts he was better left alone.)

Gershwin's next concert-hall compositions, the *Three Piano Preludes*, are as sure-fire audience pleasers as the *Rhapsody*. Lasting little more than six minutes in all, they are in the usual fast-slow-fast format. The first is bold and brassy, with big chords, leaps, and—of course—syncopation. It ends with a delicate fade-away scale in fourths followed by a crashing B-flat chord and final root note. (Gershwin is nothing if not tonal!) The second Prelude is a gentle, languid blues whose melodic outlines are similar to those of many Gershwin songs. It has a fade-out arpeggio that ends with a mild dissonance against the final C-sharp tonic note. The last of the three, as has been pointed out, is a sister to Debussy's *Golliwogg's Cake-walk*—the same key (E-flat), same rhythms, same chord combinations. It is nevertheless completely, idiomatically American.

Gershwin composed concert arrangements for solo piano of several of his songs. Quite virtuosic and rhythmically very interesting, they have nevertheless not found the concert-hall acceptance granted the *Preludes* or the *Rhapsody*. This is true as well of his 1932 arrangement for piano and orchestra of *I Got Rhythm*. The *Concerto in F* is the most extended and technically skilled "serious" work by Gershwin featuring the piano (his 1935 opera, *Porgy and Bess*, is usually regarded as his major serious work). Obviously his experience writing the *Rhapsody* and his pre- and post-*Rhapsody* studies with Rubin Goldmark, Wallingford Riegger, and Cowell had honed his abilities in structure and orchestration. The concerto had been commissioned by Walter Damrosch, conductor of the New York Symphony Orchestra, which gave it its premiere in Carnegie Hall in 1925. More admired by classical critics than Gershwin's previous efforts, the *Concerto in F* is no less full of typical Gershwinisms—jazzy syncopations, blue notes, and that combination of the casual and the energetic that makes it sound so American. Damrosch felt that, with this work, Gershwin had accomplished the miracle of bringing "Lady Jazz" to the level of acceptance by musical circles. He "dressed her up in concert garb without detracting from her personality," said Damrosch.[14] The Concerto is also replete with the conservative characteristics that have been cited as criticisms of all Gershwin's concert works: reliance on tonic-dominant harmony, symmetry of phrasing, and melodic repetition. None of these "faults" seems too dire in the light of the acceptance of minimalism and neo-Romanticism that has occurred in recent decades.

Gershwin wrote very few analytical or critical essays, so the brief paragraphs he contributed to *American Composers on American Music* are worth quoting. Giving his definition of folk music, which he felt was the true foundation of art music, he said,

> Jazz, ragtime, Negro spirituals and blues, Southern mountain songs, country fiddling and cowboy songs can all be employed in the creation of American art music. . . . Jazz I regard as an American folk-music, not the only one, but a very powerful one which is probably in the blood and feeling of the American people more than any other style of folk-music. . . . I believe it can be made the basis of serious symphonic works of lasting value, in the hands of a composer with talent for both jazz and symphonic music.[15]

On the other hand, Gershwin, in *The Composer in the Machine Age*, an article written in 1930, said, "An entire composition written in jazz could not live."[16] Gershwin resolved this apparent contradiction to his own, and many listeners', satisfaction.

To contemporary critic David Ewen, Gershwin's music was "the voice of the frenetic and convention-shattering 1920s."[17] By the time he was thirty years old, Gershwin was, according to *The Grove Dictionary of Music and Musicians*, "America's most famous and widely accepted composer of concert music."[18] It is doubtful that anyone since has usurped that position.

The Harlem Renaissance

The end of World War I saw a burst of creativity in the arts and sciences all over the Western world, and the United States participated fully in that surge of individual achievement. Poets Ezra Pound and Vachel Lindsay; novelists F. Scott Fitzgerald, Edith Wharton, Ernest Hemingway, and Sinclair Lewis; playwrights Eugene O'Neill and Maxwell Anderson—to name only some of the most famous—were responsible for an unprecedented flowering of American letters. Advances in the treatment of such ailments as yellow fever and improvements in methods of surgery brought Nobel Prizes to American medical pioneers, and the invention of the submachine gun (the Tommy gun) by John Thompson, a retired U.S. army officer, proved American technical know-how. While truly adventurous painting and sculpture were still a largely European, or more specifically Parisian, undertaking, Jerome Kern, Irving Berlin, Cole Porter, and George Gershwin were creating a genre most congenial to the American psyche, the musical comedy. At the same time "serious" composers like Gershwin, Charles Ives, Henry Cowell, Aaron Copland, and the others we have already discussed were making American concert music a distinctive and respected art form.

All of the above-named artists were part of the mainstream white culture, but during the decades of their great successes a parallel artistic awakening with similar brilliant achievements was occurring in Harlem, a section of northern New York City with a name reminiscent of the city's former Dutch owners. These enormously productive years—from 1920 until a few years after the 1929 stock market crash—became known as the Harlem Renaissance.

Many factors combined to create the Harlem Renaissance. First was the Great Migration, a voluntary relocation of hundreds of thousands of Southern, rural blacks to such Northern and Western cities as Chicago, Philadelphia, Detroit, and above all New York. This mass exodus was prompted in part by hideous, and in some Southern states legally permissible, lynchings and other forms of brutality. Even where such violence was not condoned, widespread Jim Crow laws and customs confined most

Southern blacks to second-class citizenship. In addition, better job opportunities began to lure African Americans northward and westward.

One can trace the beginnings of the Great Migration to the Reconstruction Era, which followed the Civil War. Starting as a slow trickle and
gradually gathering momentum, the migration was vastly accelerated by
the armaments buildup leading up to and during the United States' participation in World War I, which brought a sudden increase in the number
of factory jobs up North just when there were fewer white men to fill them.
This situation forced integration in many previously segregated Northern
plants. For this reason, the years 1915 to 1920 saw the greatest swell in the
migratory movement.

New York City was the natural destination for many in the Great Migration. There had always been, from its founding, a black presence in the
city, and by 1910 there were 95,000 African Americans in the five bor-
oughs.[1] The majority of these men and women were, of course, just plain
folk, but a considerable number who had been attracted by the black
theater and the incipient recording and publishing industries were professional performers and writers. This vibrant nucleus naturally attracted
others similarly inclined, and New York became a magnet for the African
American elite.

As Manhattan became more and more densely populated, the borough's
population spread northward. For a while the area around West 53rd
Street was the hub of African American activity, but constantly rising real
estate values forced the less affluent communities to relocate, and there
was really only one direction in which to go. By 1923 the African American
population of Harlem numbered somewhere between 180,000 (the figure
arrived at by the federal census) and 300,000 (Information Bureau of the
United Hospital Fund).[2] Whatever the correct figure, clearly Harlem had
become the black capital of America.

The achievements of Harlem Renaissance writers, painters, and musicians are the most visible manifestations of that fertile period, but there
were also serious political and philosophical underpinnings that deserve
attention. The principal question debated by such thinkers as James
Weldon Johnson, W. E. B. DuBois, and Alain Locke was how militant or
conciliatory the African American community should be regarding civil
rights. Could the community at large, if it spoke in a unified voice, wield
enough political power to make a difference in legal and de facto segregation? A concomitant issue was the formation of a black identity that would
lead to self-awareness and self-esteem. Pamphlets, magazines, and newslet-
ters were written and published in an effort to make the average Harlem
resident, as well as blacks throughout the country, active participants in
these debates. As we now know, these early efforts were not terribly successful, and it was not until the Civil Rights movement of the 1960s that many
of the goals espoused by Harlem Renaissance thinkers were achieved.

Among the prominent black writers of the period three names stand out: poets Langston Hughes (called "the dean of Negro writers") and Countee Cullen, and novelist Zora Neale Hurston, all of whose works are still in print and widely read. The outstanding painters of the era were Romare Bearden and Horace Pippin, both of whom chronicled the black experience in vivid detail. But, of course, it was the musicians—the jazz musicians—whose genius made the era what it was in Harlem.

With the exception of Langston Hughes black intellectuals tended to disdain jazz as a genre. They conceded only that it was a form of folk music that might at some future time inspire a "serious" composer to create great symphonic or operatic works in the European tradition. Jazz was a possible source of art, but not art in itself.[3] They focused their musical hopes on William Grant Still (1895–1978), who, like them, felt that the task of the "New Negro" was to prove the black person's right to respect by creating works that would measure up to those produced by their white counterparts.[4] As historian Nathan Huggins explains, America in general felt provincial vis-à-vis European art, and the African American community felt itself a province within that province.[5]

If Hughes was the dean of black writers, Still was the dean of black composers, producing eight operas, several ballets, many orchestral suites, tone poems and symphonies, and choral and chamber works over a long career. He was equally at home in the worlds of pop and jazz, working with "father of the blues" W. C. Handy on the arrangements of some of Handy's most famous blues (*Beale Street Blues* and *St. Louis Blues* among others) and playing oboe in the orchestra of the Noble Sissle–Eubie Blake hit show *Shuffle Along*. He prepared special arrangements for Sophie Tucker, Paul Whiteman, Artie Shaw, and Donald Voorhees, and—after moving to California in 1934—wrote music for the movies.

Still boasted many "firsts" in his career: the first black composer to have a symphony performed by a major orchestra, the first black composer to have an opera produced by a major white company (City Opera in New York City), the first black composer to receive a string of important commissions (CBS, the World's Fair, the League of Composers), the first black man to conduct a white radio orchestra, and so forth. His successes continued long after the Harlem Renaissance had faded into the past, but his mind-set remained very much that of the intellectual and creative African American of that period. He wanted to—and did—play in what had been the white man's turf, that of the concert hall and opera house, thereby changing the perception held by so many of the capabilities of his people.

The first composition by Still to break into the highest echelons of the world of classical music was his *Afro-American Symphony,* which received its premiere in 1931 under the baton of well-known white conductor Howard Hanson with the Rochester Symphony Orchestra. This piece, his most famous, remained in many orchestra repertoires through the 1940s and 1950s. Like so many of Still's works, its primary source of inspiration was the blues, which Still felt to be more indigenous to African Americans than spirituals. As the titles of this symphony and so many other Still compositions will attest, the composer never denied or tried to hide his black identity. The names of the symphonic poem *Darker America* (1924), the orchestral works *From the Black Belt* (1926) and *Africa* (1928), and his later *And They Lynched Him from a Tree* (1940) for chorus and orchestra bear testament to his involvement with the political and sociological difficulties facing the black community in America.

Still played several instruments, and his main talent seems to have been orchestral color and effects. Not having studied the piano, he did not find writing for keyboard as natural as writing for orchestra, but in the 1930s, deeply in love with the pianist Verna Arvey—who became his second wife—he did compose a small body of short piano pieces. As Albert Dominguez, the pianist who in 1987 recorded these pieces for the William G. Still label, writes in his program notes, "These piano pieces are rather like love notes scrawled in the margin of his talent."[6]

The most effective of these little pieces—none lasts more than about five minutes—is *The Blues,* an arrangement by the composer of the first movement of his ballet *Lenox Avenue.* There is an infectious swing to the rhythms Still uses here, especially the thoroughly pianistic languidly moving boogie bass. While not terribly innovative or original, all these pieces succeed in conveying the moods suggested by their titles, although like those of Mendelssohn's *Songs without Words* or Debussy's *Préludes,* the titles came after the composing was done. For example, the first of the *Three Visions, Dark Horsemen,* does have an apocalyptic fury to it, while *Mystic Pool,* the second of the *Seven Traceries,* is quietly contemplative. Throughout the piece, one finds interesting chord combinations and progressions and more than a hint of modality. Many influences can be traced—from Native American music (*Summerland,* the second of the *Three Visions*), "kitten-on-the-keys" type novelty pieces (*Quit Dat Fool'nish*), and Impressionism's concentration on atmosphere (*Cloud Cradles, Seven Traceries* no. 1).

In the opinions of historian Huggins and poet Hughes, despite Still's undeniable contributions to both the symphonic literature and the hopes of Harlem Renaissance leaders intent on forging the "New Negro," the freely improvised efforts of the jazz musicians of the era were far more important. Hughes, without worrying about its status in relation to classical music, loved to listen to jazz and sensed the genius of its practitioners.[7]

Huggins, whose 1971 *Harlem Renaissance* looked back after almost a half-century of appraisals and reappraisals, felt that the "serious" art created by African Americans during the Harlem Renaissance—the literature, painting, and concert music—was hamstrung by the desire to measure up to or surpass standards created by white culture. Describing in considerable detail many of the best-known Harlem Renaissance novels and poems, he finds little originality even where the subject matter—the black experience—is new. For him, the creators of jazz, who did not have to worry about comparisons with European or white American predecessors, and who found white musicians coming to them for inspiration and instruction, were the only free, and therefore the only truly innovative, artists of the period.[8]

Whether or not one accepts Huggins's evaluation of the other Harlem Renaissance artistic creations—there is, after all, still much interest in the writing of Hughes, Hurston, and Cullen as well as in the paintings of Pippin and Bearden, and as recently as the 1990s there has been a spate of performances of Still's works—one cannot deny the power and excitement of 1920s jazz. Innovative improvisatory music making was going on in black communities all over the United States, and New York was the primary venue in which to play it and hear it. This was especially true in the realm of piano playing, where a virtuosic kind of "stride" piano became known as the *New York style*.

Stride piano evolved from ragtime. Like its precursor, the newer genre consisted largely of four steady bass notes to a bar, the first and third separated by two or even three octaves from the usually unstressed second and fourth. Standard stress relationships in a $\frac{4}{4}$ measure require the heaviest accent on the first beat, a less heavy but still decisive accent on the third, and lighter second and fourth beats. The first and third beats were usually single notes or octaves (root notes), while the unstressed second and fourth beats were usually chords. Above this regular left-hand pattern, highly imaginative right-hand figurations, full of syncopations and pianistic flourishes, were played.

The main differences between stride and ragtime were the degree of virtuosity demanded by the latter, the speed at which it was usually played (ragtime tended to be on the *moderato* side), the complexity of its figurations, the frequent polyrhythms set up between the two hands, and the fact that stride was basically improvisational while ragtime was notated. To watch a stride pianist's left hand insouciantly leaping from one position to another while playing the most difficult figures in the right—often while smoking a cigar or beating a counter-rhythm with his feet (Jelly Roll Morton's specialty)—is a mesmerizing experience, especially when one realizes that all this dazzling music is being created on the spot.

Stride pianists often got their on-the-job training by playing at "rent parties." Even in the glory days of the Harlem Renaissance many residents had trouble finding rent money month after month, so the tradition of rent parties sprang up. A pianist would be hired for a minimal amount, the host and hostess would prepare some simple food, and friends and neighbors would pay a small amount of money to enjoy the evening. It is interesting that even people living so close to the edge of financial instability had pianos in their homes! Part of the rent-party scene was the "cutting contest," an informal competition in which Harlem pianists would try to best one another's efforts. The only prize—and only criterion—was the appreciation of the listeners. These were far from solemn occasions; the guests were drinking, eating, and dancing, but they were also listening, and they knew what they were hearing.

Acknowledged star of the first generation of stride pianists was James P. Johnson (1891–1955). This seminal figure devised countless variations on the standard "oom-pah" ragtime rhythm by occasionally accenting the ordinarily weak beats in the left hand while the right hand continued its habitual syncopations. This complex rhythmic shifting, with its double syncopations, was hard enough to duplicate much less to beat, and Johnson was king of the cutting contests. Particularly admired and imitated by other Harlem pianists was Johnson's version of *Carolina Shout* (his signature piece), which Duke Ellington and others notated from the piano roll and learned note for note.[9]

Johnson was the first stride pianist to make piano rolls, beginning in 1916. He then (1921) went on to record many of his hit numbers, some of which are available in reference collections (the complete Blue Note sessions have been released on the Mosaic Records label). It is easy to see what made other pianists gasp when listening to J. P. His crystal-clear technique, with complete independence of the two hands, effortless double thirds (would that we could hear him rip through Chopin's double-third etude—it would have been child's play for him!), and brilliant scales and complex figurations, all delivered with an almost insolent up-tempo insouciance, make one chortle with pleasure. His renditions of blues numbers tend to be slow and sexy—eliciting another sort of pleasure—with lots of tremolos in the right hand to fill ends of melodic phrases. His enormous inventiveness is proved by the different takes on record of the same tune—he seems never to have done anything in exactly the same way twice. Along with *Carolina Shout, Scouting Around, Snowy Morning Blues, Mule Walk Stomp, Arkansas Blues, Caprice Rag*, and *Improvisation on Pinetop's Boogie Woogie* continue to astound. Like most of the Harlem stride pianists, Johnson was a trained musician. He wrote an opera, *De Organizer*, with Hughes as librettist, and a string quartet, now lost, called *Spirit of America*.

Of course, a stride style like that of Johnson's did not suddenly materialize without predecessors who bridged the chasm between his playing and that of straight ragtime performers like Scott Joplin. The two best known of these precursors are Charles Luckeyeth "Lucky" Roberts (1890–1968) and James Hubert "Eubie" Blake (1883–1983). Lucky, as well as being a superb pianist (he played in Carnegie Hall in 1939),[10] was an elegant composer; his *Moonlight Cocktail*, for instance, is an urbane, sophisticated song still in the repertoire of cabaret singers. Johnson, Lucky, Eubie, Willie "the Lion" Smith, Fats Waller, Duke Ellington—they all knew one another and interacted on many planes, from rent-party cutting contests to the vibrant black theater scene on Broadway. As mentioned above, William Grant Still played in the orchestra of Eubie Blake and Noble Sissle's *Shuffle Along* (1921); Duke Ellington wrote a musical *Portrait of the Lion* as a tribute to Willie; Fats Waller (1904–1943) collaborated with J. P. Johnson on a less successful sequel to *Shuffle Along* called *Keep Shufflin'* (1928) as well as writing his own inimitable *Ain't Misbehavin'*. The profusion of African American musicals in New York, while outside our purview, was a vital component of the Harlem Renaissance.

With Johnson as a mentor—either live or through his records—just about all the Harlem pianists played at least some stride. In an effort to distinguish themselves from the rest, they often developed identifying idiosyncrasies: Willie "The Lion" Smith—the nickname referred to his legendary heroism while fighting in France during World War I—sat sideways at the piano so that he could more easily chat with his listeners while playing;[11] Fats (Thomas Wright) Waller was known for telling jokes while he played; Jelly Roll Morton, né Ferdinand Joseph Lamothe, (1891–1941), specialized in beating time with his foot loud enough to suggest a rhythm section. Morton was only sporadically part of the New York scene, but he was too interesting a character and pianist to go unmentioned. To the annoyance of other jazz artists he credited himself with single-handedly (or perhaps double-handedly under the circumstances) creating jazz out of ragtime, blues, and spirituals, and played in all styles from Dixieland to boogie-woogie. He was equally peripatetic, living for many years in his native New Orleans, working in New York in the 1910s, moving to California, and then shuttling back and forth between the two coasts. Never completely abandoning the freely improvised style of early New Orleans jazz, Jelly Roll began to sound old-fashioned when the more structured work of swing-oriented musicians became popular. For this reason he unfortunately outlived his success.

There was obviously much more to these pianists than amusing shticks. In a recording called *Fats Waller and His Buddies,* we hear intricate piano riffs both as solos and within the ensemble. *Minor Rag,* for instance, has brilliantly executed Johnson-inspired cross-rhythms and a strangely abrupt ending—it just stops short. This was characteristic of Waller and others—Jelly Roll liked the sudden stop as well; Roy Harris attributed this avoidance of final cadences and obvious closures to a "national aversion to anything final."[12] *Harlem Rag* has a strong boogie-woogie bass below end-of-phrase-filling tremolos, while *Lookin' Good while Feelin' Bad* has comical vocal effects, undoubtedly contributed by the band members themselves. *Willow Tree,* recorded with the Louisiana Sugar Babes, shifts from major to minor modality at a relaxed tempo, while Waller does his glittering riffs in the higher registers of the keyboard. *Please Take Me Out of Jail* is an amusing romp in the inimitable Waller style.

Waller studied piano with J. P. Johnson and exhibits many of the same stylistic devices. His playing does, however, tend to be a bit smoother with fewer improvised variations. Like Johnson, Waller was a trained musician; *London Suite* for solo piano, one of his extended concert pieces, includes movements that depict Piccadilly, Chelsea, Soho, Bond Street, Limehouse, and Whitechapel. Waller was also a virtuoso on the organ and played that un-jazzlike instrument in many arrangements. *Thou Swell,* for instance, features organ as well as piano in both takes, which differ quite a bit from one another, and *Fats Waller Stomp* uses organ as the only keyboard instrument. As is obvious from the last-named piece, Waller, like so many of the Harlem pianists, often used popular tunes for their jazz interpretations, causing some dismay among purists.

Count Basie, Earl "Fatha" Hines, Fletcher Henderson, Duke Ellington, and many others played stride, but in the opinion of many the finest stride player of them all was Art Tatum (1910–1956). Tatum's recordings with Louis Armstrong—*Liza* is an outstanding example—show a natural virtuosity that outdoes even J. P. Johnson in its fluidity, speed, and originality of harmonic variation.[13] His hyperkinetic rendition of the usually bland *Tea for Two* and his unique take on the ubiquitous *Get Happy* show an innate pianistic ability that must be the envy of any classical virtuoso. He represents the summation of ragtime, stride, pop, and jazz piano with generally up-tempo performances that reflect the "brash spirit . . . and optimism" of the age.[14] There were certainly many fine Harlem pianists during this exciting time, but as they themselves admitted, "you can't imiTatum."[15]

With all the "kings," "empresses," and "counts" in the jazz world, no one bore his honorary royal title more aristocratically than the Duke, Edward Kennedy Ellington (1899–1974). His posture, his speech, the way he wore his tuxedo—all bespoke the cultivated gentleman. Handsome and charismatic, Ellington always lived up to his image. Ellington was the musician to whom the ambiance of the Harlem Renaissance was most nurturing. He and his band, the Washingtonians, came to New York from the District of Columbia in the early 1920s for an appearance at the Kentucky Club, but when in 1927 he moved the group to the famed Cotton Club, he knew that he had found his true home. He stayed there until 1931, gradually increasing the ensemble to twelve players. In this segregated Harlem landmark, where blacks played and whites danced, ate, and drank, he reigned supreme. When affluent whites did "go to Harlem in ermine and pearls," it was more often than not specifically to see and hear Ellington at the Cotton Club.

Duke Ellington is included here among the stride pianists because he did indeed play in that style, but his range as a creative musician—he is credited with over one thousand compositions in many genres[16]—makes any such label inaccurate and ridiculously confining. In the popular vein Ellington wrote and played everything from novelty pieces like *Diga-Diga-Doo,* with its comic, growly trumpet passages, to the touching *Blue Feeling*, a slow, rather melancholy piece with a remarkable clarinet solo. Ellington was generous in offering opportunities for the members of his band to shine in riffs of their own, content to take his turn as featured pianist and otherwise stay in the background. Many of Ellington's original songs have become classics: *Sophisticated Lady*, *Satin Doll*, *Don't Get Around Much Anymore*, *Do Nothin' 'til You Hear from Me*, and of course his signature *Take the A Train*.

At the Cotton Club, his principal venue in New York, Ellington was famous for what was called "jungle music," in which muted horns imitated jungle animal sounds—all to a steady, danceable $\frac{4}{4}$ beat. Incorporating Cuban and Latin rhythms and forms, with facility, he was a master of the "big band" style, in which structured, notated arrangements assured smoothness, while individual riffs within the planned composition gave variety and spontaneity. It is said that he used his piano as others used a baton, conducting from the keyboard by force of his playing rather than by hand motions.[17] His extended concert pieces—*Black, Brown and Beige*, *Symphony in Black*, *Rhapsody of Negro Life*—and the suite from the film score *Paris Blues* were perhaps the most respected and admired of any of the African American jazz musicians who also worked in that field.

While Ellington, unlike J. P. Johnson, Fats Waller, Jelly Roll Morton, or Art Tatum, had no serious impact on the art of piano playing per se, he did write one clever and amusing piano duet, which he and Billy Strayhorn recorded (published by Monzino Records in 1987). Like many of the Duke's pieces, lasting just three-and-a-half minutes as required by the capacity of a shellac record, the duet is called *Pianistically Allied*. Full of syncopations and cross-rhythms, its harmonies are very like those of Poulenc with a little of the wryness of Stravinsky's own *Five Easy Pieces for Piano Four Hands* for flavoring. If it weren't for the relentlessly steady $\frac{4}{4}$ beat in the secondo part (who plays top and who plays bottom is unstated in the record notes), the piece is quite classical and would make a delightful and surprising encore for a four-hand recital.

It is undeniable that the pianists of the Harlem Renaissance and other African American pianists around the country had an influence on American classical composers, but it was the French—particularly Satie, Poulenc, Milhaud, Ravel, and Stravinsky in his French period—who were most smitten with the new sounds of jazz. Those black American jazz musicians who moved to Paris in the 1920s had the most immediate impact, since Parisians could hear them live, but records of those who stayed at home became available in France, and, as we shall see, they too played their part in the transcontinental exchange of musical ideas.

8

America in the 1930s

The WPA and Federal Music Project, Roy Harris, John Cage, Lou Harrison, Paul Bowles, Carl Ruggles, and Harlem after Its Renaissance

nd then, with a crash heard 'round the world, it all came tumbling down—the New York stock market debacle began in October 1929. The 1920s had been a period of jubilation over the successful conclusion of World War I, supposedly the war to end all wars. In addition to the emotional relief, there was an economic surge and, at least in the major cities, an astonishing relaxation of Puritanical social and sexual strictures. For the first time Americans had become aware of their great industrial potential and had watched it rescue Western civilization from tyranny. No longer a junior member of the community of nations, the United States was now a power to be reckoned with. No wonder there was a general feeling—a veritable certainty—that good times were here to stay.

The following decade could not have been more different. Bracketed by the onset of financial disaster on one end and World War II on the other, the 1930s were one of the dreariest periods in American history, and yet creative artists, as is their wont, continued to do what they always do—create. In the face of the crippling fiscal problems caused by the sudden disappearance of major fortunes among the rich and widespread unemployment among the working classes, this creativity was made possible to a considerable extent by programs instituted by the federal government, primarily the WPA (Works Progress Administration) and its affiliated subsidiaries. Particularly pertinent to our study is the FMP (Federal Music Project), which received special attention from Harry Hopkins. Hopkins had been chosen to head the entire undertaking by President Franklin Roosevelt, who was influenced by his wife, Eleanor.[1]

At first the 1929 stock market crash appeared to hurt only over-extended speculators, but the trickle-down effect soon proved to be devastating. By 1933, twelve thousand of the fifteen thousand musicians in New York were out of work.[2] This downward spiral had been begun five years earlier with the advent of "talking" motion pictures, which were drawing audiences away from music halls, clubs, cabarets, and concerts. The depression then made attending any entertainment venue an extravagance. Every industry suffered, but none was hit harder than live music.

By 1935 it was clear to the Roosevelt administration that measures of vast scope would have to be taken to bring the country back to normalcy and, at the same time, to preserve its cultural life. At Roosevelt's urging, Congress allocated an astounding $27,000,000 to the Federal Art Project on October 8th of that year.[3] This would be the equivalent of an unimaginable sum in modern-day terms, and an equally unimaginable act of generosity toward the arts in the current political atmosphere.

The appointment of well-known conductor and composer Nikolai Sokoloff as head of the FMP guaranteed its conservative viewpoint. While it tried to be inclusive, the FMP's clear bias was toward classical music and classically trained performers; for example, the ability to read music was a sine qua non. Sokoloff and his staff believed that classical music had a beneficial effect on all who heard it, and were determined to spread their gospel. "Music is a public right and obligation," said Sokoloff,[4] and enough powerful people in Washington agreed with him to enable him to act on his convictions.

The FMP hoped that subsidizing the formation of symphony orchestras all over the country would not only save hundreds of musicians from starvation, but eventually would create an intelligent, interested public willing to support these institutions after federal aid was phased out. In many instances this really did happen. Program administrators knew that they had to avoid charges of radicalism or Communist tendencies, for there were plenty in the government who still distrusted the arts and dreaded "subversive" attitudes. Administrators dictated that only U.S. citizens could be hired, and any hint of scandal canceled a program or ousted a player. Orchestras and choruses were segregated, with some of the African American groups scoring the biggest success in terms of tickets sold and revenue brought in.

Sokoloff wisely determined to connect established listening habits and the newly formed orchestras. Rather than holding stand-alone orchestral concerts, Sokoloff had the ensembles participate as part of traditional events—July Fourth celebrations, Armistice Day parades, and the like.[5] Popular favorites were included in most concerts, with Stephen Foster, George Gershwin, and John Philip Sousa getting more than their fair share of hearings. By 1938, worries over the war threatening Europe and a weakening hold over the American public caused President Roosevelt's enthusiasm for the entire WPA project to wane. Yet by that time, the FMP had sponsored over 57,000 performances, which had, in the aggregate, attracted 34,496,117 viewers/listeners. There had been almost three thousand radio broadcasts, attracting many more millions, and widespread community acceptance of the idea of classical concerts.[6] Aside from the radio broadcasts, these presentations usually were not free, but fifty-cent seats were often available and the general cost of tickets was kept to a minimum. Every performer was paid, and many concerts generated a profit.

Perhaps the most lasting contribution of the FMP was its support of American composers. Many paid commissions were meted out, and public performances were arranged of the new works that were written. As noted in previous chapters, well before the establishment of the FMP there had been a slow but steady increase in the number and independence of contemporary American composers. The problem was less that of individual creativity than of public acceptance, for with the exception of Gershwin and some of Copland's more "populist" music, the preferred classical programs were—and still are—made up of standard European works. From 1919 to 1925 only 5.3 percent of the works performed by the thirteen privately run symphony orchestras in the United States were by American composers.[7] The majority of soloists and conductors were European and knew little of the growing American repertoire. By the end of World War I the necessity of studying abroad for an acceptable pedigree had eased, but a European reputation was still de rigueur in opera houses and on orchestra podiums. Even today, when American soloists are welcomed all over the world, it is still difficult for an American conductor to claim a major post at home.

By the time the WPA and its subdivisions had run their course, 17,332 compositions by 2,258 American composers had been featured by FMP orchestras.[8] This figure is all the more astounding in light of Sokoloff's natural European—and specifically German—bias. Just how many of these works eventually found their way into the permanent repertoire is hard to say, but the general level of familiarity, understanding, and acceptance of art music by Americans was certainly raised. The FMP-sponsored Composers' Forum was organized to meet the needs of composers and to "remove the barriers between composers and public," airing over New York's radio station WQXR of more than one thousand new works by some sixty-six composers. These programs were very popular and led to similar Forums in other cities.[9] Audiences were attracted to the more rhythmic and quicker-paced music written by Americans, which seemed so appropriate to the rapid tempo of contemporary American life.

Prior to the creation of the FMP, several American composers had tried to promote their own and their colleagues' music. The most active and most public spirited of these was Aaron Copland. In 1925 Copland returned from his studies in France convinced that Americans had to be trained to listen to contemporary classical music and that it was the composer's responsibility to help. He felt that listeners tended to lump all modern music together and were sure even before hearing a new piece that they were not going to like it. Copland devotes one chapter of his *What to Listen for in Music*[10] to an explanation of the aims and perceptions of some of the best-known composers of the day, trying to differentiate among them to guide prospective listeners to those composers they were most likely to enjoy.

Copland recognized that the most important step toward liking a piece was to hear it—not once, but several times. He began a concert series in New York reminiscent of the informal concerts he had seen, heard, and played for in Paris, in which composers performed their works for each other and for small audiences and welcomed on-the-spot critiques from those present. Composer Roger Sessions was his steadiest partner in these intimate New York recitals. The Yaddo Festivals, begun in the summer of 1932, in which Copland, Sessions, Marc Blitzstein, Walter Piston, Roy Harris, and the composer-author Paul Bowles participated, were an outgrowth of the Copland-Sessions programs.

The Composers' Collective was also formed during this period, with Blitzstein as secretary and Cowell, Elie Siegmeister, and Charles Seeger among its active participants. "Dedicated to finding a socially useful music," the Composers' Collective sought to make new music simpler and more accessible rather than exposing the public to the unfamiliar, often difficult modern sounds and styles typically promoted by the Copland and Sessions. Under the guidance of the Workers' Music League, and with advice from the Communist Party, composers in the Collective employed folk and other vernacular music as a basis for their compositions.[11]

Copland was not a member of the Collective, but eventually he came around to a similar point of view. The ballets *Appalachian Spring, Rodeo,* and *Billy the Kid,* which became his most popular works, were all based on folk and popular idioms. Only a few years earlier, in *American Composers on American Music* (1933), he had stated, "There is a certain incongruity inherent in the attempt to place simple, popular themes in sophisticated harmonic settings, and it is even more difficult to build with them a large and compact symphonic edifice."[12] The suffering caused by the crash and depression had obviously prodded composers like Copland to greater social awareness and concern, and, of course, this influenced their work. Nevertheless Copland did compose his completely abstract and quite difficult Piano Sonata from 1939 to 1941, and it is one of the most interesting American solo piano works to come from this era.

Roy Harris, Copland's friend and fellow Boulanger student, played a part in the populist movement of the decade. Although better known for his symphonic works, he also composed a small body of music for solo piano that deserves examination. His first work for piano, his Opus 1, was a Sonata written in 1928 while he was in Paris. Played as one continuous movement, its four sections are distinguishable by definite changes of mood and tempo. The first, marked *Maestoso,* has some savage outbursts but no distinctive melodic content. The second is a long lyrical section that shows the influence of Erik Satie in its gentle simplicity. The *Scherzo* that follows has some tricky contrapuntal writing and a long *sostenuto* bass under a *con brio* cadenza. The use of the *sostenuto* pedal to hold bass notes under two-hand passages was to become a favorite Harris device. After the rather nice fugue that ends the *scherzo* section there is a coda in which some of the ferocity of the first section is once again heard. When it premiered at the Yaddo Festival in 1932, this Sonata made a very favorable impression, but today one finds it modestly successful at best.

It was ten years before Harris wrote another work for piano. By that time he had married a pianist who would influence and introduce his piano works in the years that followed. The piece in question was the *Little Suite* of 1938, which consists of four miniatures, each depicting a specific mood. The following year Harris began a more extended Suite, which he completed three years later. The first of its three sections is a fanfare marked *Ringing*, with trumpet-call broken triads, very American-sounding sonorities, and little melodic content—a bit like Copland's *Fanfare for the Common Man*. The second section is a theme and variations; the thematic material is based on a traditional Irish tune, but is somewhat diffuse for the subject of a set of variations and the result is rather formless. The last of the three segments contains snatches of reveille and children's games, *London Bridge Is Falling Down* prominent among them, and communicates a child-like innocence and joie de vivre. *New York Times* critic Noel Strauss heard "children imitating their elders" in the section, but it seems to this listener more like an adult imitating children.[13]

Harris's most popular piano music, *American Ballads*, was written in the early 1940s, yet exemplifies the populist spirit of the 1930s. Harris, like Cowell, hailed from California and grew up on a farm, and his use of folk music may be traced to this early exposure. *American Ballads* begins with an extended treatment of the Western folk tune *The Streets of Laredo*, with waltzlike sections alternating with a somber, moody segment. *The Streets of Laredo* pops up again in Harris's Sonata for Violin and Piano in the movement originally entitled *Dance of Spring* (Harris dropped the titles of these formerly discrete movements when he put them into sonata format).

Harris wrote in total less than an hour's worth of keyboard music, perhaps recognizing that the orchestra better suited his talents. His complete piano works, including the Sonata for Violin and Piano, can be heard on an Albany Records CD of 1993 featuring pianist Richard Zimdars. The most interesting aspect of this admittedly limited music is its consistently Western flavor: none of the urban concerns of Blitzstein's *The Cradle Will Rock*, for example; none of the hustle and bustle of city life as in Gershwin's *American in Paris*. Compared to Ives, Harris's use of Americana is straightforward—one tune at a time. It well represents a frame of mind prevalent among serious composers of the era and deserves its niche.

In 1933 a new voice tentatively made its presence known—that of John Cage (1912–1992). Cage's choice of texts for his first published work, three settings of poems by Gertrude Stein, immediately announced his preference for the new and daring. The piano pieces that followed, especially *Metamorphosis* (1935), were even more avant-garde. Cage had studied with Arnold Schoenberg soon after the Austro-Hungarian composer immigrated to the United States, and his early piano compositions expanded Schoenberg's twelve-tone system into rows of twenty-five or more notes.

An avid student of Eastern cultures, the more immersed in Zen philosophy Cage became, the more he valued silence as an expressive means. His most famous piece for piano solo is undoubtedly his aleatory *4' 33"*, for which the pianist sits at the keyboard for the stated period of time, then rises and bows. The idea was that the tension created as the audience watches this pantomime, and the ambient sound randomly occurring during the performance would combine into a valid musical experience. This ultimate iconoclast also introduced the "prepared piano" to the concert world; the piano is "prepared" prior to the performance by placing various objects, such as screws, between its strings, drastically altering the sounds produced by the instrument.

Cage was also among the first to experiment with electronic instruments. In 1939 he produced *Imaginary Landscape I*, which featured two turntables running at different speeds. His most influential work came in the 1940s and 1950s, but his potential was evident and noticed prior to World War II.

Another West Coast musician to come under the influence of Henry Cowell was Lou Harrison (born in Oregon in 1917). He first came to know Cowell while attending the older composer's course in what is now known as World Music. As a mature composer Harrison was known for the intensely percussive nature of his music, his interest in experimental and electronic instrumentation, and a fascination with music of other civilizations. Paradoxically, he was also a fine melodist whose lyric gifts made themselves apparent even in his most experimental and percussive compositions.

Harrison's pleasant and simple piano works were mostly written while he was a young, inexperienced composer. His three little *Piano Waltzes* owe much to Virgil Thomson and Erik Satie. The most adventurous of his piano pieces is probably the *Polka,* which displays some interesting polytonality. These pieces, as well as his suites for violin and piano and cello and piano, may be heard on a recent Koch recording devoted to Harrison.[14]

Although better known today for his literary works than for his music, Paul Bowles (1910–1999) was considered an important young composer in the 1930s. Born in New York, Bowles studied at home and in Paris with Copland, Thomson, Roger Sessions, and Boulanger. His fascination with the exotic led him to travel with Copland to Morocco, where he remained for many years until his death. Bowles exemplifies the Franco-American amalgam so common at the time. His *Picnic Cantata,* for example, scored for quartet of female voices and two pianists, boasts the spiky dance rhythms dear to Copland, Blitzstein, and like-minded composers, while the libretto has the surrealist flavor of Cocteau or Apollinaire. In the piece, four women sing minute descriptions of trivia, each little segment seeming to make sense, but the whole never becoming a coherent story. While hardly a standard of the repertoire, this odd piece has recently begun to appear in concert.

Apparently indifferent to or oblivious of the populist sentiments rife in the art and music worlds of the 1930s was one of the truly independent and original American composers, Carl Ruggles (né Charles Sprague Ruggles, 1885–1961). Ruggles, like his friend Charles Ives, was a New Englander who preferred to write without concern for public performances or acceptance. His output was small—eight published works plus several compositions left unfinished. It was not unusual for him to rework the same piece over decades, often leaving the prospective performer with multiple choices depending on which manuscript he or she consulted. His music is difficult to perform and difficult to absorb, so it is not surprising that there have been few performances and even fewer recordings of his works.

Having studied in Berlin, the most obvious leanings of Ruggles's work are toward the Germanic. Far from being drawn to German Romanticism, however, Ruggles showed more affinity for the atonality and serial techniques of the Second Viennese School (Arnold Schoenberg, Alban Berg, and Anton Webern). He independently developed his own type of atonality, deciding to repeat no tone before seven to ten others had been sounded, a technique which sometimes led to a Schoenbergian twelve-tone row. Following his own dictates, he was one of the few Americans to write uncompromisingly serial music. Nevertheless there is a clear and important difference between the music of Ruggles and that of the Second Viennese School—a typically American emphasis on forceful and aggressive rhythms.

In *American Composers on American Music,* Roy Harris observed that "Our [i.e., American] rhythmic impulses are fundamentally different from the rhythmic impulses of Europeans; and from this unique rhythmic sense are generated different melodies and form values." Harris explains that Americans think less symmetrically and in smaller units than Europeans, which allows for either real improvisation or an improvisatory feeling. "This asymmetrical balancing of phrases," continues Harris, "is in our blood; it is not in the European blood. . . . The rhythms come to us first as musical phraseology, and then we struggle to define them on paper." [15]

Harris's remarks are an apt introduction to *Evocations,* the one large work for solo piano written by Carl Ruggles. Ruggles began this massive, four-part composition in 1937 and continued to revise it well into the 1950s. It is difficult to tell whether the last version is definitive, or whether Ruggles just arbitrarily gave up working on this craggy, rugged work at that point.

Each section of *Evocations,* which is subtitled *Four Chants for Piano,* is dedicated to a person who was important to Ruggles in his private or professional life. The first is inscribed to his most generous patron, Harriette Miller, and the second to John Kirkpatrick, his principal interpreter. Kirkpatrick, who also championed the music of Ives, was Ruggles's musical heir, "reconstructing" many of Ruggles's unfinished works after the composer's death so they could be performed. The third section is dedicated to Ruggles's wife, Charlotte, and the last to Ives. Each section has its own character, and although certainly not traditionally Romantic, Charlotte's section is markedly more tender than the others.

Alban Berg was one of Ruggles's favorite composers, and he seemed to expand upon the older composer's techniques in this piece. In general *Evocations* is characterized by extreme dynamic contrasts and an uncompromising rejection of tonality. In this respect it is far starker than, for example, Berg's only major solo piano work, his Sonata, Opus 1, of 1906–1908. *Evocations*'s dissonances also seem harsher than those favored by Berg, with minor seconds, major sevenths, and minor ninths in even greater abundance. Yet to counterbalance the cluster-like quality of the chords in *Evocations,* there is a clear resonance to its "singing, winging polyphony"[16] and a spaciousness to its textures.

While Ives included all of Americana in his music, Ruggles gives no references, musical or extra-musical, in his own compositions. What he does offer are highly developed climaxes which evolve naturally, if somewhat obtusely, from striking central ideas. "A mystic in a non-religious society,"[17] he creates other-worldly sounds by the use of harmonics, allowing some strings to vibrate by depressing keys so the dampers are raised while playing harmonically related notes or chords in deeper registers. This tricky device was mentioned earlier and is not easy for the pianist to achieve.

With his dense chromaticism, use of tone rows, and abjurance of tonality, Ruggles earned his reputation as a forbidding, cantankerous old Yankee. But when he was about seventy years old, a different musical persona seemed to have emerged through his *Valse lente* (1945–1950). Pianist Donald Berman included this piece in a recent recital of Ruggles's complete piano works, and the reviewer commented that the *Valse* "veered between French salon music and Ivesian dissonance."[18] A deathbed conversion to Romanticism, or a delightful aberration?

The FMP aimed to be inclusive, but Director Sokoloff's preference for classical music and segregationist attitudes throughout the nation meant that black musicians benefited least from the program. Eleanor Roosevelt was far more concerned with racial inequities than her husband, and tried to promote African American participation. To some extent she succeeded, at least where classically trained blacks were involved. In 1939, the Daughters of the American Revolution infamously refused to allow the world-famous black contralto Marian Anderson to perform in Constitution Hall in Washington, D.C. The First Lady resolutely resigned from the organization and personally saw to it that Anderson performed on the steps of the Lincoln Memorial.[19]

All-black performances were given—for segregated audiences only—and ranged from the surprisingly popular and profitable *Aida* and *Il trovatore*, to stereotypical minstrel shows. Even this far into the Great Migration there were far more African Americans below the Mason-Dixon Line than above it; Mississippi, for instance, was still 50 percent black. Yet even in the South, all-black choruses, specializing in spirituals, patriotic songs, and standard ethnic material, drew record crowds and box-office takes. New York City was then only 3.3 percent black, yet had three black FMP units; undoubtedly this was because so many of the musically trained African Americans had gravitated to the city during the Harlem Renaissance.[20]

With or without the FMP and the instant millionaires of the Jazz Age, Harlem musicians played on. The 1930s were the years of maturity and mastery for Duke Ellington and Louis Armstrong in particular, as both musicians toured the United States and Europe as featured soloists with their own ensembles. Ellington was brilliantly adept at turning blues, ragtime, and stride into the smoother swing style that was preferred in this decade, when dancing to the big bands was a favorite pastime for the young and not-so-young alike. His ever-popular song *It Don't Mean a Thing if It Ain't Got That Swing* was a statement of fact for many listeners.

Armstrong, on the other hand, was the great popularizer, turning Tin Pan Alley, theater, and novelty songs into jazz by the power of his improvisatory genius. "Singing was more into my blood than trumpet," wrote Armstrong,[21] and this strong vocal sense was a major factor in his transforming the jazz of the early 1920s into the smoother sounds of the 1930s. In pure Dixieland everyone improvises, but in an Armstrong performance his solo instrument, be it voice or trumpet, dominates. The other musicians are "back-up," supporting Armstrong's flights of fancy. Even when Armstrong shares the spotlight, as he did with Sidney Bechet on some memorable recordings, there is a clear distinction between the back-up group and the two soloists. This necessitated more harmonic planning and coordination than was the norm in the earliest jazz.

In his *Jazz Modernism from Ellington and Armstrong to Matisse and Joyce*, Alfred Appel, Jr., calls Armstrong, Fats Waller, and others of their ilk "alchemists who have 'jazzed' the ordinary and given it new life." He points out how Waller "deconstructs" a ditty like "Jingle Bells" (rechristening it

"Swinging Them Jingle Bells") by first playing it with "respectful restraint," admonishing himself in a schoolmaster's tone "not to swing them jingles, son," and then proceeding to do just that; converting "language-bound song into pure music."[22] According to Appel, Armstrong was the only jazz performer to enter the canon with as secure a place as a Hemingway, Faulkner, or Fitzgerald. Ellington, by contrast, was placed in that exalted company because of his compositions.[23]

The events of Duke Ellington's personal life were reflected in his music. After his mother's death in 1935, he wrote a long mood piece entitled *Reminiscing in Tempo*,[24] which was followed by *Diminuendo and Crescendo in Blue*. These compositions and others of a similarly somber nature show innovative orchestration far beyond the usual scope of jazz: the brass were muted, the sonority thick with polytonality, the chords laced with dissonance. Ellington indeed tried to distance himself from the jazz—or any other—label so that his works could be heard without preconception.

An autodidact in compositional technique, Ellington relied on his experience as a pianist and conductor when writing his concert pieces. His full-bodied, resonant, tonally, and dynamically varied piano sound is thus reflected in his large-scale orchestral works. Even in his shorter song-and-dance tunes, his piano introductions, riffs, and postludes usually set the tempo and mood and then—after giving way to semi-improvised solos by members of his band—keep things moving. Good examples of this are *I Let a Song Go out of My Heart* and *Do Nothin' 'til You Hear from Me* from the Sony Music CD *Duke Ellington's Sixteen Most Popular Songs* (CK 57901), a rerelease of material recorded from the 1930s on.

Discussions of the relationship between jazz and classical music usually focus on the influence of the former on the latter, but many Ellington works show that the influences went both ways. The little piano duet called *Pianistically Allied*, brilliantly recorded by Ellington and Billy Strayhorn, has harmonies that echo those favored by Poulenc as well as discernable references to Stravinsky. Extended mood pieces like *Sophisticated Lady*, as heard on the Sony CD mentioned above, capture some of the harmonically created atmosphere so often found in Debussy. Augmented chords, unresolved sevenths, and ninths became the stock-in-trade of jazz as well as classical compositions, and it is not always possible to tell which came first.

Like most artists of the 1930s, Ellington was aware of the socio-political consequences of his work and knew that every African American who achieved either renown or notoriety affected the way in which white Americans perceived the people as a whole. He accepted the challenge that represented, saying "I think the music of my race is something which is going to live, something which posterity will honor in a higher sense than merely that of the music of the ballroom today."[25]

Other pianists with different characteristics also blossomed in the late 1920s and early 1930s. Count Basie, with his witty, blues-based style, liked simple riffs with lots of space to breathe. Perhaps as a reaction to the super-kinetic James P. Johnson and Art Tatum, Basie was a sophisticated mini-malist. Another important transitional soloist who helped move jazz piano from stride to swing was Earl "Fatha" Hines. Like many of his predecessors and contemporaries, Hines often used tremolos rather than elaborate figurations to fill in the measures at ends of phrases. His melodic lines, often doubled in octaves, were freer of ornamentation than those of the great striders.

The prominence—or perhaps even predominance—of white ensembles was certainly one of the major differences between swing and its predecessors. *Let's Dance* (1934–1935) and *Camel Caravan* (1936–1939), the live network broadcasts of Benny Goodman's band, are sometimes said to have been the real beginnings of the Swing Era. Many of the big bands still used arrangements by Fletcher Henderson, William Grant Still, and other African Americans, and many had integrated personnel. However, the majority of the famous bandleaders of the time—the Dorsey brothers, Glenn Miller, Woody Herman, Artie Shaw, Harry James, Claude Thornhill—were white. They played extroverted, exuberant music that was great for dancing, but the raw, unbridled quality of so much earlier jazz had been calmed down and "domesticated." These bands played written arrangements, but in order to put back some of the vitality that arises from improvisation, many employed vocalists who were able to fit the expressivity of the blues into the swing rhythms of the groups.

As the swing bands made their mark, the older styles of Dixieland, rag-time, blues, and stride continued to charm listeners and influence serious composition. Even composers like Copland who had ostensibly eschewed jazz as a viable element in concert music were affected by the rhythmic freedom and generally accelerated pace of the jazz players. As we shall see, French composers and critics of the 1920s had embraced jazz with more affection and respect than had most American traditionalists, but in the 1930s a few American critics and musicologists began to take jazz seriously enough to examine and write about it. Winthrop Sargeant's *Jazz, Hot and Hybrid* of 1938 offered some cogent analysis, and others followed suit. Like it or not, in the long run jazz and popular music could not be ignored by classical composers.

9

Paris in the 1920s, Part I

Non-Parisians in Paris: African American Jazz Men;
Jean Cocteau, Maurice Ravel, Darius Milhaud

While the mood in the years immediately following World War I
ranged from relief to euphoria in the United States, feelings in
France were mixed. There had been many American casualties once the
troops landed in Europe, but four years of horrifying battles and endless
trench warfare between the French and German armies had cost an incred-
ible number of young French lives. A period of mourning was inevitable.
Equally inevitable was the determination to shake the grief, to put sorrow
aside, to enjoy life once again. There was a sort of frenzy to the pleasure
seekers, a wish to make up for lost time, to try whatever was new and daring
that might erase or at least dull the pain of the past.

Americans played a considerable part first in the city's return to normalcy and then in the reincarnation of Paris as the center of the art, music,
and literary worlds. Affluent tourists, either blessed with "old money" or
newly flush from stock-market speculations, resumed their "Grand Tours,"
filling restaurants, cafés, and hotels. American initiative and financing
created the American Conservatory of Music at Fontainebleau, a small
working-class town about a half-hour train ride from Paris. There Nadia
Boulanger reigned, helping Aaron Copland, Roy Harris, Marc Blitzstein,
Virgil Thomson, and many other young American composers to find their
own compositional voices. F. Scott Fitzgerald, Ernest Hemingway, John
Dos Passos, Archibald MacLeish, and Ezra Pound were among the American writers who found the atmosphere in Paris and favorable exchange
rate congenial to their muses. Sylvia Beach, a young American woman
who loved books and their creators, opened a bookstore, Shakespeare &
Company, which rapidly became the center for American literary life as
well as a favorite hangout for all artistic expatriates in the city.

Americans were not the only expatriates to enliven the Parisian scene.
James Joyce wrote and published *Ulysses* there, largely through the good
offices of Sylvia Beach. Sergei Diaghilev brought his Ballets Russes to

Paris and stayed. Igor Stravinsky soon followed, shocking music lovers and critics with the scores Diaghilev commissioned from him for his troupe. Pablo Picasso, Amedeo Modigliani, Constantin Brancusi, and others opened their *ateliers* in the more Bohemian sections of the city, where they soon wrenched the avant-garde banner from the Impressionists and post-Impressionists.

No single group had a more pronounced influence on French music—classical as well as popular—of the period than the contingent of African American jazz musicians who joined this lively Parisian mix. This transatlantic migration occurred during the Harlem Renaissance, and was minor in comparison to the Great Migration from the Southern states to New York and other Northern metropolises. It might seem strange that these musicians would choose to go abroad when so many opportunities for professional fulfillment were available to jazz players at home, yet beginning with World War I itself, many possible explanations can be found.

"The War to End All Wars" began in Europe in 1914. The United States was reluctant to become embroiled in European affairs, and did not begin to arm itself in any significant way until May 1917, when the first draft law since the Civil War was passed. Up to that point, those in the government who foresaw the necessity for America's eventual entry into the conflict had relied on voluntary recruits. The response to the call for volunteers was lukewarm at best. Blacks were particularly wary of enlistment, given that the strictly segregated branches of the armed forces consistently relegated African American troops to menial jobs. In fact, this practice persisted in the U.S. military until the last year of World War II. Chief of Staff Tasker Bliss institutionalized this prejudice through his recommendation of "Plan 6," in which black regiments were to receive only minimal training before being sent to France, where they would be used exclusively in "service," that is, nonfighting, capacity.[1]

These Jim Crow attitudes are hard to understand in light of the history of African Americans in the U.S. Army. During the Civil War some 180,000 blacks, in 150 all-black regiments, fought in the Union Army. In 1866, immediately following the Civil War, four black regiments were authorized by Congress for combat in the Indian Wars. These soldiers, dubbed "the Buffalo Boys," draped buffalo skins over their inadequate uniforms to protect against the cold.[2]

There were some twenty thousand African American volunteers despite these problems, which was invaluable for practical and propaganda reasons since a draft had not yet been enacted. Among these volunteers was orchestra leader James Reese Europe. Europe and his band had worked closely with the popular dance team of Irene and Vernon Castle, and when British-born Vernon enlisted in his country's air corps, Europe decided that he should volunteer for the U.S. Infantry. However, the savvy white officer Colonel William Hayward of the Nebraska National Guard had a better idea. He ordered Europe to form an all-black marching band—a jazz-oriented marching band—to entice other African Americans into the army.[3]

It worked. Some two thousand black men enlisted in what became New York's 15th Infantry Regiment, later part of the 92nd Division of the 369th Regiment. As decreed in Plan 6, military training was minimal. The government issued them no rifles, so many of the men joined shooting clubs in order to buy their own. They succeeded in obtaining only 250 rifles, and the rest of the men drilled with broomsticks. No Armory space was allotted to the Regiment and the soldiers marched instead in the Lafayette Dance Studio or in the city streets. Proper uniforms were almost as scarce as the rifles—during these marching drills only soldiers on the ends of the rows wore mufti.[4]

On New Year's Day, 1917, the Harlem regiment was shipped to France on the *S.S. Pocahontas*. The New York State flag flew high above the vessel, an appropriate symbol for the men on board but probably illegal—eventually the Stars and Stripes took its rightful place when the men were permitted to fly it. The arrival in France brought to light a complex situation, however; African Americans were legally forbidden to fire at any white person, and this would necessarily include the German enemy.[5] General George Pershing, chief of the American armed forces in France, was therefore forced to "lend" these soldiers to the French. Incredibly, this group, dubbed the Harlem Hellfighters because of their ferocity in battle, became the most decorated in the entire fighting force. For the last few months of the war even the band members joined the fighting. The first troops to reach the Rhine, the men collectively and individually earned medals, including the Croix de Guerre, and accolades from all sides.

The one privileged segment of the Harlem Hellfighters was "Big Jim" Europe's band. The group numbered over fifty members, nearly twice the regulation size. Europe's band became General Pershing's personal envoy,[6] performing for Allied conferences at headquarters and touring the country to boost morale.

Audiences went wild over the new American music. Recordings made shortly after the Armistice reveal a style unknown in any other marching band, military or otherwise, with wah-wah trumpet effects, sliding and swooping trombones, percussion sounds to mimic tap dancers, bent notes, blue notes, syncopations, and a totally unique joie de vivre. The band's basic beat, a steady $\frac{4}{4}$, was marchable, but nothing else about it fit the stereotype of a military ensemble. It was brash, fun, and even funny, and as American as the Statue of Liberty (which was, of course, made in France). It made the listener want to dance, not march, and it was just what the general ordered to raise everyone's spirits.

One of the songs in the Harlem Hellfighter band's repertoire, *How Ya Gonna Keep 'em Down on the Farm after They've Seen Paree*, proved frighteningly prophetic after the war. Returning black troops were greeted in many areas of the United States by the threat of lynchings and race riots, which had begun to proliferate before the war and became even more common in the years that followed. Revival of the Ku Klux Klan was encouraged in several Southern states "to meet the 'peril' of returning colored veterans who might have been infected with foreign ideas of liberty, equality and fraternity."[7] In France African Americans were accepted as equal human beings, and none was made to feel more welcome than the members of the band. French women, many of whose husbands and lovers had been killed in the carnage of the trenches, fell in love with these strapping military-musicmen. There were romances, marriages, and—after the fighting had ceased—plenty of cabaret gigs for small combos and individual jazz players. French critics took their music seriously, French audiences wanted to hear them, French musicians wanted to learn from them. Most importantly, there seemed to be—at least in the majority of Frenchmen—an absence of the racial bias so common in the United States. Inevitably many ex-GIs of color either stayed in France or returned after their release from the service.

Most black expatriates settled in the area known as Montmartre, a hilly section of Paris nicknamed *La Butte*, or the Mound. The neighborhood nestled under the gaze of the enormous white church of Sacré-Coeur, but there was nothing sanctimonious in its aura. The home of artists and con artists, bohemians and brigands, Montmartre offered drugs, sex, and the liveliest cabarets in the city. Tabarin, Monaco, Le Rat-Mort, Le Royal-Souper, Mirliton, Le Chat Noir, and, most famous of all, Le Moulin Rouge were all there, and *tout Paris* flocked to them. Somewhat akin to the Harlem Renaissance scene, ladies in ermine and pearls and their formally attired escorts could regularly be seen crowding into the clubs.

There were some very famous singers and instrumentalists among the African American entertainers holding forth in Montmartre clubs. Among these was the brilliant doubler Sidney Bechet (1897–1959), who played clarinet and soprano saxophone. For Bechet, going to France was like going home. His parents had been part of the French-speaking Creole community of New Orleans, where Sidney had been born and raised. Indeed, he was among the few black expatriates to make France a permanent home, settling there in 1951 and remaining until his death eight years later.

Bechet and Louis Armstrong, another New Orleans product, moved jazz away from the dissonant, raucous sound of Dixieland's group improvisation, toward the more coordinated style of individual improvisations over ensemble accompaniment. Their riffs were like spontaneously conceived cadenzas—free, virtuosic, and dazzling. Even when the still smoother big-band swing style began to displace primarily improvised solos in popular taste, Bechet stuck to his standards, saying "There ain't no one can write down the feeling you have to have. That's from inside yourself, and you can't play note by note like something written down."[8]

Bechet went to Europe at the same time as the ex-GIs were settling in after the war. In 1919 he was invited by composer-bandleader Will Marion Cook to join the latter's Southern Syncopated Orchestra, which was about to play London. Swiss conductor Ernest Ansermet heard him there and was moved to write, "There is in the Southern Syncopated Orchestra an extraordinary clarinet virtuoso who is, so it seems, the first of his race to compose perfectly formed blues on the clarinet. I wish to set down the name of this artist of genius; as for myself I shall never forget it, it is Sidney Bechet."[9] In 1925, when he was featured in *La revue nègre* (The Negro Revue) starring American expatriate Josephine Baker, every music-loving Parisian came to know that name.

Bechet's trademark was a particular kind of tight vibrato, with which he ended many phrases. Vibrato cannot, of course, be imitated on the piano, but other Bechet characteristics—the fluency of his long, legato melodic lines and the intricacy of his arpeggiated figures—could be and were translated into pianistic terms.

There were other celebrities among the African Americans in Montmartre in the 1920s. Divas Florence Mills, Alberta Hunter, Bricktop, and, above all, superstar dancer Josephine Baker all made a huge impression on Parisians and American tourists alike. Bandleader Billy Arnold was well known at the time and had a major influence on such avant-garde composers as Darius Milhaud, who went to hear him regularly.[10] Drummer Louis Mitchell had arrived in Paris a little earlier than the rest, and first appeared at the Casino de Paris in 1917. He was so successful in that venue that the management sent him back to New York to recruit an entire band. He came back with two combos—Mitchell's Jazz Kings and Seven Spades—that became the most sought-after groups in the city. "The big attraction at the *Casino Theater* here and the big attraction at every Parisian theater that can bid enough for his services is Louis A. Mitchell, who just drummed his way to Paris and into the hearts of Parisians," wrote one reviewer.[11] Mitchell commanded seven thousand francs per week, about ten times the salary of a French Cabinet member at the time.[12]

When the World War I influx began, black entertainment was not completely new to Paris. As early as 1836 a blackface minstrel show headed by T. D. Rice, composer of the song that gave *Jim Crow* its definition, played Paris. In 1878 a banjo virtuoso named Horace Weston portrayed "Uncle Tom" in the city, using the popularity of Harriet Beecher Stowe's novel as a springboard. In the last quarter of the nineteenth century the Fisk Singers, a chorus specializing in Negro spirituals and other ethnic material, toured Europe several times. Toward the end of the century many minstrel shows—some black and some blackface—entertained Parisians with "coon songs," ragtime, and the cakewalk.[13]

John Philip Sousa toured France several times in the first decade of the twentieth century, creating a veritable craze for the cakewalk and its ragtime music when he featured them in his performances at the Paris Exposition of 1900. This undoubtedly accounts for Debussy's *Golliwogg's Cake-walk,* composed a few years later. There were cakewalk classes and contests all over Paris, and whether played by blacks or whites, its syncopated music was called *la musique nègre* (Negro music).

The difference between these earlier black and white American arrivals in France and the post–World War I migration was twofold: size and staying power. Previously isolated groups were welcomed as visiting novelties, but after 1920 there was an entire community of American black musicians living and working in Paris on what appeared to be a permanent basis. Suddenly it seemed that the jazz music played by these newcomers—and if it was American and black it was called jazz, whether or not it would meet the definition of purists—had taken over the city. One of the hit songs in Paris in 1920 was in fact called *Jazz partout* (Jazz everywhere), with lyrics such as "They're jazz bands by day, by night / They're jazz bands everywhere / It's all the rage in Paris, it makes men crazy."[14]

As that last line suggests, some French listeners saw jazz as a breath of fresh air that would revitalize the nation's music, while others saw it as the end of civilization. Music had become a political issue in France at the end of the Franco-Prussian War. It still was a political issue in 1920, but now with a different focus. In 1870 the aim of the nationalistic composers in France was to avoid German influences; in the 1920s Americanization was seen as the problem. As the French saw it, there were two facets to the problem as the French saw it—the mechanization of American society and its arts, and the perceived primitivism of *la musique nègre*—and plenty of Frenchmen wanted no part of either. Regardless of these minority opinions, which could also be heard in different forms back home, it was clear that the jazz age had come to Paris, and there was no stopping it. The Parisian public wanted to hear Americans—especially black Americans—playing their music, and entertainment impresarios were determined to oblige.

They say that nothing can stop an idea whose time has come, and American jazz came to Paris at just the right moment. If French composers wanted to shake the influence of German Romanticism at the end of the Franco-Prussian War, after World War I they were more determined than ever to reject what they saw as the grandiose, overly orchestrated Germanic styles of Wagner, Bruckner, and Mahler. They wanted a leaner, meaner style, one that would allow for astringent chords, angular rhythms, and unpretentious dimensions. They liked the irreverence of jazz, its perceived primitivism and savagery. They liked its brevity, precision, clarity, and wit—time-honored French traits. In a populist spirit not too different from that in America in the 1930s, they wanted to attract the musically naive as well as the traditional concertgoer. They wanted audiences, especially young audiences, to have fun at their concerts.

Among the composers most receptive to the new music were Ravel, Milhaud, and other avant-garde musicians. This young group gathered around their twin idols, surrealist writer Jean Cocteau and iconoclastic composer Erik Satie. Cocteau (1889–1963), himself a semi-serious composer, caricaturist, and painter, was the instigator of many multimedia projects. The ballet *Parade* was one such project, a collaborative effort for which he wrote the text, Satie composed the music, and Picasso designed the sets. Completed in 1917, *Parade* is periodically revived by New York's Metropolitan Opera as part of a triple bill with Ravel's *L'enfant et les sortilèges* (The child and the spells) and Poulenc's *Les mamelles de Tirésias* (The breasts of Tiresias). Satie's score was the first extended work to include African American music, albeit in only one brief vignette of an American girl dancing to a rather lugubrious ragtime. Although its musical value is slight, this amusing piece makes its composer a true pioneer.

True to the tenets of surrealism, Cocteau turned out texts whose line-by-line dialogue is always comprehensible but whose plot lines make no sense. A prolific poet, dramatist, writer of fiction, and even distinguished film maker, his most famous novel *Les enfants terribles* (literally "Terrible children," but known in English as *Children of the Game*) was written in 1928. Like *Parade* and so many of his other works, it caused a scandal. Objections to *Les enfants terribles* became even more vociferous in 1949, when it was turned into a film. Cocteau could hardly have been surprised at condemnations from conservative quarters, for the protagonists were an incestuous sister and brother.

Avant-garde French composers pursued the study of American jazz as they would have any other compositional style or technique: they listened to its practitioners and sought training from them. Most methodical in the pursuit of this knowledge was the most serious and experienced of the group, Maurice Ravel. Ravel arranged for weekly meetings with Leo Vauchant, a twenty-year-old French jazz trombone player whom he first heard at the famed artistic hangout *Le Boeuf sur le Toit*. Vauchant, a classically trained cellist, had taught himself to play jazz by listening to the Louis Mitchell band.[15] These tutorial sessions went on for four years, from 1924 to 1928.[16]

Vauchant's written accounts of the weekly lessons are instructive: what Ravel most wanted to know, he recorded, was the secret of improvisation. At Ravel's suggestion the two musicians took turns, one playing the straight man while the other improvised around the melodic line or the harmonic structure. Vauchant explained the idea of the flatted third and seventh in a major scale: an E flat above a C chord is "the augmented ninth. Since you have a tenth it could be a flatted tenth. You have both intervals but you have to say raised, although it's really flatted because you get off it and come back, but it doesn't lead upward."[17] Ravel grasped this technique immediately. He found in it a similarity with the music of George Gershwin, whom he admired greatly. In fact, when Ravel visited the United States in 1928 the one person he was most anxious to meet was Gershwin; the admiration was clearly mutual, for Gershwin wanted to study orchestration with Ravel, but the desired lessons never took place. About these flatted thirds and sevenths in the major scale, Ravel asked Vauchant "Where did [Gershwin] get it from?" Vauchant replied that they came from the blues.

Ravel quickly incorporated the new stylistic devices—principally blue notes and jazzlike syncopations—into several major compositions. The first Ravel composition to manifest these new elements was the charming one-act opera *L'enfant et les sortilèges* of 1925. Ravel based his score on the wistful, nostalgic fantasy by Colette, which was thoroughly compatible with the composer's own view of how a child learns compassion and humanity. This little opera is not entirely outside the purview of our study, for its instrumentation includes a nonsoloistic piano part.

Ravel's Sonata for Violin and Piano, published in 1927 but begun in 1924, came next. According to musicologist Wilfrid Mellers, its middle movement, entitled *Blues*, "distills the mood of a generation into something rich and strange."[18] It is the most consistently jazzlike section in the piece and, indeed, in Ravel's output. A strumming effect for violin, accomplished by double pizzicati, is first heard over the piano's very jazzy support. (The equality of the parts in this composition precludes the term "accompaniment.") To imitate the "bent" notes of jazz players, the violin sometimes slides from pitch to pitch, but the effect is quite unlike the Romantic slide now shunned by most classical fiddlers. The mood fluctuates between cheerful and jocose.

The sonata's opening movement, which is relatively quiet, is notable for the independence of the two instruments, which seem to go their own ways, meeting only often enough to provide coherence. Sometimes the moods of the players seem at odds with one another, the piano jovial and jaunty while the violin is lyrical. The *scherzando* third movement begins with the violin's flight-of-the-bumblebee buzzing. This is, of course, a twentieth-century bumblebee, whose independence from the piano part leads to considerable dissonance. A glissando or two for the piano remind us of Ravel's earlier solo piano oeuvre. In addition, there are motoric sections of the finale that are reminiscent of the *Toccata* movement of *Le tombeau de Couperin*, but here Ravel is more astringent and more percussive than he was in the earlier works.

Many classical composers who incorporated jazz in their concert works have been criticized for merely borrowing the clichés of that idiom to spice up their output. While there are some fairly obvious jazz references in the *Blues* movement of the Ravel Sonata for Violin and Piano, especially in the keyboard part, at least in this piece the composer seems to have made jazz style his own. The jazz elements are clear, but the music is still totally Ravel's and there is no jarring disruption between movements: the *Blues* does not stand out awkwardly but leads convincingly into the Scherzo. Because the violin became such a vital part of French jazz, while remaining peripheral to its American counterpart, the *Blues* seems to be a particularly French manifestation of jazz-influenced classical music.

Four years after the Sonata for violin and piano, the two concerti for piano—the D Major for left hand alone (composed for Austrian Paul Wittgenstein, a pianist who had lost his right arm in World War I) and the two-hand G Major—were published. Of the two, the G Major is more obviously jazz-oriented, especially in its first movement. Lazy blues and jazzy syncopations override effects such as the characteristic glissandi from Ravel's earlier works. The brass often carries the tune while the piano plays figurations around it, and touches of Latin rhythms and oriental scale patterns are in evidence.

The Concerto's second movement owes far more to Satie than it does to jazz; one might easily mistake parts of it for a newly discovered *Gymnopédie*. The endlessly meandering melody over steady $\frac{4}{4}$ chords in the extended piano solo is, like those in Satie, markedly modal. The final movement keeps the piano busy with virtuosic figurations. It includes music-hall chord sequences, military-style trumpet calls, and fairly obvious references to Stravinsky's *Petrushka,* in homage to the Russian-born composer. While less tightly structured than his solo piano pieces, the movement hangs together in a coherent fashion. It is said that Ravel wanted to premiere this work himself but found the piano part too difficult; he settled for conducting the first performance.

When the Violin and Piano Sonata and the Concerto in G were first heard, most critics found them "insignificant" in comparison to the extraordinary body of music Ravel had already composed, though perhaps because of its uniqueness and raison d'être they were more accepting of the Concerto for the Left Hand. Ravel himself admitted that, "Fascinated as I am by this idiom, I cannot possibly feel as if I were an American. It is to me a picturesque adventure."[19] Nevertheless, despite these modest disclaimers, the frequency with which these pieces are performed today clearly obviates critical cavils of the past.

Although several songs with interesting piano parts followed, the Violin and Piano Sonata and the concerti were Ravel's last major efforts featuring keyboard. To understand fully the jazz influence on these compositions, one must review the piano pieces that preceded them. Beginning in 1893 with his first published piano solo, *Sérénade grotesque* (Grotesque serenade), and continuing until the last, *Le tombeau de Couperin* (literally "Couperin's tomb" but generally translated as "Homage to Couperin" [1917]), Ravel had developed a highly original approach to the keyboard. One of its key elements was the use of modal melodies and harmonies, thus imparting a characteristic antique flavor to such pieces as *Menuet antique* (Antique minuet, 1893), *Pavane pour une infante défunte* (Pavane for a dead princess, 1899), the first movement of the *Sonatine* (1905), and all but the last movement (*Toccata*) of *Le tombeau de Couperin*. Like his teacher Fauré, Ravel rarely ended a piece or a section with a traditional dominant-seventh/tonic progression, preferring the whole-step interval (B-flat to C in the key of C) or the so-called Landini cadence (C–B–A–C). Incredibly, no matter how Dorian, Phrygian, or Pentatonic the melodies and harmonies, this persistent modality never obviates diatonic tonality. Unlike Debussy, with whom he is inevitably paired, Ravel never substitutes whole-tone for diatonic scales even when incorporating chords of augmented fifths, a favorite "Impressionist" sound.

From *Jeux d'eau* (1901) onward Ravel explored the use of glittering cascades of notes, glissandi, trills in double thirds in high registers (the unresolved double-third trill at the end of *Menuet* from *Tombeau de Couperin* is especially telling), and sweeping arpeggios that encompass the entire keyboard. The effects created, which are extremely difficult to achieve, bring to mind sunlight on water (*Jeux d'eau*), gushing fountains, turbulent oceans (*Une barque sur l'océan* from *Miroirs*), whole flocks of birds in flight, or an army of harpists. The right-hand descending/left-hand ascending black-note glissandi in the piano part of *Paon* (The Peacock), the first song in the cycle *Histoires naturelles*, the glissandi in double thirds in *Alborado del gracioso* from *Miroirs*, and arpeggios executed simultaneously by the two hands in different keys continue to be innovations which stretche the techniques of even the most seasoned virtuosi.

Ravel is known as a great melodist, albeit rarely in the nineteenth-century Schubert-Chopin-Schumann vein. His innovations include figures which initially seem to be ornamental, but which then metamorphose into melodic fragments that appear, disappear, and reappear throughout the composition. The listener has to work a bit to grasp the melodic content in a piece like *Une barque sur l'océan* from *Miroirs*, for example. Ravel was a master of special effects that are always in the service of the tight structures and highly organized general scheme of a composition. One of the most salient examples of this technique may be found in the *Gibet* movement of *Gaspard de la nuit* (1908), where a single repeated note, a B-flat, is used as an interior pedal point; as the harmonies around the B-flat change, the note is in turn dissonant, or consonant with the sounds that surround it. Its unrelenting presence endows the somber movement with foreboding and inevitability. As the title of the movement, *Gibet*, means "gallows," we can assume the hapless Scarbo will be hanged.

As Jack Sullivan points out in *New World Symphonies*, both Ravel and Debussy were moved and inspired by the poems and stories of American writer Edgar Allan Poe (1809–1849). "I spent my existence in the House of Usher," said Debussy, who worked for years on an unfinished opera based on Poe's story. Ravel is quoted as proclaiming, "My teacher was Edgar

Allan Poe."[20] The French knew Poe through translations by poet Charles Baudelaire, another ardent fan. Valuing him much more highly than did most American critics, they saw in his writing musicality, unity of mood, and a subtle sense of the sinister, the same qualities one finds in Ravel's *Scarbo*. The hallucinatory quality of "The Pit and the Pendulum" or "Descent into the Maelstrom" is also part of *Scarbo*'s effect.

Of particular interest to pianists who enjoy playing duets is Ravel's delightful *Ma mère l'oye* (Mother Goose Suite, 1908). While not entirely free of technical challenges, the music is enchanting and neither part presents the formidable difficulties of so much of Ravel's piano oeuvre. The five-movement suite opens with a *pavane* for a beautiful princess in an enchanted "sleeping" forest. The music is quiet and stately—no prince has come to awaken her as yet. Next comes a rather sedate Tom Thumb (*Petit poucet*); the *secondo* plays scale figures in thirds to prepare for the *primo*'s modal melody. The tempo remains moderate. *Laideronnette, Impératrice des pagodes* (Little Homely One, Empress of the pagodas), which follows, is played entirely on the black keys and includes one of Ravel's infamous black-key glissandi, best accomplished with the finger tips of an open hand; the effect is oriental as well suits the Empress of the pagodas. Beauty and Beast have a dialogue in the fourth section, the beast growling away deep in the bass while Beauty floats high above. *Le jardin féerique* (The Fairy Garden) ends the suite with the sweeping ascending and descending glissandi—now on white notes—so dear to its composer.

The hiatus in piano works between *Le tombeau de Couperin* and the Violin and Piano Sonata and the concerti has puzzled musicologists. Was it the lack of opportunity caused by Ravel's military service during World War I? Did the composer feel that he had said everything he had to say for the instrument? Clearly the composer's interest in jazz sparked a new period of creativity for him.

Although Ravel was a respected part of the group that met every Saturday night for jazz at Le Boeuf sur le Toit, he was more or less an anomaly—an established genius and a reserved middle-aged man. The other regulars were at least a generation younger than he and at the start of their careers. The club's surrealist name (The Ox on the Roof) was borrowed from the ballet that Darius Milhaud (1892–1974) had composed in 1919, and it was Milhaud around whom the group centered. Most of the others in the inner circle, including Swiss-born composer Arthur Honegger (1892–1955) and Jean Wiéner, the club's principal pianist, had been Milhaud's fellow students in André Gédalge's prewar composition classes. Friends for more than a decade when the club opened, they were comfortable with one another and with the painters and poets of their generation.

"Le boeuf sur le toit" ("O boi no telhado" in the original Portuguese) was the name of a popular Brazilian song Milhaud had heard during his year-and-a-half tour of duty in Brazil. Brazil was the first Latin American country to ally itself with the anti-German forces, and many French were sent there to help the war effort from abroad. While serving as secretary to poet Paul Claudel, who had been appointed French ambassador to Brazil during World War I, Milhaud led a rich musical life. He was exposed to touring performers like Artur Rubinstein, Enrico Caruso, and the Ballets Russes—but what really interested him was the native music he heard around him every day.

Arriving during Carnival, he and Claudel were immediately swept up in the excitement. "I was fascinated," wrote Milhaud in his autobiography,

> by the rhythms of this popular music . . . imperceptible pauses in the syncopa-
> tion, a careless catch in the breath, a slight hiatus that I found very difficult
> to grasp. So I bought a lot of maxixes and tangos and tried to play them with
> their syncopated rhythms, which run from one hand to the other.[21]

He described the playing of Ernesto Nazareth as an "elusive, mournful, liquid way of playing [that] gave me deeper insight into the Brazilian soul."[22]

Happy as Milhaud was to return to France at the end of the war, Brazilian music had made an indelible impression upon his creative mind. "Still haunted by my memories of Brazil, I assembled a few popular melodies, tangos, maxixes, sambas, and even a Portuguese fado, and transcribed them with a rondo-like theme recurring between each two of them. I called this fantasia *Le boeuf sur le toit*."[23] Milhaud had originally thought of his score as an ideal musical background for a Charlie Chaplin film. However, when Cocteau heard it he claimed it for a project of his own, writing a ballet scenario to fit the music. Despite Milhaud's light-hearted intentions, the piece was taken by critics and public alike as a manifesto for the new, postwar aesthetic, and Milhaud was henceforth regarded as one of the leaders of the postwar generation. Since Satie had contributed some music for the three scheduled performances—*Le boeuf* was not a full-length production—he was hailed as the father and mascot of the new group, which was soon to be dubbed Les Six (The Six). The lesser-known Georges Auric (1899–1983) had also written something for the occasion. The sensation and scandal that the work caused seemed to genuinely surprise Milhaud, but the boos and cheers drowning out the music, and the now-requisite police intervention had become typical responses to most projects associated with Cocteau.

Perhaps the most interesting products of Milhaud's Brazilian period in the pianistic literature are the two books of *Saudades do Brasil* (Memories of Brazil). These comprise twelve short sketches—only one lasts over two minutes, and several are barely one minute long—which he composed during the 1920–21 season. Each title refers to a section of Rio, many obscure (e.g., Sorocabo, Botologo, and Tijuca), but some have been made familiar by popular songs (such as *The Girl from Ipanema*). For listeners unacquainted with indigenous South American music and unfamiliar with the city of Rio, it would be difficult to identify the native styles that inspired Milhaud. All twelve pieces are attractive and obviously Latin American in flavor, however, with sinuous and insinuating rhythms, dissonant chords, and often unresolved endings. Milhaud creates interesting clashes by allowing a chord pattern to continue after the melody has passed to another tonal center. These pieces are fun, novel, charming, and pianistic. If there seems to be a hint of jazz in them, it is only a reflection of later developments: Latin elements in jazz became pronounced in the 1930s and 1940s, but has no connection to *Saudades*.

Milhaud wrote several more short pieces for solo piano, but his most familiar work for keyboard is certainly the delightful *Scaramouche* for two pianos. This irresistible three-movement work, written much later in 1939, revisits Brazilian rhythms in a more assimilated fashion. The slow middle movement, *Modéré*, is simple and melodic, while the two outer sections, *Vif* and *Brasileira*, are joyous rhythmic romps. A real novelty is Milhaud's 1948 six-movement suite for four pianos. While fun to hear and play, it shows that multiple pianos are really rather redundant: two sets of eighty-eight keys can do just about everything four or more sets can.

Meanwhile, back at the club named after *Le boeuf* French composers and civilians were listening to jazz. This club had previously been called *La Gaya*, but Milhaud and Cocteau had granted permission to use the name *Le Boeuf* after the club's owner moved it to larger quarters to accommodate the crowds. The combo playing there night after night included Vauchant, the trombonist who so intrigued Ravel, and the French pianists Jean Wiéner and Clément Doucet. Wiéner, as we mentioned, was a former classmate of Milhaud and was a serious and well-trained classical musician. He had taken the club job out of necessity but turned it to great advantage. He and Doucet were skilled improvisers alone and as a four-hand team, moving easily from American popular music to Bach preludes and fugues.[24] They were usually joined by African American banjo and saxophone player Vance Laurie and various drummers. The moderately skilled Cocteau occasionally sat in on drums.[25] The atmosphere was casual, and many customers dropped in to see the celebrities rather than to hear the music.

Wiéner (1896–1982) also led the band, and the 1950s and 1960s recordings based on his work at Le Boeuf during the 1920s and 1930s show a relaxed, affable personality at home in many styles. He characteristically begins each session with a cheery *Bonjour, tout le monde* (Hello, everyone) and ends with *À demain* (See you tomorrow). There are medleys of his spontaneous arrangements of American pop tunes (such as *Tea for Two; Smiles; Oh, Lady, Be Good!* and *My Blue Heaven*) done in what is now pure cocktail-pianist style; fairly intricate, witty, jazzed-up forays into the Baroque styles of Bach and Handel; slow, lazy rags and blues; Latin-inspired tangos; a bit of boogie-woogie; some stride—in short, the whole potpourri of American vernacular music.[26] A feeling of originality or cutting-edge audacity is missing from the recordings, but evidently his adventurous work was enough to intrigue avant-garde French composers.

Wiéner and his band were certainly not the only jazz French avant-garde composers heard. When Milhaud and Cocteau went to London for a performance of *Le boeuf sur le toit,* they listened to Billy Arnold's jazz band, which was then causing a sensation with its fresh New York style. In their performances Milhaud found

> a very subtle understanding of the art of timbres: the use of the saxophone, destroyer of dreams, of the trumpet, alternatively languorous or dramatic, of the clarinet, often high in the upper register, of the lyrical trombone bending the notes a quarter of a tone with the slide on the crescendos. . . . Meanwhile the piano, together with the drums, whose complete and subtle punctuations provided an inner pulse indispensable to the life of the music, held this diverse but never disjointed ensemble together. Their constant use of syncopation in the melody was done with such contrapuntal freedom as to create the impression of an almost chaotic improvisation, whereas in fact, it was something remarkably precise requiring daily practice. I got the idea of using these rhythms and timbres in a work of chamber music, but first I needed to go more deeply into this new musical form, whose techniques still troubled me.[27]

Wiéner organized a series of concerts at La Salle des Agriculteurs (Farmers' Hall) to present all kinds of avant-garde music. He featured the Billy Arnold Orchestra, and followed that rousing success with a performance of Schoenberg's *Pierrot lunaire* (Pierrot of the Moon), which Milhaud conducted. The series was nothing if not eclectic!

Milhaud visited New York in 1922, listening to all genres of American vernacular music. He dismissed Paul Whiteman as "pedestrian and predictable," especially when compared with "the broken, twisted," percussion-driven rhythms he heard in Harlem. When a black woman sang the same melody over and over, with "dramatic, despairing expression," to constantly changing accompaniments, Milhaud felt that he had witnessed "the most obscure elements of the black soul."[28]

The most significant result of Milhaud's fascination with jazz was *La création du monde* (The creation of the world). A ballet inspired by African creation legends, the piece astounded the American classical music establishment. Like *Parade, Création* was a collaboration of genius, with poet-novelist Blaise Cendrars (1887–1961) providing the stories and Fernand Léger (1881–1955) designing the sets. It was produced by the Ballets Suédois, a company which briefly rivaled Diaghilev's Ballets Russes, and which had also produced *Le boeuf sur le toit.*

Milhaud's choice of instrumentation was heavily indebted to the Harlem ensembles he had heard, featuring the sounds of the saxophone, piano, percussion, flute, clarinet, trumpet, and trombone. The double bass carries the all-important blues theme, which then turns into a fugue. As in so many orchestral scores that include piano, the keyboard plays a significant part, often taking a solo riff. The music begins slowly, somberly, as though the depths of some inchoate entity were just beginning to stir. It then builds to bright, jazzy, syncopated, Dixieland-inspired sections in which individual brass instruments go their own way in pseudo-improvisational style. There is a return to the dirgelike opening, but the up-beat, jazzy mood always comes back around. Complex syncopation, raucous Bronx-cheer smears, glissandi and slides, shocking modulations, and astringent dissonances abound. At one point the sober and the upbeat are heard simultaneously. Despite its complexity, it all adds up to a boisterous, fun-filled tour de force. In its use of Afrocentric themes, its brashness, its incorporation of jazz rhythms, and its instrumentation as well as its unfettered spirit, the piece is typical of the mood and methods of so many Parisian composers of the 1920s.

10

Paris in the 1920s, Part II

Les Six, The Clubs, Shakespeare & Company, George Antheil, L'École d'Arcueil

*U*pon Milhaud's return from Brazil, his Paris apartment became a frequent Saturday night meeting place for his group of friends to exchange their newly written music and poetry. Following these intimate weekly recitals, the group would remove themselves to dinner at some neighborhood bistro. Milhaud soon reconnected with another old friend, Jean Wiéner, who was playing nightly in La Gaya, a club on the rue Duphor, in order to support his wife and child. When the recital crowd grew too large for Milhaud's apartment he was glad to move the whole coterie to La Gaya.

As Eveline Hurard-Viltard writes in her *Le Groupe des Six ou le matin d'un jour de fête* (The Group of Six, or the morning of a festival day), "Everybody came: [author André] Gide, kings, Mistinguett [famous cabaret singer], the Rothschild set, and naturally the Saturday regulars."[1] Composers Arthur Honegger and Jacques Ibert had been part of the gatherings from the beginning, as were many poets and novelists. Word of the celebrities and music to be found at La Gaya spread, and eventually its owner, an astute entrepreneur named Moyses, decided to open a larger, more elegant place on the rue Boissy d'Anglais. It was for this new *boîte de nuit* that he asked to use the name Le Boeuf sur le Toit.

Although the composers and writers who met at Le Boeuf were intensely independent, a few combined efforts began to come of all these friendly get-togethers. A collection of piano pieces by Georges Auric (*Prélude*), Louis Durey (*Romance sans paroles* [Song without Words]), Arthur Honegger (*Sarabande*), Darius Milhaud (*Mazurka*), Francis Poulenc (*Valse*), and Germaine Tailleferre (*Pastorale*) was published shortly after the war, a point made by Jean Cocteau in his manifesto *Le coq et l'arlequin* (The Cock and the Harlequin).[2] Such collaboration was not without precedent. In June 1917, while the war still raged and Milhaud himself was still in Brazil, a concert featuring works by Auric, Durey, Honegger, Tailleferre (the only woman in this almost exclusively male world), and Erik Satie had been given in Paris. Before this program, Satie made a speech presenting the young musicians, announcing that they all "viennent de constituer le groupe des Nouveaux Jeunes" (had just begun to constitute the group of New Youth).[3] It was rumored that Satie had invited Ravel and beloved teacher and respected composer Charles Koechlin (1867–1951) to join the New Youth, but both declined. The birthdates of those who eventually became Les Six, as well as their relative standing as composers, shows the anachronism the inclusion of the two older composers would have posed:

Durey	1888–1979
Honegger	1892–1955
Milhaud	1892–1974
Tailleferre	1892–1983
Poulenc	1899–1963
Auric	1899–1983

In an article entitled "Un livre de Cocteau: Les cinq russes et les six fran-çais" (A book by Cocteau: The five Russians and the six French) that ran in the paper *Comédia* on January 16, 1920, music critic Henri Collet "baptized" the musicians named above as Le Groupe des Six. The Cocteau book in question was the aforementioned *Le coq et l'arlequin*. The five Russians, who had previously been linked by many other critics and musicologists, were Nikolai Rimsky-Korsakov, César Cui, Alexander Borodin, Mili Balakirev, and Modest Musorgsky.

As a début effort the little collection of piano works was definitely weak. Said a contemporary critic,

> The *Prélude* of Auric is dry and of a deliberate poverty; the *Romance sans paroles* of Durey, despite its cloak of dissonance, is essentially Romantic; the *Sarabande* of Honegger overcharged and clumsy; the *Mazurka* of Milhaud, fresh and of a repressed primitivism; Poulenc's *Valse* deliberately banal, aggressive, and obviously based on the rhythms of Stravinsky; and Germaine Tailleferre's *Pastorale* inoffensively amiable.[4]

This less than enthusiastic reception was not unique to this singular critic. Yet the publication of the volume and the attention it received were perceived as a plus for these mostly unknown composers. And, ironically, the very elements attacked by the critic were an essential part of the aesthetic espoused by at least five of these composers. In other words, the critic didn't misconstrue the music, he just didn't like it.

With the exception of Honegger, who differed from the others in many significant ways (not least his Swiss parentage and education), Les Six did share an aesthetic vision for a period of time. Harking back to Emmanuel Chabrier, whom they regarded as their spiritual grandfather, and Satie, whom they acknowledged to be their ever-present sire, they aimed for simplicity, brevity, and accessibility.

Chabrier and Satie, albeit in quite different ways, deliberately kept their melodies simple and often borrowed popular or folk tunes for their compositions. Instead of elaborate modulations, they favored strings of juxtaposed chord blocks; rather than hour-long symphonies or tone poems, they opted for shorter formats. Chabrier liked virtuosity—he was a wild and wonderful pianist—but Satie preferred an apparent although sometimes deceptive ease of execution. Banality was not to be avoided—it was part of the modern music-hall experience and perfectly suitable for the concert stage. Satie thought of his compositions as ephemeral and aimed to please the public that existed rather some unknown future audience. Therefore, he held that a work need not endure through the ages to be successful, and posthumous fame did not tempt him.

For the most part, again with Honegger as the exception, members of Les Six found these parameters satisfactory and usually worked within them. Perhaps the most stunning deviation from these "Sixish" characteristics is Poulenc's great opera, *Dialogues des Carmélites* (The dialogues of the Carmelites), a long, austere, passionate expression of its composer's religious convictions. The opera describes the spiritual development of a young aristocratic girl, brought up in privilege, who takes the veil in the final days of the French monarchy. The nuns of the convent are sentenced to the guillotine by the French Revolutionary forces for harboring priests within their walls. At the moment of supreme crisis, after initially running away, she finds the strength to sacrifice herself along with the other nuns. The swishing of the guillotine's blade occurs fourteen times at irregular and hence unexpected intervals in the slow, hymnlike music to which the nuns march to their doom, creating one of the most chilling moments in all of opera. Although the melodies in Poulenc's *Gloria*, another religious work, are recognizably within his style, this work too has a seriousness of purpose quite distinct from most of his—and most of Les Six's—oeuvre.

If Poulenc wrote the least characteristic work of the group, he also seems to have written the most characteristic—his *Mouvements perpétuels* for piano. These three little pieces, which together take just under five minutes to perform, enjoyed an enormous vogue among pianists and audiences throughout Europe and the United States. Composed in 1918, two years before Collet gave Les Six its official title, they clearly show how Poulenc, had developed the style that later identified these composers as a group. In her book on Le Groupe des Six, Hurard-Viltard writes:

> If there is one "Six" piano work, if ever the "Six" aesthetic was made incarnate, it was in the *Mouvements perpétuels* of Poulenc. . . . [H]ere are three concise and gay little pieces . . . the melodies remain clearly tonal or adopt a simple mode . . . the second section turns on itself, *à la* Satie, monotonous and of a

lovely gray . . . although the fairground is missing, the music-hall bursts forth unbridled in the third movement . . . [an] admirable triumph of the little piece that does not seek to be a great accomplishment.[5]

By the time he turned fifteen, the precocious Poulenc had studied the scores of Debussy's *Pelléas et Mélisande*, Stravinsky's *Petrushka*, Schoenberg's earliest twelve-tone pieces for piano, and all that was new, exciting, and controversial in the musical world. He apparently rejected Schoenberg's innovations for his own compositions, but the other three composers, with the addition of Satie, remained his idols and inspiration.[6]

The influence of Stravinsky on Poulenc may be heard in the opening chord blocks of his charming Sonata for Piano Duet, also of 1918. These rhythmically insistent and percussive chords are the legitimate offspring of *The Rite of Spring*. The bright, saucy, nonchalant melody above these brusque chords could have come from a music-hall number. The middle movement of the miniature Sonata—the whole piece lasts but a few minutes—is reminiscent of Satie. Marked *Rustique*, it is pleasant, simple, melodic, and pastoral in nature. The brisk finale is replete with little five-finger exercises, scale fragments in the primal key of C. Repeated notes in the bass create a pulsating rhythm that recalls the opening passages of the first movement, syncopated ninths over the dominant pedal point and a final unprepared and unresolved chord in the combined keys of C and G-flat—twin sister of the *Petrushka* chord—mark the last few bars. Effective, easy to play and to listen to, it is a compendium of the composers Poulenc revered and the new aesthetic he drew from them.

One of Poulenc's most successful efforts in the solo piano genre is his *Suite française*, a seven-movement work of 1935. Comparing the much earlier *Mouvements perpétuels* to this later Suite, one finds many of the same stylistic characteristics: the sections are very short—*Pavane*, with its dignified and stately pace, is the longest at just over two and a half minutes—and the melodies are simple and unpretentious. As is appropriate to a suite dedicated to the sixteenth-century French composer Claude Gervaise, four of its movements are in dance forms: two *Bransles* (a dance, one from Bourgogne and one from Champagne), a *Sicilienne*, and a *Petite marche militaire* (Little military march). Side by side with its modal references to antiquity are music-hall figures and cadences. There are the inevitable wrong-note or wrong-tonality final chords and nary a tonic-dominant final cadence in sight.

Poulenc wrote dozens of compositions for piano solo; he was the only one of Les Six who had developed a virtuosic keyboard technique, and it was his instrument of choice. More in the footsteps of Chabrier than Satie, he occasionally wrote a brilliant passage or even an entire piece—the fifth of his *Eight Nocturnes*, the *Presto in G Minor*, the first of his *Quinze improvisations* (Fifteen improvisations), for example—that veers away from the group's usual self-imposed ease of execution. Almost embarrassed by these "lapses," he explained that his fingers wrote those passages.[7]

Poulenc was a very prolific composer, and his keyboard music alone would keep most pianists sufficiently occupied. Nevertheless the piano accompaniments to some of his many songs are well worth attention as well, for they are often beautiful, with evocative harmonies that measure up to those used by Debussy or Henri Duparc in their vocal works. Two of the best and most popular are *Violon* (Violin) and *Les chemins de l'amour* (The ways of love), and fortunate is the accompanist whose singer wants to perform them.

Every member of Les Six wrote music for piano solo, but only in the oeuvres of Milhaud and Poulenc do we find keyboard works still programmed today. The work of Germaine Tailleferre, little known and scarcely published in her own lifetime, has been revived by pianists hoping to spark interest in women composers. A 1980 Musical Heritage release with pianist Virginia Eskin, for example, features works by Louise Talma, Grazyna Bacewicz, Amy Beach, and Marion Bauer, and ends with Partitas and the *Perpetuum mobile* by Tailleferre.[8] The selections by Tailleferre are charming and pleasant, the perpetual motion sections lively and—unlike those of Poulenc—quite tender. In these pieces Tailleferre tends to favor the upper registers of the keyboard, which adds to the lightness and grace of the music.

Georges Auric's very successful Hollywood movie scores have by and large eclipsed his concert music, and recordings featuring the latter are rare. Most that do exist contain works by all members of Les Six—music for flute and piano or clarinet and piano by members of the group, for example—or their one collaborative production, *Les mariés de la Tour Eiffel* (The newlyweds of the Eiffel Tower). Those lucky enough to have caught a performance of an Auric work such as *Alphabet,* his impish mini song-cycle to poems by Cocteau's doomed lover Raymond Radiguet (1903–1923), know how delightful and humorous his music can be and regret the difficulty of hearing more of it. The sheet music for this work is still available and worth a look for a pianist interested in working with singers.

Radiguet's childlike texts proceed quite logically from A to Z with the first letter represented by the quatrain entitled *Album.* Auric begins his setting with the musical equivalent of the letter A, the key of C major, but after a single introductory chord in that key he gives us wildly unrelated harmonies. The tonalities never cease to jump about in a carefree, anti-academic fashion from then on. Radiguet was sixteen years old when he wrote the poems, and Auric just four years older, so both were entitled to the youthful abandon one hears in the cycle. When Radiguet was only fourteen he had a passionate affair with a woman whose husband was serving at the front. He turned this true story into *Le diable au corps* (Devil in the flesh), one of the most widely read and scandal-provoking works of fiction to emerge from World War I. Unfortunately the young author did not have much time to enjoy the success of his book, for he died in 1923, the year of its publication.

A master of brevity and wit, Auric stated his aesthetic—and that of Les Six—in an article in *La nouvelle revue française:* "The jazz-band and the circus are as boring as cathedrals and sunsets, but one finds less pretension in them."[9] His own best-known version of "jazz-band" music, *Foxtrot: Adieu à New York* (Foxtrot: Farewell to New York), was composed in 1919. With this little piece Auric said *Adieu* not only to New York, but to his interest in African American jazz as well.[10]

Honegger's piano music, like all of his compositions, is quite different from that of the other members of Les Six. It is darker, more heavily atmospheric, more difficult to play and to hear. His *Esquisses* (Sketches), for example, is a lovely, lyric, big—almost ten-minute-long—piece, while his *Toccata et variations* is virtuosic and important-sounding. There is no trace of the music-hall nonchalance so characteristic of Poulenc and Auric in these pieces, which owe more to Debussy and the German Romantics than they do to Satie or Chabrier. As though in deliberate contrast to Tailleferre, Honegger often emphasizes the deep bass registers of the keyboard.

Honegger is better known for his orchestral works than for his keyboard music. Most often performed today is his symphonic tone poem *Pacific 231* (the name of a train locomotive). The popularity of this composition was a mixed blessing for its creator, who would have preferred his fame to rest on his more abstract compositions. He insisted that he intended the piece, whose title he claimed was an afterthought, more as an impression than as a description of a locomotive and that it was a viable symphonic work without extra-musical references. In the words of *New York Times* critic Bernard Holland, "the whooshes of steam, the slow chugs, the gathering momentum and the braking to a stop are all there,"[11] so one can hardly blame audiences for considering it an example of program music and enjoying it as such. Other orchestral works by Honegger—*Pastorale d'été* (Summer pastorale), for example—are more lyric, more evocative of the countryside, and more indebted to Beethoven's Sixth Symphony than to modern machinery. Yet *Pacific 231* pointed the way to the mechanistic works of Antheil and Varèse, while *Pastorale d'été* is merely lovely to listen to.

Louis Durey, the oldest member of Les Six by several years, was the first to quit the group. He alone refused to participate in their one true joint effort, *Les mariés de la Tour Eiffel.* Even in his submission for the early album of their piano pieces, *Romance sans paroles* (Song without words), he was going against the grain, borrowing the title and mood from Felix Mendelssohn's *Songs without Words* (the title annoyed Cocteau greatly!). Durey wrote some lovely songs, which can be found on a Hyperion CD A67257, featuring baritone François Le Roux with pianist Graham Johnson. The piano parts are usually rather spare and reminiscent of Satie's style of keyboard expression. Best known of his song cycles is *Bestiaire* (Catalog of animals), published the same year as Poulenc's cycle of the same name.

None of the piano works discussed above owes much to jazz. Of course, there are syncopations throughout, but syncopation is as old as music itself; the distinctive jazz characteristics—blue notes, bent notes, and the like—by and large are missing. Ironically the only significant compositions by members of Les Six that are notably indebted to jazz are Milhaud's *La création du monde* and Honegger's *Concertino for Piano*. The irony lies in the facts that Honegger was the most "serious" of Les Six, and Paul Claudel, Milhaud's most important literary influence, was among those who found jazz trivial and uninteresting.[12] In a letter to Milhaud dated March 6, 1951, Poulenc wrote, "Now I like *Création* from which my phobia against jazz previously alienated me."[13] Obviously most of the time for most of Les Six it was the aesthetic of the circus, the fairground, and the French music hall that resonated.

By 1924, without any defining event or moment, whatever cohesiveness Les Six had had disintegrated. Musicologists continued to refer to the six composers as a group, and if not for their brief affiliation with it, the names Durey, Auric, and Tailleferre would by now be dim memories. At about the same time the interest Milhaud and Honegger had taken in jazz as a revitalizing element in classical music faded. As we have noted, American Aaron Copland continued to incorporate jazz in his concert works a little longer—the Piano Concerto of 1927 is still quite indebted to jazz—but then he too turned away from it until he composed the 1948 clarinet concerto for Benny Goodman.

The use of jazz in concert music on the part of most French and American composers was diminishing, yet interest in American music for its own sake—jazz, pop, or "serious"—had never been keener than it was in Paris in the mid-1920s. The 1925–26 season was particularly rich in American-flavored events, with Josephine Baker's spectacular debut in *La revue nègre*, brilliant concerts by American bass-baritone Paul Robeson, Charlie Chaplin's wildly successful movie *The Gold Rush*, an ever-increasing number of African American jazz clubs and dance bands, and a program of American concert music produced by Nadia Boulanger. Included in the Boulanger program were a string quartet by Copland and some piano pieces composed and performed by Virgil Thomson. Parisian critics found this American music, much of which had been conceived under the tutelage of their own Boulanger, "distressingly modern," with "no ethnic quality" to give it a "claim to the title American."[14] "Ethnic" may be seen as a code word for African American; evidently French critics, who continued to value jazz as an important art form, looked for its influence in all American compositions and were disappointed when they did not find it.

Although serious concerts created a stir, it was the combos at the clubs that really popularized American or American-style music in Paris. Parisians, tourists, and expatriates wandered from place to place, but many clubs had their own loyal regulars. Le Boeuf sur le Toit, one of the older *boîtes*, seemed to attract well-known painters and writers. Situated in the fashionable 8th Arrondissement, which also boasted the Arc de Triomphe and L'Avenue des Champs-Elysées, its address at 28 rue de Boissy d'Anglais right off La Place de la Concorde suited Picasso, Diaghilev, Tsara, and the other celebrities who frequented it. Another group of celebrities— F. Scott Fitzgerald, the Duke of Wales, the Aga Khan, Cole Porter, and others—seemed to prefer a small cabaret in Montmartre called Le Grand Duc, located at the corner of the rue Fontaine and rue Pigalle.

Le Grand Duc was opened in 1924 by Eugene Jacques Bullard (1895–1961), a fascinating African American whose life story has only recently been rediscovered.[15] Bullard was the seventh of ten children born to a poor family in southern Georgia. His school days were over at age eleven when he ran away from home. Steadily working his way north he managed to get to Norfolk, Virginia, where he stowed away on a German liner and wound up in Scotland. Still on the move, in England he joined a traveling vaudeville troupe, Belle Davis's Freedman's Pickaninnies, and become part of the emerging black expatriate movement. In 1914 he found himself in Paris where, on his nineteenth birthday (October 9, 1914), he enlisted in the French Foreign Legion to fight the advancing Germans. Wounded at Verdun, he was awarded the Croix de Guerre, the first of fifteen medals he garnered fighting in the two world wars. Even more astounding than the medals, at a time when "common wisdom" decreed that black men were genetically incapable of flying, he was trained by the French as a fighter pilot. Their confidence in him was rewarded: he flew some two dozen missions and reportedly shot down several enemy aircraft. His career as a fighter pilot was abruptly terminated when white American officers complained of this distinctly anti–Jim Crow situation.

Although Bullard occasionally played drums for jazz combos, his talents were more those of an impresario, and his timing was perfect when in 1924 he opened Le Grand Duc. There were by that time quite a few African American expatriates living in Montmartre, and they immediately made Le Grand Duc one of their principal meeting places. For a while poet Langston Hughes worked as a dishwasher there, and when such luminaries as Louis Armstrong came to town, it was to Le Grand Duc that they flocked after their paid gigs.

Among Bullard's best ideas was to invite the singer-hostess Bricktop (née Ada Beatrice Queen Victoria Louise Virginia Smith) to leave her New York job to preside at Le Grand Duc.[16] Bricktop—so named for her red hair and freckles—rapidly transformed the little *boîte* into the center of Montmartre's musical life. Singing now and then—Cole Porter thought she was a superb interpreter of his songs—she regularly devoted more time to chatting with her star-studded roster of regulars. Most of her "guests" were white, but any well-dressed person with ready cash was welcome. At the Cotton Club in Harlem, where she had sung before moving to Paris, the entertainers were all black and the customers all white. Eventually Bricktop opened her own club, called simply Bricktop's. F. Scott Fitzgerald's melancholy portrait of Montmartre after the U.S. stock market crash and before the impending Nazi invasion, *Babylon Revisited*, mentions only Bricktop's club by name: "He passed a lighted door from which issued music, and stopped with the sense of familiarity; it was Bricktop's, where he had parted with so many hours and so much money."[17]

At the height of *le tumulte noir* (the black tumult), as the Montmartre African American scene was known, there were dozens of clubs in the area featuring black jazz. The clubs were so numerous and so close together that it became the custom to start one's evening at one, order a drink and stay for a while, then leave with drink in hand to go on to the next. It was a mark of savoir faire never to end up at the bar where you started. The musicians who worked the clubs wandered too, jamming in impromptu combos for one another after closing time, which was usually early in the morning. These indefatigable performers were largely responsible for the spread of real black jazz, which was quite different from the sweeter, gentler, more insipid music played by Wiéner and his band at Le Boeuf sur le Toit.

American tourists made up a considerable percentage of the customers at Bricktop's, Moulin Rouge, Chez Florence, and the other Montmartre *boîtes*, but native Parisians and expatriates from other countries were equally enthusiastic patrons. Drinking, dancing, and listening to music made friendly exchanges easy, and social sets from both continents mixed freely. There was another venue—a far more sedate one—where similar international camaraderie was fostered: Sylvia Beach's Shakespeare & Company.

Sylvia Beach, an energetic young woman from New Jersey, fell in love with Paris while on a prewar visit with her parents. After the hostilities ended in 1919, she returned to Paris to open a bookstore, Shakespeare & Company, which carried only English-language publications.[18] A lending library as well as a store, the warm and welcoming shop on the rue Odéon almost immediately became a magnet for the British and American writers who went to Paris for extended stays in the 1920s—Hemingway, Fitzgerald, Dos Passos, Cummings, Wilder, MacLeish, and Pound the most famous.

Perhaps the best-known and certainly the most frequent visitor to the shop was James Joyce, whose *Ulysses* was published in Paris due to the good offices—and financial support—of Beach. No English or American printer would touch the novel, which the establishment viewed as obscene. Yet Parisian typesetters, not understanding a word of James's almost indecipherable manuscript, had no such scruples. Readers who scrutinize every syllable of the punning, neologism-laden work might be bemused to know that Joyce was almost blind when he proofread the galleys, that he wrote with an easily smudged pencil, and that most of the manuscript was typed by whoever came into Shakespeare & Company with an hour to spare, including Beach's mother.[19]

While most of Beach's celebrity clients were writers, a fair number of expatriate composers also became subscribers to her lending library. Most of Boulanger's American students—Copland, Thomson, and others— borrowed and bought books from Shakespeare & Company, enjoying its warm fire in the chilly Parisian winters and relishing the chance to speak English with one another. The two rooms above the store were often a refuge for struggling young writers or musicians who needed a place to camp out for a while.

One of Beach's longest-staying "guests" (she charged him the equivalent of $17 a month and welcomed his girlfriend as well) was the American composer George Antheil. Drawn to Paris by the music of Stravinsky, who was then living and working there, Antheil was "a fellow with bangs, a squished nose and a big mouth with a grin in it. A regular American high school boy."[20] Today Antheil is known primarily for his music for Hollywood movies, but for over a year (1923–24) he was the musical toast of Paris, sweeping Beach, Pound, and the whole Shakespeare & Company entourage into the vortex of Paris musical life.[21]

Antheil's first big splash in that sophisticated town was at a solo concert of his own piano pieces, *Airplane Sonata* and *Sonata Sauvage* (Wild [or savage] sonata), both written in Trenton, New Jersey, shortly before his first trip to Paris. Held at the prestigious Théâtre des Champs-Elysées on October 4, 1923, the performance of these wildly percussive, pseudo-primitive pieces played in Antheil's idiosyncratic, near-hysterical style (supposedly he kept a loaded pistol in his piano when he played) caused a sensation. Although both his attitude and his music would change dramatically in the 1930s and 1940s, these piano works embodied Antheil's principal aesthetic theory at that time. He held firmly that twentieth-century music must reflect the cacophonous civilization in which it was being composed. This theory entailed eschewing two of the three elements long considered essential to Western music, melody and harmony, and concentrating exclusively on percussive, mechanistic, motoric rhythms, conveyed by a veritable arsenal of noise-making implements.

Listening to these works today it is clear to see why Antheil became known as "The Bad Boy of Music." Such is the title of his 1946 autobiography and of the CD featuring much of his piano music, as played by the heroic Marthanne Verbit and produced by Albany Records (Troy 146). The first of the two early sonatas on the disc, the so-called *Airplane,* is six minutes long; nowhere in its three brief movements does one hear a tune or a recognizable harmony. Even the slow section, which features some Webernesque bloops and bleeps, maintains a fiercely nontonal stance. This is not twelve-tone music; this is music without any tonal scaffolding. The outer sections are raucous, energetic, and full of jazz rhythms, the finale sounding more like Stravinsky than Stravinsky himself. As becomes apparent when hearing more of Antheil's compositions of the 1920s, the glissando is one of his favorite devices: a perfect expression of his ideas, in itself it denies pitch, the primal building block of Western music. We see this device again when the protagonist of Thomas Mann's *Doctor Faustus* decides to "take back" Beethoven's *Ode to Joy* because he has been tricked by the Devil, composing a piece beginning with shrieking descending glissandi of human voices and thus denying pitch and speech, two decidedly human elements. Antheil's second sonata is more of the same, although now and then a melodic idea seems to intrude, only to be squelched as soon as possible. Here we have scale passages as well as glissandi, and motoric chords both reminiscent of Stravinsky's *Rite of Spring* and predictive of Prokofiev's piano technique, though Prokofiev usually interrupts and intertwines beautiful melodies with the percussive passages.

Antheil had also composed one major orchestral work, his First Symphony, before leaving Trenton. It is far less raw and raucous than the contemporaneous piano pieces, as is no doubt inevitable when full string sections are involved. Its most interesting feature is the wonderful jazz rhythms Antheil has these somewhat conventional orchestral forces perform, making it one of the earliest examples of symphonic jazz, a short-lived subgenre of concert music (Gershwin's *Rhapsody in Blue* dates from 1924).

Using some of the material from the early piano pieces he had already played in his Parisian debut, Antheil began work on his principal Parisian product—the composition for which he is best known—*Ballet mécanique* (Mechanical ballet, 1924). He began this effort with the encouragement of poet Ezra Pound, with whom he had become friendly at Beach's shop. Pound, a tone-deaf music lover and would-be composer who had not yet begun to manifest his infamous political leanings, firmly believed in Antheil's aesthetic proposition that only mechanistic music was appropriate for modern times. Together, Antheil supplying the music and Pound providing much of the hype, they treated Paris audiences to what they loved best—a riot-inciting concert. The French concert-going public hadn't had so much fun since the 1913 premiere of Stravinsky's *Rite of Spring*.

Ballet mécanique was based on an austere and harsh aesthetic: no melody, no harmony, just mechanical sound. The effect, which one might expect to be stark and unattractive, is anything but. It is surprisingly gay, exuberant, and at times downright funny. Such somber analytic notes as "The second part begins with a martial tattoo on the pianos and glockenspiel, accompanied by an aeroplane propeller pedal point" seem—however accurate—absurd. Equally odd is the list of instruments used in this 1953 version of the piece: eight pianos, glockenspiel, small airplane propeller, large airplane propeller, gong, cymbal, woodblock, triangle, snare drum, tambourine, small electric bell, and large electric bell. This wildly innovative orchestration results in a joyous masterpiece. Xylophones, pianos, and glockenspiel hurl glissandi into space, while vaguely oriental intervals make up tiny snatches of melody. Delicate Webernesque interludes interrupt the louder sections, while adumbrations of Gershwin's *Fascinating Rhythm* set the toes to tapping.

It is difficult to understand why audiences took offense at this amusing, light-hearted, charming novelty piece. Part of the fuss was no doubt extramusical: a great deal of publicity, including false reports of the composer's disappearance in darkest Africa where he had supposedly gone in search of authentic primitive rhythms, preceded its premiere. Then too there was the shock of the instrumentation: Antheil's original scoring called for, among other sundries, player pianos, whistles, and that aforementioned airplane propeller. Evidently it was not possible to fit a real propeller on the stage of the Théâtre des Champs-Elysées, so several electric fans were set up as a substitute. When Vladimir Golschmann, the conductor of the premiere, gave the signal for the fans to begin whirring in front of the loudspeakers, they created such a wind current that a gentleman in the second row lost his toupée, or so the newspaper accounts of the event reported. There was the predictable riot, with

> Man Ray [Dadaist artist] punching somebody in the nose in the front row, Marcel Duchamp [painter of the notorious *Nude Descending a Staircase*] arguing loudly with somebody else in the second row. In a box nearby Erik Satie was shouting 'What precision! What precision!' and applauding. In the gallery the police came in and arrested the surrealists who, liking the music, were punching everybody who objected.[22]

Thus read Antheil's description of his great triumph. Perhaps in this case something was gained in translation for Antheil was unable to reproduce his *succès de scandale* in America. Antheil spoke not a word of French and, until Beach enlightened him was unaware of the delightful pun inherent in the title of this mechanically conceived piece: *balai,* pronounced almost exactly like *ballet,* is the French word for broom, hence *un balai mécanique* is an electric carpet sweeper. *Ballet mécanique* was booed and then dismissed by irate critics after its Carnegie Hall premiere on April 10, 1927.

The following year (1928), poet William Carlos Williams wrote a brief article for the journal *Transition* with the verbose title "George Antheil and the Cantilene Critics: A Note on the First Performance of Antheil's Music in New York City: April 10, 1927." In the article Williams lambastes the critics for ignoring the music in favor of snide, superfluous, and superficial remarks on Antheil's personal appearance and stage presence, attributing their failure to respond to the music itself to a natural hostility to anything new. He rebuts the critics' assertions that most of the audience left in the middle of the concert, noting that the vast majority remained till the end and gave the last piece, which he calls the *Jazz Symphony,* "wild" applause. His own reason for valuing the music is very interesting in view of the way the volume of most music—especially the popular—has increased in the last few decades: going directly from Carnegie Hall to the subway he finds that the noise of the trains had been "mastered, subjugated" by Antheil's music. In *Ballet mécanique,* Williams continues, "Antheil had taken this hated thing life and rigged himself into power over it. . . . [B]y hearing Antheil's music, seemingly so much noise, when I actually came upon noise in reality I found that I had gone up over it."[23]

Despite Williams's defense of his work, the virtually unanimously hostile critical reaction in his own country to *Ballet mécanique* and other works eventually sent their composer to the sunnier critical climes of Hollywood. He certainly did not stop composing concert music, however. Max Ernst's surrealist collage novel *La femme cent têtes,* which may be strictly translated as "The woman [of] one hundred heads" but which sounds something like *La femme sans tête* or "The woman without [a] head" inspired him to compose forty-five piano preludes, each of which portrays one of Ernst's etchings. A few years later, Antheil attempted to forge a typical American style with an opera called *Transatlantic,* which had its premiere in Frankfurt, Germany, in 1930. The protagonist of this piece was a rich, corrupt American politician. The opera, like so many contemporary works of Copland and Milhaud, makes evocative use of Latin American rhythms, in this case the seductive pulsations of the tango. In the 1940s Antheil composed a delightful group called *Eleven Valentine Waltzes* as a gift for a friend. This nostalgic and gently ironic work has close affinities with some of Poulenc's most popular songs, such as *Le violon* and *Les chemins de l'amour,* as well as fond references to Ravel's works in waltz time.

For many years after *Ballet mécanique* Antheil was relegated to a footnote of music history. A late flowering of productivity in the 1940s and 1950s resurrected his reputation somewhat, as may be ascertained by the relative sizes of entries under his name in the *New Grove Dictionary of Music,* and by recent commentaries on his work. Contemporary music historian Kenneth Bindas, for example, sees Antheil as the first American composer who "tried to recreate and define musical composition in relation to the changes brought about by the machine and technology."[24] Regardless of his own prominence as a composer, Antheil's theories were themselves influential in his own time and in later decades, perhaps serving as the guiding principles of what later became known as *musique concrète.*

Antheil was the composer most closely associated with Shakespeare & Company, but others came and went. Ezra Pound himself, despite his documented inability to carry a tune, tried his hand at composing in the mid-1920s. The success of this venture may be summed up by the title of musicologist Richard Taruskin's review of a recording of Pound's music in the *New York Times:* "Ezra Pound, Musical Crackpot." Nevertheless, some of Pound's theories resonate today. He regarded poetry as a performance art rather than a form of literature, valuing above all its sound, and agreed with the Greeks that music and poetry were inseparable. Copland borrowed a few books from the lending library, but complained that his studies with Boulanger kept him too busy to read. Milhaud was made part of the inner circle because of Beach's fondness for his wife, Madeleine Milhaud, and Poulenc was similarly included because of his friend Raymonde Linossier. There were other native French men and women on Beach's lending-library subscription list, but none was as anomalous an aficionado as Erik Satie.[25]

Satie met Beach through her French friend and companion, Adrienne Monnier, whose all-French bookstore was a short distance from Shakespeare & Company. In Beach's words, "He called me 'mees,' the only English word he knew, I imagine, and turned up regularly, always carrying an umbrella, rain or shine; no one had ever seen him without one!"[26] As antic in his own way as Antheil, he fit right in with the group. It is hardly surprising that he cheered *Ballet mécanique* at its riotous premiere performance, for his own use of sirens, typewriters, airplane propellers, and other unconventional instruments in *Parade* had preceded the Antheil work by several years. (Sirens seemed to be de rigueur for Parisian composers at that time; as we shall see, Edgar Varèse included one—specifically a New York firehouse siren—in his *Amérique.*)

Satie died in 1925, his most important work having been done between about 1895 and 1919. Nevertheless his influence on the younger generation continued long after his death. In addition to Les Six, whose members never wavered in their respect and regard for him, there was another less well-known coterie even more dedicated to the master, the so-called École d'Arcueil (School of Arcueil). Typical of his idiosyncratic lifestyle, Satie lived in an unfashionable industrialized suburb of Paris called Arcueil; Henri Sauguet and the other acolytes in L'École, Roger Désormière, Maxime Jacob, and Henri Cliquet-Pleyel, used the place-name to align themselves publicly with the older composer, who was often referred to as *le maître d'Arcueil* (the master of Arcueil).

Sauguet's principal successes were his scores for ballets, particularly those like the Diaghilev commissioned *La chatte* (The Female Cat). *La chatte* ran for over one hundred performances and probably would have had even more were it not for Diaghilev's death in 1929, which effectively put an end to the Ballets Russes. Sauguet was extremely prolific, composing many light operas that were also quite popular at the time, symphonies, a violin concerto, three piano concerti, and even a work for harmonica and chamber orchestra. His music, as befits a disciple of Satie, was unpretentious and spontaneous, polished and without ambitions toward profundity.

Including his two suites for children, all of Sauguet's piano works display typical Gallic wit and ingenuity. He obviously enjoyed the sonic possibilities inherent in music for two pianos and wrote several works in that genre, the most extended of which is *Les jeux de l'amour et du hasard* (Games of love and chance, inspired by the delicate play of that name by Pierre Marivaux). *Les jeux* was composed in 1932; *Valse brève* (Short waltz), another piece for two pianos, was written eighteen years later, but it still shows the same charm and insouciance characteristic of Poulenc and others of Les Six. Like Samuel Barber's *Souvenirs* for two pianos (1952), which may in its debt, *Valse brève* was composed for and recorded by the two-piano team Gold and Fizdale. Both works are sweetly nostalgic, looking back to the more genteel days of tea dances in elegant hotels (Barber placed his suite at the Plaza Hotel in New York).

As for the other members of L'École d'Arcueil, Roger Désormière is better remembered as a conductor and orchestrator than as a composer in his own right, yet was successful when he joined Auric in composing for films. Maxime Jacob was a friend of Milhaud's. When still a young man he entered a monastery, thereby ending his musical career before achieving true mastery. Prior to this life change, however, he successfully collaborated with Sauguet on *Viñes aux mains de fée* (Viñes of the magical hands) of 1925, a two-minute, fifteen-second tribute to Spanish pianist Ricardo Viñes, who was the first interpreter of so much important French music. Sauguet composed the *primo* part and Jacob contributed the *secondo*, but the two fit well with no dissonance to speak of. Of the four members of L'École d'Arcueil, Henri Cliquet-Pleyel seems to have left almost no impression on posterity, making him perhaps the ideal Satie disciple.

In March 1928 George Gershwin went to Europe, accompanied by his sister, Frances, his brother Ira, and Ira's wife. In Paris the Gershwins heard the French premieres of *Rhapsody in Blue* at the Théâtre Mogador and *Concerto in F* at the Théâtre des Champs-Elysées. The concerto was conducted by Vladimir Golschmann with Dimitri Tiomkin at the piano. Critics and audiences alike were ecstatic about both works, all agreeing that they had heard attractive, listenable, thoroughly successful amalgams of jazz and symphonic music. Gershwin was inspired by his first acquaintance with the city, and bought real French taxi horns for performances in the United States of his newly begun *An American in Paris*.[27] The rapport between French and American composers and listeners seemed to grow more and more solid.

Edgar Varèse and Igor Stravinsky

o one exemplifies the intertwining of French and American music better than Edgar (sometimes spelled Edgard) Varèse. He was born in Paris in 1883, and after many transatlantic comings and goings he settled in New York City, where he died in 1965. For most of his adult life he felt himself to be a quintessential New Yorker, and loved his bohemian surroundings in Greenwich Village.

Varèse studied with Vincent d'Indy at the Schola Cantorum (1903–1905) and then at the Conservatoire, but the greatest influences on his early musical development were Claude Debussy and Igor Stravinsky. He knew Satie, Apollinaire, Picasso, Duchamp, and others of the Parisian avant-garde but was not part of their or any other school. A long period of study in Berlin (1907–1913) led to his acquaintance with the structural innovations of Arnold Schoenberg, who became another seminal influence. In 1913 he brought some Schoenberg scores back to Paris with him and was the first to introduce Debussy to this new kind of music. The French master's comments on this German newcomer were ambiguous: "Take the music of Arnold Schoenberg, for instance. I have never heard any of his works. My interest was roused by the things that are written about him, and I decided to read one of his quartets, but I have not yet succeeded in doing so."[1]

Schooled as an engineer specializing in the science of sound (he said he preferred the phrase "organized sound" to the term "music"),[2] Varèse was fascinated by the early experiments with electric instruments then taking place in Paris. Throughout his life he tried to find or invent new instruments through which to express the sounds of modern civilization.

In 1915, after serving for several months in the French army, Varèse went to the United States where he helped to found the International Composers' Guild. He introduced much modern music to American audiences through this organization, yet most were not terribly receptive to it. He was back in Paris in time for the much touted premiere of George Antheil's *Ballet mécanique,* the best-loved scandal of the 1923–24 season. His own *Amérique,* begun in 1921 but revised throughout the decade, has much in common with the Antheil piece.

Much has been written about *Amérique*. To Henry Cowell it was "a Frenchman's concept of America," hence the French spelling of the title. It is "acrid and telling, with a magnificent hardness of line," continues Cowell. "Varèse breaks no rules of ordinary harmony; they do not come into consideration at all." In his article on Varèse, published in *American Composers on American Music*, Cowell also passes the rather curious judgment that Varèse's work "has nothing in particular to do with America," a statement countered by many who find in it the very heart of New York City.[3] But in the 1920s and early 1930s, to portray America in sound was to recreate the atmosphere of the wide open spaces, the mountains and the prairies, as Copland and Thomson did. This is the very nostalgia Varèse eschews. To a more recent critic *Amérique* combines "the monumentality of Europe's Romanesque cathedrals with the noise, vulgarity and anxiety of American life,"[4] an assessment easier to agree with. Varèse himself said that *Amérique* symbolized "New Worlds on earth, in the sky, or in the mind of men."[5]

Listening to *Amérique* is a taxing experience. In its definitive version it is scored for 125 musicians including a twelve-person percussion battery. Its rhythmic complexity stems from Varèse's decision to deemphasize melody and harmony, both of which he considered inappropriate to representations of modern life. This is an aesthetic attitude which he shared with both Antheil and Pound. Whatever references to melody do occur are interwoven in continuously evolving polyphony, with as little repetition as possible.

The piece begins in a deceptively quiet, wistful mood. A flute passage reminds the listener of Debussy, especially the evocative solo-flute passage that begins the older composer's *L'après-midi d'un faune*. Soon, however, brass and massed strings interrupt the idyllic sounds (interestingly enough, Debussy encouraged Varèse to find his own sounds, even to use noise if that's what he needed to do). Harp glissandi return Debussy to mind, and a sort of agon between the two opposing strains ensues. There is what seems to be the sound of a quacking duck, but the affect is not comical, nor are the intermittent siren sounds amusing. There is something primordial, elemental, and stormlike in the music. Syncopations of all kinds abound, but perhaps the strangest rhythmic element is a harsh waltz time that seems incongruous yet somehow inevitable. This is a composition of great originality and, congruent with Antheil's theories, harshly cacophonous. Nevertheless the use of large string sections, which is definitely not typical of Varèse's later output, keeps it in the realm of traditional symphonic music. Despite the passage of time and exposure to so much modern music, audience reaction to *Amérique* at a New York Philharmonic concert in June 2003 was one of stunned disbelief. The piece was eighty years old at the time, yet because it cannot be duplicated on a CD, and the composition is rarely programmed, these twenty-first century listeners were not prepared for the assault on the ears created by this live performance. Whether painful or

pleasurable, appalled or attracted, one cannot deny the skill and originality of the composition. Its juxtaposed blocks of sound might be deemed
the musical equivalent of Cubism, the style of painting introduced in 1911
by Picasso, Braque, and Gris, and in fact later works by Varèse have been
associated with the "action painting" of Jackson Pollock.

Varèse's thirst for new ways of portraying modern life in sound was
not quenched by the astonishing effects he achieved in *Amérique*, so he
turned to the new but burgeoning field of electronic instruments.[6] As
early as 1910 Ferruccio Busoni (1866–1924), the prolific German-Italian
composer with whom Varèse had studied for a time, was interested in a
crude synthesizer-like device called the Dynamaphone. Other mechanical
means of making music like the trautonium and the theremin were fash-
ioned and then largely forgotten in the years following World War I, and
the quest went on. Varèse in particular was looking for "an instrument that
can give us a continuous sound at any pitch," saying that "the composer
and the electrician will have to labor together to get it."[7]

In 1928 a French cellist and radio telegrapher named Maurice Martenot
received a patent for an electronic keyboard he called the ondes martenot
(*ondes* is French for "waves"). The first successful electronic instrument, it
is still in use today and has become very much part of modern performing life. In addition to producing the standard pitches of regular pianos,
which made the instrument easy for any pianist to master, the ondes martenot can duplicate vibrato and eerie, seamless glissandi. In addition, by
manipulating a control panel above the keyboard, the player is able to vary
the timbre and character of the tones he or she is producing.

Varèse was one of the first to incorporate this machine into a symphonic
composition, writing *Ecuatorial* (1932–1934) for two ondes martenot, regular piano, organ, trumpets, trombones, low-voice male chorus, and a plethora of percussion instruments operated by six players. Since the traditional
piano has a major role in this fascinating piece, we may feel justified in
exploring it in some detail.

Varèse had expressed his desire to reproduce the sounds of the urban
jungles of machine and manmade skyscrapers and noise in which he felt
so at home. *Ecuatorial*, on the other hand, portrays the "beautiful and sinister landscape of South America,"[8] with its deeply resonant forest canopies
and mysterious animal and bird sounds. But Varèse's is a jungle in which
man is always present. In it are jungle drums and deliberately artificial
birdcalls quite different from the realistic ones simulated by Olivier Messiaen or imitated by Beethoven in the *Pastoral* Symphony. The use of a
chorus singing words—speech being one of the principal factors distin-
guishing man from the other animals—confirms the composer's desire to
include mankind in his equatorial landscape.

Ecuatorial opens with a brief piano figure followed immediately by a
blaring trumpet. Tremendous outbursts of sound, supplied by the brass,

organ, and drums, alternate with quiet moments in which one hears the piano, wood blocks, and the ondes martenot. The text of the piece is a poem based on an ancient Mayan invocation to the Spirit of the Earth and Sky as interpreted by Guatemalan poet Miguel Asturias. The chorus, used primarily in its lower registers, in turn sings, speaks, whispers, or intones these words. Although the Varèse work is far more austere and innovative, at times *Ecuatorial's* use of the chorus is similar to that in Carl Orff's *Carmina Burana,* which was composed only one year later. After so much volume and intensity, *Ecuatorial* fades away, with only solemn snare drums and softly swooping ondes martenot remaining. The Sony CD featuring Pierre Boulez and the New York Philharmonic (SMK 68334) gives a most effective reading of this unique composition.

Varèse's later compositions strayed further and further from traditional instrumentation. *Ionisations,* was scored for two sirens and thirty-seven percussion instruments. Composed prior to *Ecuatorial* during one of his periodic stays in Paris (1928–1933), it is perhaps his best-known work. It was the first European composition to be almost completely devoid of pitched sounds, which figure only in the coda. After *Ecuatorial* Varèse fell silent for twenty years, perhaps awaiting the technological advances that would allow him to create *Déserts* (1954), a piece which may be described as "a collage of taped sounds." This work is often cited as being the one that earned its composer the title "father of electronic music," but as we have seen, his pioneering efforts came long before.

The 1954 edition of *Grove's Dictionary of Music and Musicians* identifies Igor Stravinsky (1882–1971) as an "American composer of Russian origin." Both the Russians and the French might take issue with this statement. In truth, Stravinsky's life divides itself into three more or less equal parts: the first third as a young man in Russia, studying law but at the same time composing under the guidance of fellow law student Rimsky-Korsakov; the next third achieving fame in Paris; and the final segment—due to the Nazi threat —living and working in the United States. Stravinsky's influence was surely felt earlier in Paris than elsewhere, for his best-loved and most seminal works, *L'oiseau de feu* (The firebird, 1910), *Pétrouchka* (Petrushka, 1911), and *Le sacre du printemps* (The rite of spring, 1913) were first heard in Paris.

These three compositions had been commissioned by Sergei Diaghilev (1872–1929) for his Ballets Russes, which had its home in Paris.[9] The Ballets Russes, ironically enough, never performed in Russia. The formation of the troupe was the inevitable but hardly foreseen outcome of Diaghilev's many presentations of ballets starring Russian dancers. The year after the premiere of *The Rite of Spring,* World War I broke out, making travel impossible, and three years later the Russian Revolution occurred, making travel to his homeland undesirable for an elitist group like Diaghilev's.

Through commissions like these, Diaghilev became a major figure in the cultural life of Paris, simultaneously reviving interest in the art of ballet, introducing Russian composers to the French, and giving avant-garde French composers a sparkling venue for their works. He entered Paris as the head of a show of Russian art held at Le Grand Palais that dealt primarily with painting and sculpture, but there was no branch of creativity foreign to him. By 1907 he was presenting concerts featuring Russian composers at Le Théâtre des Champs-Elysées. His instinct for the superb led him to import the great Russian bass Fyodor Chaliapin in 1908 for the first Paris performance of Musorgsky's opera *Boris Godunov*. The following year he gave the Parisians excerpts from Glinka's *Ruslan and Ludmila* and Borodin's *Prince Igor,* Rimsky-Korsakov's *Ivan the Terrible,* and assorted ballets. Anna Pavlova, Nijinsky, Fokine, Bakst, Petipa—all the great choreographers, designers, and dancers—took part in his glittering presentations. Not only did Picasso design the sets for *Parade,* another Diaghilev project, but he also designed many of the front curtains for new Diaghilev productions. How did this Russian émigré accomplish all this? "I am first a great charlatan, though with brio," Diaghilev explained in a letter to his stepmother; "secondly a great *charmeur;* . . . a man with a great quantity of logic, but with very few principles."[10]

Whatever Diaghilev's principles, or lack thereof, there was no denying his willingness to take a chance, as he did by commissioning the little-known Stravinsky to write a score for a ballet based on a Russian folk tale about a magic bird. The ballet and score were both resounding successes, bringing the young Stravinsky to Paris and launching him on an international career that lasted over half a century. Then came *Petrushka,* equally appealing to critics and audiences despite its daring use of bitonality (the famous C/F-sharp chords). Stravinsky arranged this score for solo piano, and it is devilishly difficult. The last of the compositional triumvirate, and effectively the end of Stravinsky's Russian period, was *The Rite of Spring.*

Diaghilev had a knack for attracting scandal, which seemed only to help the box-office receipts. His production of Nijinsky's choreography to Debussy's *L'après-midi d'un faune,* for example, caused a near riot because of its overt autoeroticism. But no scandal outdid that caused by *The Rite of Spring.* So violent was the audience's reaction at the premiere that Stravinsky threatened never to compose for ballet again. Diaghilev persuaded him to continue and, until Diaghilev's death, Stravinsky composed score after wonderful score for the Ballets Russes.

The Rite of Spring is not, of course, for piano, nor is there an authorized piano reduction for recital purposes. Stravinsky did, however, write a two-piano version of the work, which was to be used only for rehearsals of the corps de ballet. That piano score was long lost, but a few years before his death Stravinsky found it in an auction house, bid on it himself, and reacquired it. It has since been recorded, and although there are tedious moments—segments when the orchestra has little to do behind the dancers—it offers instructive insights into the original composition. The raw primitivism that was so shocking to audiences is considerably blunted by the sound of the two pianos, which are, after all, highly civilized instruments. On the other hand, the intricate rhythms are easier to follow and even more fascinating in this bare-bones fluoroscope of the piece.

Even when considered only as an orchestral score, this work, with its insistent percussiveness and its "primitive" rhythms that take precedence over melody or harmony, influenced many keyboard compositions. Poulenc's sonata for piano duet, whose opening chords are clearly derived from it, has already been mentioned. In subtler ways much of what we hear in the piano music of Antheil, Prokofiev, Bartók, Khachaturian, and others from all over the world may be traced to this seminal work. In fact, it may be fair to say that the modern era in music really begins in 1913 with *The Rite of Spring.*

Petrushka's resemblance to *The Rite of Spring* is obvious even in its original orchestral setting, but in its piano arrangement, robbed of its instrumental colors, the intensely percussive rhythmic nature it shares with the slightly (two years) later work is highlighted. The stories the two ballets convey are, however, quite different. *The Rite of Spring* portrays a primitive rite of sacrifice, and *Petrushka* tells the story of the puppet whose name it bears. (*Petrushka* is the Russian equivalent of Pierrot. Interestingly, Schoenberg's *Pierrot lunaire,* another seminal work, was composed just one year later.) Because the eponymous hero of *Petrushka* experiences the modern angst of loss and loneliness, Stravinsky's score includes lyric and mournful moments, and because it is based on folklore it is full of recognizable Russian folk tunes. The virtuoso pianist can reproduce these elements, but the fuller, more aggressive orchestral sections are difficult for ten fingers on eighty-eight keys to duplicate. Robert Lubin, the pianist on the Bridge Records disc (BCD 9051) of Stravinsky's piano music, does a creditable job of it. If memory serves, a live performance by Artur Rubenstein was an astonishing feat.

His arrangement of *Petrushka* is more extensive and impressive than any of the works Stravinsky actually composed for keyboard. He did, though, write two sonatas for solo piano, the first in 1903–1904, the second twenty years later, the Sonata for Two Pianos in 1943, a Concerto for Two Pianos (1935), two sets of *Easy Pieces* for piano duet (1915 and 1917), and a few short solo works. Among the more interesting of this rather subsidiary group of compositions is *Piano Rag Music* of 1919.

In *Jazz Away from Home,* Chris Goddard states that Stravinsky was the only one of the Parisian composers attracted to jazz who was able to make the idiom his own, rather than merely borrowing clichés from it to spice up his own compositions. Stravinsky "dress[es] ragtime syncopation in his own unique style," says Goddard. "The harmonic dissonances are clearly

Stravinsky, but they are also extensions of the things which Earl Hines and J. P. Johnson were to do ten years later."[11] It is possible that these two brilliant jazz pianists were influenced by Stravinsky, but it is equally possible that the influence ran in the other direction, that the ostinato and incremental repetitions found in jazz (and Russian folk music) were at least partly responsible for the sheer physicality of *Rite of Spring, Petrushka,* and *Piano Rag Music.*[12] Jazz and Stravinsky, each in its own way but hardly without connection, used rhythm to merge the primitively ritualistic and the urbanely sophisticated.

Stravinsky's introduction to jazz did not come through hearing one of the Paris-based African American combos, but came rather by seeing a page of a jazz score brought to him in Switzerland by conductor Ernest Ansermet.[13] This visual rather than aural initial acquaintance had two effects on Stravinsky's interpretations of jazz: on the one hand, he had no idea how jazz musicians made the music "swing" and how impossible it was to notate their subtle rhythmic adjustments; on the other hand, he was free to make those rhythms his own. Stravinsky did eventually become an aficionado of live American jazz, attending Charlie Parker's concerts at New York's Birdland club in the early 1950s. After having written the *Ebony Concerto* for jazzman Woody Herman in 1946, Stravinsky had become "an icon of jazz fans" and was treated with great deference at the clubs.[14]

In the performance of *Piano Rag Music* on the Bridge Records CD mentioned above, there is a definite rigidity to the rhythms which separates it from a more familiar free-wheeling jazz. Ordinarily one might blame the performer, but Stravinsky's square conducting of his own *Ragtime for Eleven Instruments* (1918) exonerates the pianist on the recording. Roy Harris may have put his finger on the difference between European and American composers' use of jazz in an article entitled "Problems of American Composers."[15] As noted in chapter 8, he wrote, "Our [i.e., American] rhythmic impulses are fundamentally different from the rhythmic impulses of Europeans." American composers, less steeped in the tradition of two- or four-bar phrases "answered" by phrases of equal length, tend to aim for asymmetrical balances. For Americans, Harris felt, the rhythmic impulses come first, while for Europeans they follow melodic or harmonic ideas. Harris gives as examples the "blues" movement of Ravel's Sonata for Violin and Piano, whose rhythms he finds "studied" rather than integral to the music. In contradiction to Goddard's assessment, he hears in Stravinsky's *Les noces* (The wedding), to cite another example, "an imbroglio of rhythmic patterns" in which the melody is "submerged."

Even without American "swing," Stravinsky's rhythms in *Piano Rag Music* are clearly jazz-based, with highly complex cross-syncopations. The music is percussive, with "run-along" figurations interrupted by banging chords. There is an occasional and unexpected music-box effect, and in general the piece is fragmented and varied. Like so many jazz pieces it doesn't really come to an end—it just stops.

Les cinq doigts (The five fingers) and the two sets of *Easy Pieces* for piano four-hands are teaching pieces. The former is a set of five-finger exercises that go from very simple to quite challenging, manifesting Stravinsky's typical astringent harmonies, complex tonal relationships, and repetitive chords. They are comparable to Bartók's first book of the *Mikrokosmos*. The four-hand pieces give the student an opportunity to participate in some sophisticated material, for the *secondo* (teacher) parts are full and rich. They also force the student—and the teacher—to count with absolute accuracy if they want to reach the double bar at the same time.

L'histoire du soldat (The soldier's tale) and *Les noces* (The wedding) were composed in Switzerland, where Stravinsky had taken refuge during World War I. *L'histoire* was first performed in 1918, and *Les noces* was staged by Diaghilev in 1923. Together they form a sort of postscript to their composer's Russian period (the soldier in question is, of course, Russian, and the wedding is that of Russian peasants) while pointing in different directions. At this juncture non-Russian elements—some old and some new—begin to take precedence in Stravinsky's musical thought.

L'histoire and *Les noces* may thus be regarded as transitional, for while their subjects come from the master's mother country, they also exemplify Stravinsky's jazz-oriented style. Scored for four singers, chorus, percussion, and four pianos, *Les noces* eschews orchestral color. Like *L'histoire*, whose full instrumentation is influenced by that of the jazz combo (violin, double bass, clarinet, bassoon, cornet, trombone, and percussion, not to mention three actors and a mime), it is concise and spare. When performed by violin, clarinet, and piano, as it most often is, its keyboard part is rich, energetic, and virtuosic. It is primarily the pianist's responsibility to keep the steady "walking" pace that indicates the soldier's long trek, while the clarinet and violin work around the beat. In its fourth movement we hear Stravinsky's interpretation of tango, waltz, and ragtime, all of which he makes uniquely his own. As usual the tango lacks sensuality, the waltz is deliberately anachronistic, and the ragtime tempo is too rapid even to suggest the languor of a Scott Joplin piece. Like his three most famous ballets, *L'histoire*, despite its astringent harmonies, has become one of the few twentieth-century compositions popular with audiences.

The Piano Sonata of 1924 adumbrates Stravinsky's neoclassical period, which is usually said to have arrived the following year with his ballet *Pulcinella*, which he based on music then attributed to the eighteenth-century composer Giovanni Battista Pergolesi. The seldom-heard Sonata begins with a perpetual-motion figuration with interesting rhythmic interruptions. After much dissonance and polytonality, a major chord comes as a surprise ending to the section. The Sonata continues with a slower but still quite virtuosic section with an insistently rhythmic bass. The music here is dry and deliberately not pretty, featuring lots of trills and scales in the style of Mozart, but to completely different effect, yet there is an unexpected touch of tenderness in its final bars. A third section returns to the scampering momentum of the opening, once again ending with a startling major chord. Non-*legato* bass notes dominate another section which begins slowly and gently; the *legato* line in the right hand never actually blooms into the melody it seems to promise.

Far lighter in mood are Stravinsky's *Tango* for piano solo and *Circus Polka,* originally written for orchestra but arranged by its composer for keyboard (1940 and 1942, respectively). Even in the *Tango,* that most seductive of dances, there is a marked lack of sensuality in most of the music, and when a touch of the sensuous does creep in, it seems reluctant, as though the composer could not help it. The *Circus Polka* includes a bit of tango too, along with bugle calls and its own infectious polka rhythm, and here Stravinsky does relax his usual austerity.

Two major Stravinsky works for piano and orchestra, the Concerto of 1924 and the *Capriccio* of 1929, complete the composer's contributions to the keyboard literature until his much later serial-style *Movements.* After a somber introduction for piano and brass, characterized by ominous dissonances and a funeral-march rhythm, the Concerto bursts into a gay and lively *Allegro.* A brutal percussiveness lies behind the high spirits of the music, and the abrupt rhythmic changes seem arbitrary and unpredictable. Reminiscences of *Petrushka* and *The Firebird* waft through the long sections of relentless motoric force. The slow movement is only intermittently lyric—the many single notes for the pianist's right hand promise melody, but none really emerges. The harmonies tend to be gloomy, and there is not a trace of Romanticism in the section. The finale is once again lively, with scampering piano figures in almost constant motion. These figures seem not only separate from but unaware of the melodic fragments offered by the orchestra, except for an occasional and startling meeting of the two. This kind of polyphony—characteristic of Stravinsky—is governed by vertical, harmonic considerations only at these junctures; for the most part the ruling impetus is horizontal.

As one would expect from its title, the *Capriccio* is lighter and gayer than the Concerto. The opening is abrupt, and is followed by a charming interaction between the piano and piccolo, and the music is bouncy and alive with rhythmic verve. Here the touches of tango rhythm—again deprived of their customary sensuality—merely add to the overall spirit. A slower, somewhat ominous section, introduced by a crashing chord, breaks the insouciant mood for a while. Then there are grotesque moments, brief references to Baroque-style polyphony, a bit of music-hall aesthetic—a constant variety. Similar to what we have heard in the Concerto, the piano and orchestra sometimes seem oblivious of one another, only to join forces at defining cadences.

While audience and critical assessments of the works from Stravinsky's Russian period are almost unanimously positive by now, there is less agreement about his jazz-based and neoclassical compositions. For Wilfrid Mellers, for example, a work like *Piano Rag Music* "order[s] into art the uncompromising harshness of texture, the dislocated rhythmic energy of the New Orleans blues player and band."[16] Yet as we have seen, Roy Harris thought it unlikely that any European would be able to capture the rhythmic subtlety that is so inborn in the American composer—both the classical and the popular—and he makes no exception for Stravinsky.

Stravinsky's neoclassical style was seen as a new form of modernism—dry, astringent, and nonmelodic. In it the composer turns his back on ethnic color and jazz, occasionally offering witty incongruities in the form of "wrong-note" dissonances to enliven his otherwise austere compositions. Although he occasionally brought both of these elements back into his music, his enthusiasm for both had by then faded. "I like jazz," he said, "when it is the simple expression of *la musique nègre;* I like it a great deal less in its Anglo-Saxon transcriptions."[17] Perhaps, having little connection to the Anglo-Saxon world, the Russian-French-American Stravinsky exempted himself from this judgment.

Paris in the 1930s

Messiaen, La Jeune France, Ibert, Le Hot Club

livier Messiaen's *Vingt regards sur l'enfant Jésus* (Twenty gazes on the infant Jesus) is widely considered the most important composition for piano solo of the first half of the twentieth century. The work lasts about two hours and ten minutes, and was not premiered until 1944. However, like that of two other major works involving piano by Messiaen— *Visions de l'amen* (Visions of the amen) for two pianos and *Le quatuor pour la fin du temps* (Quartet for the end of time) for piano, violin, clarinet, and cello, its gestation undoubtedly began before Messiaen was drafted into the French army in 1939.

Messiaen (1908–1992) could not have been more different from the members of Les Six, Satie, Cocteau, and so many other creative people who set the often frivolous tone in Paris between the two world wars. A passionate Catholic and mystic, Messiaen revered equally the natural and the supernatural. He was an ardent ornithologist who used authentic birdsongs as part of his musical vocabulary, which also included Ravel- and Debussy-inspired sweeping piano figures, Gregorian plain chant, church modes, and ancient Greek and Hindu rhythms.[1] In 1936 he formed the group La Jeune France (The young France), with composers André Jolivet, Yves Baudrier, and Daniel Lesur. The stated objectives of the group— "sincerity, generosity and artistic good taste"—show his serious nature and that of the musicians for whom he felt an affinity.

Vingt regards is a daunting composition for both performer and audience. Its sheer length means that nothing else can be programmed with it, and its complexity makes intense concentration essential for appreciation. While the individual sections are clearly demarcated, some characteristics pervade the work: the impression of tonality despite the use of tone clusters rather than identifiable triads; the at times hypnotic repetition of single notes or chords; the exploitation of the entire keyboard and its full range of dynamic possibilities; long pauses within sections preceding abrupt conclusions; hard-to-track rhythmic patterns; a deliberate lack of harmonic progression; and—with but few exceptions—an unrelieved aura of seriousness.

Messiaen does not aim to portray Jesus or anyone else in *Vingt regards*. An occasional Poulenc, Ravel, Stravinsky, Debussy, or even vernacular-like moment can be heard in this original and unique composition, but in large part there are few passages that point to any other composer, and the only possible extra-musical reference is the chimelike quality of some of the tone clusters. Markedly missing are references to the nineteenth-century Romantics; Messiaen is far more likely to look way in the past for inspiration than to the great keyboard composers of the 1800s.

The first of the twenty *regards* is that of *le Père*, the Holy Father. It is slow moving, repetitious, and solemn. Its heavy chords and octaves are static, nonmelodic, and devoid of any indication of traditional harmonic direction. After its quiet ending the crashing chords at the beginning of the next section, *Le regard de l'étoile* (Regard of the star), are startling, to say the least. The third section, *L'échange* (The exchange), is short and almost brutal, but *Le regard de la Vièrge* (Regard of the Virgin) which follows is gentle and feminine. In this five-minute segment Messiaen writes a brief melodic figure, which he then accents on each of its components in turn. This use of variation within repetition is found in various guises throughout the work. The rapidity with which the tone clusters in the treble are played does not change the static nature of the fifth section, *Le regard du fils sur le fils* (The gaze of the Son upon the Son); this unusual combination of speed and stasis is another element of Messiaen's style in *Vingt regards*.

It is not until the tenth of the twenty, *Le regard de l'esprit de joie* (Regard of the Spirit of Joy) that Messiaen injects a welcome lighter mood. Insistent, percussive bass notes accompanied by rolled chords at irregular intervals yield to a music-hall spirit, although even here we never lose the typical Messiaen sound in which every triad is compromised by notes extraneous to it. This section—and many of the others—is extremely difficult, making almost impossible demands on the performer.

While some of the sections relate well to their titles, others do not. In this latter category is the heavy *Regard des anges* (Regard of angels, no. 14), but *Le baiser de l'enfant Jésus Christ* (Kiss of the infant Jesus) which follows is appropriately tender and caressing. Here tonality prevails despite the inevitable dissonances. The many trills in the highest register of the piano hint at the composer's fascination with birdsongs. Surprisingly, toward the end of this twelve-minute section, there is a bit of cocktail-lounge piano music; a distinctly tonal final cadence ends the section.

The penultimate section, *Je dors, mais mon coeur veille* (I sleep but my heart keeps vigil), reminds one a bit of Poulenc's song settings, as Messiaen once again lightens the mood. The work ends with its longest section, *L'église d'amour* (The church of love). Beginning in lively, energetic fashion, the music of this concluding portion is as excited as it is exalted.

Touches of banality and a real melody, adorned with Ravel-like double arpeggios, gradually yield to a long, solemn section reminiscent of the opening segment.

This taxing work is unlikely to become a staple of the concert stage. The brilliant American pianist Peter Serkin has performed it from memory—an astonishing feat—and several pianists have recorded it, but opportunities to present it uncut are obviously rare, and few pianists have the technique, stamina, or concentration to master it. Nevertheless, hearing it in its entirety is an experience worth contemplating. Study of some of the individual sections would also be rewarding for pianists.

Considerably more manageable for the performers and more accessible to the audience—and hence more frequently encountered in concert—is Messiaen's *Quatuor pour la fin du temps* (Quartet for the end of time). This work, scored for piano, cello, violin, and clarinet, was composed while Messiaen was a prisoner of war during World War II. As luck would have it, the commandant of the prison in which Messiaen found himself was a music lover who was well aware of Messiaen's reputation. He saw to it that the young composer had music paper and the time and solitude to work. Imprisoned in the camp were also a clarinetist, a violinist, and a cellist, hence Messiaen's choice of instruments (Messiaen was himself a gifted pianist and a brilliant organist). The piece received its premiere in the camp on January 15, 1941, with the officers and prisoners all shivering together in the unheated space.[2] In later years the pianist Peter Serkin, clarinetist Richard Stoltzman, violinist Ida Kafavian, and cellist Fred Sherry formed the group Tashi specifically to perform this work. Their 1976 recording of it is still regarded as definitive and has been reissued on an RCA Victor CD (7835-2-RG).

In the opinion of the *New Yorker*'s music critic Alex Ross, the eight-movement, fifty-minute quartet is "the most ethereally beautiful music of the twentieth century."[3] Once again Messiaen gives us pure music, with no attempt to portray in musical terms the place or situation in which he wrote it. In fact, as is made apparent in the passages cited below, the composer's mind was on far less stark, far more ephemeral matters than the privation of a POW camp. Messiaen wrote guides for performers and listeners for each of the eight sections of the piece; the following are the descriptions of the first three sections:

I: *Liturgy of Crystal.* Between the morning hours of three and four, the awakening of the birds: a thrush or a nightingale soloist improvises, amid notes of shining sound and a halo of trills that lose themselves high in the trees. Transpose this to the religious plane: you will have the harmonious silence of heaven.

II: *Vocalise for the angel who announces the end of Time.* The first and third parts (very short) evoke the power of that mighty angel, his hair a rainbow and his clothing mist, who places one foot on the sea and one foot on the earth.

Between these sections are the ineffable harmonies of heaven. From the
piano, soft cascades of blue-orange chords [Messiaen associated sounds with
colors, and there have been performances of *Vingt regards,* for example, in
which colors are projected on the wall behind the pianist], encircling with
their distant carillon the plainchant-like recitative of the violin and cello.
III: *Abyss of the birds.* Clarinet solo. The abyss is Time, with its sadnesses and
tediums. The birds are the opposite of Time; they are our desire for light, for
stars, for rainbows and for jubilant outpourings of song!

To use more concrete musical terms, Messiaen seems to deny Time (the
composer always uses a capital T for the word) by avoiding audible rhythmic patterns; just when the listener thinks he or she can spot a likely meter
and bar-line division, the rhythm changes and the pattern is broken. The
first section opens with a duet for piano and clarinet, but the strings soon
join in. Birdcalls and trills surround nontonal chords, which provide no
harmonic motion. Crashing chords ("the power of the mighty angel")
alternate with trills and other birdsong-like figures ("the ineffable harmonies of heaven") in the second movement. Endless melismas, rather than
recognizable melody, surround the piano's ever-present chords as the section continues. The final chords seem strangely unrelated to the music
that preceded them.

The extreme contrasts heard in these opening movements are typical
of the work as a whole. The two sections of *Praise,* one for "the eternity of
Jesus" (no. 5 for cello and piano), the other "to the immortality of Jesus"
(no. 8 for violin and piano), are the most tender of the eight. Both have
seemingly endless, meandering melodic lines supported by ever-present
piano chords. They build to ecstatic climactic peaks and then fade away
until their final tonal cadences. Despite Messiaen's stated dislike of jazz,[4]
section 6 has some suspiciously jazzlike syncopations. Messiaen calls this
movement *Dance of fury, for the seven trumpets,* referring to the trumpets of
the Apocalypse, and describes it as "the most rhythmically idiosyncratic of
the set." The composer explains the rhythms as "non-retrogradable . . .
[i.e.,] a systematic use of values which, read from left to right or from right
to left, remain the same."[5] Another section is for clarinet alone, and still
others focus on either cello or violin, some utilizing the full quartet. The
piano is a constant presence in all but the clarinet solo section. The overall
effect of the Quartet is that of austere solemnity combined with religious
and carnal ecstasy, a peculiarly French confection that can also be heard in
Gabriel Fauré's late song cycle *La chanson d'Eve* (The song of Eve).

Les visions de l'amen (Visions of the amen) for two pianos is the last of
the three major works involving piano written or conceived by Messiaen at
the end of our period of study. In this fifty-minute composition Messiaen
creates an air of mystery by scoring the *primo* and *secondo* as far apart on the
keyboard as possible, reminiscent of Beethoven's wide spacing of the two
hands in his Opus 111 Sonata. The chords deep in the bass are solemn,

while the tone clusters in the treble resonate like church chimes. There is some harmonic motion, but since it seems to lack discernible direction, the effect is static. The two parts move in and out of synchronization, sometimes apparently quite unaware of each other's existence. Their independence leads to remarkably complex cross-rhythms. The second movement is livelier than the first. It ends with unrelenting, piercingly *fortissimo* chords. There are occasional melodic fragments in the gentler sections, but the ever-present interval of the second keeps one on edge. Huge build-ups often lead to sudden, startling silences. Toward the end of the last movement one hears an almost Romantic ecstasy followed by skittering Stravinsky-like passages. Of all the French compositions for two pianos we have thus far discussed, none begins to approach the scope, originality, or seriousness of purpose of Messiaen's contribution to the genre.

Messiaen had written several less ambitious keyboard works before his army and prisoner-of-war experiences. Even in these earlier compositions one can hear seeds of the massive three works discussed above. The *Fantaisie burlesque* of 1932, for example, is a light-hearted, jolly work with music-hall flavor. Nevertheless its tone clusters and constantly changing rhythms point to the more mature pieces. The brief 1936 *Pièce pour le tombeau de Paul Dukas* (Piece for the tomb of Paul Dukas) is tonal, but Messiaen's characteristic dissonances are always present. Dukas, one of Messiaen's teachers, was at one time a highly regarded composer of operas and chamber music as well as a renowned pedagogue, and is now remembered primarily for his *Sorcerer's Apprentice*. One of Messiaen's strangest keyboard works of the 1930s is *La fête des belles eaux* (The celebration of beautiful water). Written for the Paris Exposition of 1937, *Fête* featured six women in elegant white costumes, each playing an ondes martenot, the electronic keyboard used by Varèse in his *Ecuatorial*. Here, instead of slide projections of color, the music was enhanced by gushing fountains. As though to prove that he had not lost his sense of humor or capacity for fun, in 1943 Messiaen composed a charming little *Rondeau*. Like the last movement of Haydn's quartet known as *The Joke*, the *Rondeau* has several false endings after which its delightful theme returns.

Tempting as it is to follow Messiaen's later development, we have already overstepped our 1940 limit, and so shall abandon this fascinating composer in mid-career. Messiaen had many disciples in the avant-garde of the late 1940s and 1950s, the most important of whom are Pierre Boulez and Karl Stockhausen, but of the composers gathered around him in La Jeune France in the 1930s and 1940s only André Jolivet (1905–1974) produced a noteworthy body of work. Most attractive of the pieces for keyboard composed by Jolivet in the 1930s is *Cosmogonie*, a not-quite nine-minute piano prelude that is quite gentle and consonant in comparison to his *Danses rituelles* (Ritual dances) and *Mana*, two other keyboard compositions of the period. Much of Jolivet's music sounds quite a bit like Messiaen's, with constantly changing rhythms, percussive bass chords, and scampering melismatic figures in the higher registers of the piano. There is little frivolity in these ardent and arduous compositions, and although they are little known and seldom played, they are not without interest.

In general the atmosphere in France in the 1930s was considerably more somber than it had been in the previous decade. The post–World War I euphoria was replaced by a sense of impending doom as Germany rearmed. The effects of the 1929 crash of the stock market in the United States were gradually making themselves felt in Europe, as tourists stopped coming and expatriates headed for home. Satie died in 1925, and Diaghilev, four years later. The presence around town of the quirky little figure with the umbrella was sorely missed, as were the brilliant performances of the Ballets Russes, which were effectively ended by Diaghilev's death.

Nevertheless all was not sobriety and sermonizing in Paris after 1930. Poulenc and Stravinsky were composing in earnest, Cocteau was still organizing fantastic happenings, and many composers were still writing lighthearted works influenced by Satie and Les Six. In fact, much of Poulenc's keyboard music was composed in the 1930s, including *Sept nocturnes* (7 Nocturnes), the second of which—*Bal de jeunes filles* (Ball of young girls)—is in the style of Chabrier. His *Improvisations* is a series of brief sketches dedicated to famous people, from Marguerite Long to Edith Piaf, on which Poulenc worked from 1932 until 1959, and which were among his own personal favorites. Contrarily, Poulenc claimed to loathe his *Soirées de Nazelles* (Soirees of Nazelles). Finally, his *Suite française* (French suite) is based on the music of sixteenth-century French composer Claude Gervaise. Clearly, the 1930s was among Poulenc's most fruitful decades.

One of the most charming of the works from this period is Jacques Ibert's *Divertissement* of 1930. Ibert (1890–1962) was a serious Conservatoire student who earned a First Prize in composition for his cantata *Le poète et la fée* (The poet and the fairy) and then went on to become director of the French Academy in Rome (1936–1940 and 1946–1960). Yet he was nonetheless noted for his "'musical hedonism,'" the desire to combine accessibility, elegance, and humor in his concert works. In this he was following a time-honored French tradition. His particular kind of sophisticated playfulness made him the ideal composer for theater, ballet, and movies, and he composed over sixty cinema scores.

Divertissement has a most delightful internal piano part, which aids and abets the various spoofs and parodies in which the six-movement piece abounds. The *Cortège* has a ragtime march as well as irreverent references to the *Wedding March* from Mendelssohn's *Midsummer Night's Dream*. There is a lazy interlude before the wonderfully silly *Valse,* a compendium of French and Viennese waltz styles punctuated by military-band sounds. Police whistles and blaring brass accompany the toy soldiers marching in *Parade,* after which the *Finale* begins. The portentous opening of this last section soon yields to wilder and wilder tempi; pandemonium breaks loose with the piano's bold tone clusters, which owe nothing to those of Cowell or Messiaen. Everyone, including the pianist, has a great time in this piece—but the best part of all must be that of the whistle blower.

The ragtime references in *Divertissement* notwithstanding, the 1930s saw a decrease in French classical composers' infatuation with jazz as an element in serious concert music. The populace at large, however, still flocked to clubs and dance halls to listen and to dance to the African American beat. Montparnasse gradually began to replace Montmartre as the best place to hear American jazz, but some of the old clubs still held on to their loyal customers.

There had always been some resentment on the part of French popular entertainers of the African American infiltration and virtual takeover of the club scene in Paris. As early as 1922, in response to pressure from this displaced and disgruntled coterie of French players, the Poincaré government passed the so-called "10 percent law," stipulating that no more than one of every ten members of a group playing in a public venue could be foreign-born.[6] For over a decade this law was ignored. Very few clubs had ensembles of ten players or more, so enforcing the law would have meant eliminating American players altogether. Few club owners were willing to risk losing their clientele by doing that.

Enforcement of the law was inevitable by the summer of 1933, however, as unemployment increased in the European wake of the American depression. In November 1931 there were forty-six foreign orchestras in France employing 236 foreign-born players; from June 1933 until April 20, 1934, when the Willy Lewis band opened at Chez Florence, not one black jazz club was operating in Paris.[7] Since few French musicians at that time had made the jazz idiom their own, there was a decline in the quality of the music in the clubs and a concomitant decline in patronage. Black jazz withered, the Charleston and other jazz-based steps replaced by new dance crazes based on Latin beats, with which the French bands were apparently more comfortable.

It did not take long, however, for cagey club owners to find loopholes in the law that allowed them to rehire their favorite bands. Owners of clubs were permitted to play in their own places, so some proprietors gave nominal partnerships to band members. The law pertained only to "musicians," so some groups—like Willy Lewis's—called themselves "entertainers." A few affluent entrepreneurs had two bands, one all French, a smaller one all African American. This was the solution chosen by the newly opened Parisian Cotton Club, named and patterned after the famous Harlem *boîte.* The Montmartre clubs began to come back to life, but things were not the same: fewer tourists, less easy money, growing fear of the political

situation—these realities did not disappear through even the most inge-
niously configured loopholes.

Montmartre was clearly suffering. Many black players went elsewhere—
Shanghai was a favorite destination—to find jobs. Some went back to
America, and others, like Bricktop, stuck it out until the Nazi threat could
no longer be ignored. Paradoxically, during these years of attrition, several big bands from the United States toured Europe. The French had
been hearing smaller combos in person for over a decade but knew the
famous bands of the Swing Era only through the recordings, which they
bought avidly. Duke Ellington's recording of *Mood Indigo* became available
in France in 1932, and Ellington, Louis Armstrong, and Coleman Hawkins
were among those who wowed Paris in the early 1930s. Ellington's band
gave three concerts at the Salle Pleyel in the summer of 1932; Armstrong
and company followed two years later. French critics found in the performances of Ellington's band "fantasy disciplined by primitive musicality"
and couldn't get enough of it. They loved the "blackness" of Armstrong's
playing, which "put the heart, the fireworks back" after the blander symphonic jazz epitomized by Paul Whiteman.[8] These celebrated African
American visitors, rather than the resident expatriate Montmartre performers, proved to be most inspiring to French jazz players.

For many years French music critics had been writing serious analytic
articles about American-style jazz. Among the first American studies of
this nature was Winthrop Sargeant's *Jazz, Hot and Hybrid* of 1938. As a
more commercial, Tin Pan Alley sound crept into popular jazz, writers like
Charles Delaunay, publisher of *The Hot Discography,* and Hughes Panassié
urged a return to the pure sounds of Dixieland and other New Orleans–
based music. To promote his ideas, in 1932 Panassié founded Le Hot Club
de France (HCF), which was at once a place for French jazz musicians to
get together, a recording company, and a booking agency. The HCF was
the country's "premier jazz appreciation society, disseminating jazz to new
audiences across France" through its radio broadcasts and magazine.[9]

It was under the auspices of the HCF that the two most famous French
jazz players of all time, guitarist Django Reinhardt and violinist Stéphane
Grappelli, formed the historic Quintette du Hot Club. Panassié saw to it
that the Quintette played in prestigious places, booking them at the Salle
Pleyel in conjunction with the Coleman Hawkins band, whom the Club
itself had invited to Paris.[10]

There were other collaborations, usually sponsored by the HCF, between
famous French and American jazz musicians. While on tour in Paris in
1935, Armstrong appeared with Reinhardt at Bricktop's, one of the Montmartre clubs that was limping along. Coleman Hawkins and Benny Carter
made some recordings with Reinhardt and Grappelli in 1937. Ellington
was in the throes of organizing a United States tour for the Quintette when
the outbreak of World War II made such plans unfeasible.

Le Quintette du Hot Club had a truly unique sound. There were no brass and no drums, only the two soloists backed by two additional guitars and a double bass. Grappelli and Reinhardt were extraordinary improvisers, and the other players supplied the steady beat and predetermined harmonic scaffolding that allowed them to indulge their spectacular flights of fancy. A CD released by Pavilion Records in 1991, a compilation of recordings made by the group in 1936 and 1937, gives a fair sampling of their work.

Most of the songs on the CD are American standards—*After You've Gone, In the Still of the Night, I Can't Give You Anything but Love, Ain't Misbehavin'*—and all vocals are sung by an American. There are up-tempo, mid-tempo, and more leisurely numbers, but the steady beat of the backup trio allows no sentimentality in even the slower songs. Most amusing is a novelty piece called *Nagasaki,* whose lyrics, "back in Nagasaki where the women chew tabaccy and the wacky woo the wacky," must have been incomprehensible to even the most bilingual French audiences. Since country fiddlers and banjo players had been part of the earliest vernacular American music, the sound produced by the Quintette was considered by French critics to be more authentic than that of the slicker, more commercial African American groups with which they were familiar. Because of this perceived authenticity and the overwhelming skill of its two stars, the Quintette du Hot Club de France became the first European group to rival its American counterparts in the affections of French critics, audiences, and aficionados.

13

Epilogue-Envoi

*I*n an art form as dependent on continuity as music, all dates are often more or less arbitrary. Because of the particular situations in France and the United States, 1870, as I have explained, seemed a logical place to begin this study. But using World War II as a cutoff point is merely a matter of convenience, for musical life continued in France and America despite the battles and the occupation.

While in a prisoner-of-war camp, Olivier Messiaen managed to continue his creative work, and the performance of Verdi's *Requiem* at the Terezin concentration camp, as well as original works by Jewish composers sent there, all condoned and abetted by the notorious Adolf Eichmann, has been documented. The Nazis officially despised "ethnic" music, but they did not forbid jazz during the occupation of France, and in September 1941 there was a Festival of Swing at the Salon Pleyel.[1] Classical concerts of all kinds continued, although many players were torn between their love for music and their desire to perform it and their reluctance even to seem to collaborate with the hated regime (unfortunately some, as we know, were willing collaborators).

Nadia Boulanger and much of the Fontainebleau crowd, including the Casadesus family, moved to the United States to avoid the carnage; while here they taught, performed, absorbed American culture, and spread their own. Igor Stravinsky was able to join his colleagues Arnold Schoenberg and Thomas Mann in Los Angeles, where all lived fairly normal lives—there are delightful film clips of some of these august refugees playing tennis, which somehow makes them seem a little more like the rest of us. French composers Georges Auric and Arthur Honegger joined Austrian Erich Korngold and Americans George Antheil, Aaron Copland, and Virgil Thomson in composing for the movies; with their talents and tastes they made an art form out of the background music so vital to the atmosphere of a film, winning many an Oscar along the way. Quite a few composers and performers found employment at New York City's New School for Social Research, a truly liberal arts school not unduly worried about less-than-perfect English. Other universities and conservatories also tried to find room for these displaced talents.

Immediately after World War II, serialism seemed the way to go; Pierre Boulez was the leading composer in an increasingly intellectualized music. Boulanger, as she told her Fontainebleau students, thought Boulez had the most brilliant musical mind of the twentieth century, but—accepted as he was as an excellent conductor—his compositions appealed to even fewer people than had Schoenberg's most austere works. The work started by Edgar Varèse, now dubbed *musique concrète,* was continued by Frenchman Pierre Schaeffer, who worked with technologically manipulated effects, such as prerecorded bell or percussion sounds juggled on many-tracked machines.

Perhaps it was because of all this experimental composition, which most concert subscribers didn't really care for, or perhaps it was just inevitable, but after World War II classical and popular music seemed to grow farther and farther apart, with most forms of classical music—opera seems to be the exception—losing considerable numbers of their supporters. This loss was gradual, but after the introduction of "hard rock" many young and even middle-aged listeners turned away from the piano or orchestral sounds that had been part of so many popular entertainments (Who among us of a "certain age" can hear the *William Tell* Overture without thinking of Tonto and the Lone Ranger?) and that served as a bridge between lighter and more serious music. Nelson Riddle's elaborately orchestrated arrangements of the songs of Cole Porter, for example, which were at one time much admired as popular entertainment, would now seem inappropriately elaborate and "classical" to most audiences, for they lack the pulsating, pounding beat so essential to contemporary pop.

Sadly, jazz, once thought of as the quintessentially American form of music, suffered a decline in popularity comparable to that of classical music. Today it is at least as difficult, if not more so, to find a respectable jazz-oriented radio station as it is to find a classical one. Headlines like "Jazz Impresarios Try New Idea: Jazz, Just Jazz"[2] are indications of how hard it has become to keep alive this music, which was once the most popular America had produced and which was regarded as our one indigenous art form.

Had jazz, like so much twentieth-century art music, become inaccessible, or had it lost its focus? As early as the 1950s a rift developed in jazz between the purists, who saw "real" jazz as exclusively improvisational and based on the original New Orleans Dixieland sound, and those who wanted to include newer developments like bebop and rock.[3]

Even today the controversy continues, as Wynton Marsalis champions the cause of the exclusionists. Ironically, due largely to the efforts of Marsalis and his friends, jazz now has a permanent home in the prestigious Lincoln Center complex in New York City, an overdue recognition of its important place in historical and contemporary American culture.

During World War II, with American jazz—live or recorded—unavailable in France, French jazz began to develop independently. From the early days of the Quintette du Hot Club de France, the sound of the violin had been part of French jazz, with violinist Stéphane Grappelli a featured soloist in the group. The extensive use of string instruments became an identifying feature of French jazz, while it is still somewhat of an oddity—except as background in the larger swing bands—in American jazz. From the experience of one frequent visitor to Paris, the French are far from exclusionists; old-style Dixieland as well as the newest homegrown efforts can be heard on taxicab radios, and no one seems to object. There are dozens of jazz festivals annually throughout the country, plenty of players—French as well as other nationalities—to perform in them, and an avid public to patronize them. Since the French have developed their own jazz style, they seem to have accepted the idiom as part of their own culture rather than resenting it as an American incursion.

When Stravinsky wrote *The Rite of Spring,* orchestras needed dozens of rehearsals and then said it was impossible to play; now every conservatory orchestra can make a credible job of it. The same is true of many other works that seemed outrageously difficult at first, only to yield with familiarity. Mozart's *Dissonant* quartet was roundly criticized for its complexity; Beethoven's violin concerto floored the most virtuosic fiddler of his day, for whom it was written, and the deaf composer's late quartets were seen as the work of a madman. This is hardly a new phenomenon.

And so one trend not unique to this time period but worth noting nevertheless is that more pianists are now willing to tackle the really tough gems of the late-twentieth-century repertoire than ever before. As we have noted, Peter Serkin makes rather a specialty of Messiaen's titanic works, performing the French composer's formidable *Vingt regards sur l'enfant Jésus* from time to time, always from memory. A review in *The New York Times* by Anthony Tommasini discusses two concerts, given several months apart, by a young French pianist named Pierre-Laurent Aimard, on the first of which he also performed the Messiaen.[4] In the second of his concerts, Aimard played more Messiaen, but then moved on to American composers, performing works by Elliott Carter and then the monumental *Concord Sonata* by Charles Ives. Works such as these are still not programmed very often, but clearly they have become international property, to be struggled over and enjoyed by all pianists brave enough to try.

The years since World War II have seen many styles presented to the public; in fact, one can hardly imagine a style that is not being championed by someone somewhere. Serialism, neoclassicism, neoromanticism, minimalism, primitivism, world music, Eastern music, Dixieland, bebop, progressive jazz, *le jazz hot, le jazz cool*—all are out there for the listening. Not surprisingly these trends have roots in the period we have been exploring: Satie is dear to American minimalists, the work of Varèse and Antheil led to electronic music of all kinds, and Takemitsu Tōru and Peter Lieberson may justly claim ties to Ravel and Debussy. Music changes, but the continuity can be found just beneath the surface.

Notes

2. The Formation of a French Style of Composition

1. *The New Grove Dictionary of Music and Musicians*, s.v. d'Indy, Vincent.

2. For a detailed study of the songs of Fauré, Chausson, Duparc, and Debussy, see Barbara Meister, *Nineteenth-Century French Song* (Bloomington: Indiana University Press, 1980).

3. Claude Debussy, *Debussy on Music: The Critical Writings of the Great French Composer Claude Debussy*, trans. Richard Langham Smith, collected and introduction by François Lesure (New York: Alfred A. Knopf, 1977) (originally published as *Monsieur Croche et autres écrits*), p. 54.

4. Wilfrid Mellers, *Man and His Music: Romanticism and the Twentieth Century* (New York: Schocken Books, 1969), pp. 109–110.

5. Ibid., p. 111.

6. Quoted in Rollo Myers, *Chabrier and His Circle* (London: J. M. Dent, 1969), pp. 40–41 (quoted from a letter by Mme Chabrier written in 1882).

7. Ibid.

8. Quoted in E. Robert Schmitz, *The Piano Works of Claude Debussy* (London: Duell, Sloan and Pearce, 1950), pp. xvii–xviii.

9. Quoted in Gail Hilson Woldu, "Debussy, Fauré and d'Indy and Conceptions of the Artist: The Institutions, the Dialogues, the Conflicts," Jane F. Fulcher, ed., *Debussy and His World* (Princeton, N.J.: Princeton University Press, 2001), p. 247.

10. Quoted in Jane F. Fulcher, "Introduction: Constructions and Reconstructions of Debussy," in Fulcher, *Debussy and His World*, p. 2.

11. Christophe Carle, "Debussy in Fin-de-Siècle Paris," in Fulcher, *Debussy and His World*, p. 273.

12. Marguerite Long, *At the Piano with Debussy* (London: J. M. Dent, 1972), p. 6.

13. Ibid.

14. Mellers, *Man and His Music*, p. 131.

15. Jack Sullivan, *New World Symphonies* (New Haven, Conn.: Yale University Press, 1999), p. 198.

16. Debussy, *Debussy on Music*, p. 83.

17. Mellers, *Man and His Music*, p. 132.

18. Quoted in Noel Riley Fitch, *Sylvia Beach and the Lost Generation* (New York: W. W. Norton, 1983), p. 149.

19. Quoted in Sullivan, *New World Symphonies*, p. 204.

20. Quoted in Bruno Monsaingeon, *Mademoiselle: Conversations with Nadia Boulanger* (Manchester: Carcanet, 1985), p. 26.

3. The Formation of an American Style of Composition

1. Jeremy Eichler, "Crossing Old World Angst with New World Music," review in the *New York Times* of Michael B. Beckerman's *New World of Dvorak*, January 10, 2003.

2. Richard Crawford, *America's Musical Life* (New York: W. W. Norton, 2000), pp. 12–14.

3. Ibid., pp. 17–30.

4. Ibid., p. 38.

5. Ibid., p. 57.

6. William Shack, *Harlem in Montmartre* (Berkeley: University of California Press, 2001), p. 28.

7. Harold Schonberg, *The Great Pianists* (New York: Simon and Schuster, 1963), pp. 205–207.

8. Sullivan, *New World Symphonies*, pp. 196–197.

9. Quoted in Crawford, *America's Musical Life*, p. 342.

10. Schonberg, *The Great Pianists*, p. 177.

11. Crawford, *America's Musical Life*, p. 293.

12. Ibid., p. 304.

13. Quoted in *The New Grove Dictionary of Music and Musicians*, s.v. Foster, Stephen, as well as in Crawford, *America's Musical Life*, p. 213.

14. The information for this discussion was taken in large part from program notes by Steven Blier for a concert given on November 20, 2002, at Weill Hall in New York City entitled "Dvořák and the American Soul." Mr. Blier, cofounder of the New York Festival of Song and a faculty member at the Juilliard School of Music, credits Michael Beckerman, author of *New Worlds of Dvořák*, for much of the research in his notes.

15. Quoted in program notes by Steven Blier for New York Festival of Song concert, November 20, 2002.

16. Judith E. Carman, William K. Gaeddert, and Rita M. Resch, eds., *Art Song in the United States: An Annotated Bibliography*, 2nd ed., revised and enlarged (Jacksonville, Fla.: National Association of Teachers of Singing, 1987).

17. *New Grove Dictionary of Music and Musicians*, s.v. Foote, Arthur.

18. *The New Grove Dictionary of Music and Musicians*, s.v. Chadwick, George.

19. Crawford, *America's Musical Life*, p. 461.

20. Joseph Kerman, *Listen* (Berkeley: University of California Press, 1996), p. 361.

4. A Brief History of Jazz in America

1. Bill Kirchner, ed., *The Oxford Companion to Jazz* (New York: Oxford University Press, 2000), p. 5.

2. William Youngren, "European Roots of Jazz," in ibid., p. 19.

3. Ibid., p. 17.

4. Samuel A. Floyd, Jr., "African Origins of Jazz," in Kirchner, *Oxford Companion to Jazz*, p. 13.

5. Ibid., p. 12.

6. Crawford, *America's Musical Life,* p. 533.

7. Ibid., p. 416.

8. Ibid., p. 533.

9. Youngren, "European Roots of Jazz," p. 25.

10. Bob Porter, "The Blues in Jazz," in Kirchner, *Oxford Companion to Jazz,* p. 64.

11. Crawford, *America's Musical Life,* p. 407.

12. See *Yes, We Sang! Songs of the Ghettos and Concentration Camps,* an exploration of this phenomenon, by Shoshana Kalisch with Barbara Meister (New York: Harper and Row, 1985).

13. Ibid., p. 46.

14. Jeff Taylor, "The Early Origins of Jazz," in Kirchner, *Oxford Companion to Jazz,* p. 47.

15. Bob Porter, "The Blues in Jazz," in Kirchner, *Oxford Companion to Jazz,* p. 65.

16. Thomas L. Riis, *New York Roots: Black Broadway, James Reese Europe, Early Pianists,* in Kirchner, *Oxford Companion to Jazz,* p. 57.

17. Ibid., p. 60.

5. American Composers in the 1920s, Part I

1. Crawford, *America's Musical Life,* p. 519.

2. From the second edition of the score of the *Concord Sonata,* published by Arrow Music Press. There is no date or address given, nor are the plates of text numbered. This quote is found on the last page before the composer's instructions to the pianist.

3. Ibid.

4. Arthur Berger, *Aaron Copland* (New York: Oxford University Press, 1953), p. 7.

5. Ibid., p. 9.

6. Arnold Dobrin, *Aaron Copland: His Life and Times* (New York: Thomas Crowell, 1967), p. 30.

7. Arnold Shaw, *The Jazz Age* (Oxford: Oxford University Press, 1987), p. 8.

8. Barbara Meister, "Aaron Copland: A Recollection and a Tribute," *Music Magazine* (February/March 1991), p. 11.

9. Alan Kendall, *Tender Tyrant: Nadia Boulanger, a Life Devoted to Music* (Wilton, Conn.: Lyceum, 1977), p. 36.

10. Ned Rorem, *Pure Contraption: A Composer's Essays* (New York: Holt, Rinehart and Winston, 1974), pp. 72–73.

11. Kathleen Hoover and John Cage, *Virgil Thomson: His Life and Music* (Freeport, N.Y.: Books for Libraries, 1959), p. 50.

12. Mellers, *Man and His Music,* p. 259.

13. Hoover and Cage, *Virgil Thomson,* p. 133.

14. Ibid., p. 144.

15. Anthony Tommasini, "What's So Gay about American Music?" *New York Times,* October 24, 2004.

6. American Composers in the 1920s, Part II

1. Nicolas Slominsky, "Henry Cowell," in Henry Cowell, ed., *American Composers on American Music: A Symposium* (New York: Frederick Ungar, 1962), p. 158.

2. Quoted in Nicolas Slominsky, "Roger Sessions," in Cowell, *American Composers on American Music,* p. 180.

3. CD featuring works by Henry Cowell produced by the New Music Association and distributed by New Albion, NA 103.

4. Herbert Russcol, *The Liberation of Sound* (Englewood Cliffs, N.J.: Prentice Hall, 1978), p. 71.

5. Henry Cowell, "Trends in American Music," in Cowell, *American Composers on American Music,* p. 8.

6. Aaron Copland, "Carlos Chávez, Mexican Composer," in Cowell, *American Composers on American Music,* p. 102.

7. Cowell, "Trends in American Music," p. 7.

8. Ibid., p. 8.

9. Ibid., p. 13.

10. *The New Grove Dictionary of Music and Musicians,* s.v. Gershwin, George.

11. Shaw, *The Jazz Age,* pp. 44–45.

12. Wayne Schneider, ed., *The Gershwin Style* (New York: Oxford University Press, 1999), p. 179.

13. Shaw, *The Jazz Age,* p. 50.

14. Quoted in Schneider, *The Gershwin Style,* p. 181.

15. George Gershwin, "The Relation of Jazz to American Music," in Cowell, *American Composers on American Music,* pp. 186–187.

16. Quoted in Schneider, *The Gershwin Style,* p. 7.

17. Quoted in ibid., p. 51.

18. *The New Grove Dictionary of Music and Musicians,* s.v. Gershwin, George.

7. The Harlem Renaissance

1. Aberjhani and Sandra L. West, *The Encyclopedia of the Harlem Renaissance* (New York: Checkmark Books, 2003), p. 238.

2. Ibid., p. 137.

3. Nathan Irvin Huggins, *Harlem Renaissance* (New York: Oxford University Press, 1971), p. 10.

4. West and West, *Encyclopedia of the Harlem Renaissance,* p. 316.

5. Huggins, *Harlem Renaissance,* pp. 3–12.

6. *The Piano Music of William Grant Still,* WGSM 1002.

7. Huggins, *Harlem Renaissance,* p. 5.

8. Ibid., p. 11.

9. Shaw, *The Jazz Age,* p. 80.

10. Ibid., p. 84.

11. Ibid., p. 22.

12. Roy Harris, "Problems of American Composers," in Cowell, *American Composers on American Music,* p. 154.

13. Shaw, *The Jazz Age,* p. 85.

14. Mark Tucker, "Duke Ellington," in Kirchner, *Oxford Companion to Jazz,* p. 132.

15. Shaw, *The Jazz Age,* p. 85.

16. Mark Tucker, "Duke Ellington," p. 133.

17. Ibid., p. 145.

8. America in the 1930s

1. Kenneth J. Bindas, *All of This Music Belongs to the Nation: The WPA's Federal Music Project and American Society* (Knoxville: University of Tennessee Press, 1995), p. ix. (Most of the information on the FMP is taken from this extremely detailed work.)

2. Ibid., p. 1.

3. Ibid., p. x.

4. Ibid., p. 15.

5. Ibid.

6. Ibid., p. 35.

7. Ibid., p. 60.

8. Ibid., p. 63.

9. Ibid., p. 65.

10. Aaron Copland, *What to Listen for in Music,* rev. ed. (New York: New American Library, 1957; first published 1939).

11. Bindas, *All of This Music Belongs to the Nation,* p. 62.

12. Aaron Copland, "Carlos Chávez, Mexican Composer" in Cowell, *American Composers on American Music,* p. 104.

13. Program notes for *The Piano Music of Roy Harris,* Albany Records CD RO 105.

14. Koch International 3-746-2 H1.

15. Harris, "Problems of American Composers," p. 151.

16. Mellers, *Man and His Music,* p. 250.

17. Ibid.

18. Alan Kozin, "Two Yankee Iconoclasts Juxtaposed at the Piano," *New York Times,* April 10, 2003.

19. Bindas, *All of This Music Belongs to the Nation,* pp. 71–76.

20. Ibid., pp. 84–85.

21. Cited in Alfred Appel, Jr., *Jazz Modernism from Ellington and Armstrong to Matisse and Joyce* (New York: Alfred A. Knopf, 2002), p. 8.

22. Ibid., pp. 13, 26–27.

23. Ibid., p. 16.

24. Mark Tucker, "Duke Ellington," in Kirchner, *Oxford Companion to Jazz,* p. 137.

25. Quoted in ibid., pp. 146–147.

9. Paris in the 1920s, Part I

1. Arthur E. Barbeau and Florette Henri, *The Unknown Soldiers: African-American Troops in World War I* (New York: Da Capo, 1996), pp. 12–13.

2. E. B. Hogan, *The Last Buffalo: Walter E. Potts and the 92nd "Buffalo" Division in World War I* (Austin, Tex.: Eakin, 2000), p. 1.

3. Shack, *Harlem in Montmartre,* p. 12.

4. Barbeau and Henri, *Unknown Soldiers,* p. 71.

5. Shack, *Harlem in Montmartre,* p. 19.

6. Ibid., p. 18.

7. Barbeau and Henri, *Unknown Soldiers,* p. 175.

8. Quoted in an article by Carl Woideck, "Sidney Bechet: Beyond Category," in the University of Oregon publication *Le Jazz Hot* (2000), p. 40.

9. Ibid.

10. Jeffrey H. Jackson, *Making Jazz French* (Durham, N.C.: Duke University Press, 2003), p. 111.

11. Quoted in ibid., p. 18.

12. Ibid., p. 19.

13. Ibid., p. 17.

14. Ibid., p. 1.

15. Chris Goddard, *Jazz Away from Home* (London: Paddington, 1979), p. 261.

16. Ibid., p. 114.

17. Quoted in ibid.

18. Mellers, *Man and His Music*, p. 146.

19. Quoted in Sullivan, *New World Symphonies*, p. 201.

20. Quoted in ibid., p. 61.

21. Darius Milhaud, *Notes without Music* (New York: Alfred A. Knopf, 1953), p. 33.

22. Ibid., p. 75.

23. Ibid., pp. 101–102.

24. Ibid., p. 128.

25. Goddard, *Jazz Away from Home*, p. 118.

26. Released on INA Mémoire VIVE under the title *Jean Wiéner, improvisations au piano*.

27. Quoted in Goddard, *Jazz Away from Home*, pp. 122–123.

28. Ibid., p. 123.

10. Paris in the 1920s, Part II

1. Eveline Hurard-Viltard, *Le Groupe des Six ou le matin d'un jour de fête* (Paris: Méridiens Klincksieck, 1987), p. 30; all translations from this book are my own.

2. Jean Roy, *Le Groupe des Six* (Paris: Seuil, 1994), p. 5.

3. Hurard-Viltard, *Le Groupe des Six*, p. 23.

4. Quoted in ibid., p. 161.

5. Ibid., p. 156.

6. Ibid., p. 121.

7. Quoted in ibid., p. 156.

8. *Virginia Eskin Plays Piano Music of Women Composers*, Musical Heritage, MUS 4236.

9. Quoted in Barbara Meister, *Art Song: The Marriage of Music and Poetry* (Wakefield, N.H.: Hollowbrook, 1991), p. 170.

10. Jackson, *Making Jazz French*, p. 117.

11. Bernard Holland, "Recalling the Mind behind Gears and Pistons," *New York Times*, March 25, 2004.

12. Jackson, *Making Jazz French*, p. 78.

13. Quoted in Hurard-Viltard, *Le Groupe des Six*, p. 138.

14. Quoted in Fitch, *Sylvia Beach and the Lost Generation*, p. 234.

15. Most of the information on Bullard was taken from West and West, *Encyclopedia of the Harlem Renaissance*.

16. Shack, *Harlem in Montmartre*, p. 31. Most of the information on Bricktop is culled from her autobiography, entitled *Bricktop* and co-authored by James Haskins (New York: Welcome Rain, 2000).

17. F. Scott Fitzgerald, *Babylon Revisited and Other Stories* (New York: Scribner's, 1960), p. 214.

18. Most of the material dealing with Shakespeare & Company and Sylvia Beach is taken from Fitch, *Sylvia Beach and the Lost Generation.*

19. Ibid., pp. 13–14, 77–81, 87–88, 102–108, 113–114.

20. Quoted from a letter by Sylvia Beach, ibid., p. 150.

21. Ibid., p. 145.

22. Ibid., p. 157.

23. William Carlos Williams, "George Antheil and the Cantilene Critics—A Note on the First Performance of Antheil's Music in New York City: April 10, 1927," *Transition*, no. 13 (summer 1928): 236–240.

24. Bindas, *All of This Music Belongs to the Nation*, p. 61.

25. Fitch, *Sylvia Beach and the Lost Generation*, p. 150.

26. Quoted in ibid.

27. Elaine Brody, *Paris: The Musical Kaleidoscope 1870–1925* (New York: Braziller, 1987), p. 245.

11. Edgar Varèse and Igor Stravinsky

1. Debussy, *Debussy on Music*, p. 328.

2. *The New Grove Dictionary of Music and Musicians*, s.v. Varèse, Edgar.

3. Henry Cowell, "Edgar Varèse," in Cowell, *American Composers on American Music*, p. 43.

4. Quoted in Sullivan, *New World Symphonies*, p. 143.

5. Quoted in ibid., p. 142.

6. Russcol's *The Liberation of Sound* is a very good study of the development of electronic instruments.

7. Quoted in ibid., p. xix.

8. Sullivan, *New World Symphonies*, p. 150.

9. Much of the information on Diaghilev and the Ballets Russes is taken from John Percival, *The World of Diaghilev* (New York: Harmony Books, 1971).

10. Quoted in ibid., p. 12.

11. Goddard, *Jazz Away from Home*, p. 121.

12. Mellers, *Man and His Music*, p. 201.

13. Sullivan, *New World Symphonies*, p. 194.

14. Appel, *Jazz Modernism*, p. 60.

15. Harris, "Problems of American Composers," p. 151.

16. Mellers, *Man and His Music*, p. 202.

17. Quoted in Sullivan, *New World Symphonies*, p. 210.

12. Paris in the 1930s

1. Rebecca Rischin, *For the End of Time: The Story of the Messiaen Quartet* (Ithaca, N.Y.: Cornell University Press, 2003), p. 4.

2. Alex Ross, "Revelations," *New Yorker*, March 22, 2004, pp. 96–97.

3. Ibid., p. 96.

4. Sullivan, *New World Symphonies*, p. 194.

5. Notes to the Tashi recording of *Quatuor pour la fin du temps,* RCA Victor 17835-2 RG.

6. Shack, *Harlem in Montmartre,* p. 78.

7. Ibid., pp. 78–80.

8. Jackson, *Making Jazz French,* pp. 156–157.

9. Ibid., p. 7.

10. *The New Grove Dictionary of Music and Musicians,* s.v. Jazz.

13. Epilogue-Envoi

1. Jean-Dominique Brierre, *Le jazz français de 1900 à aujourd'hui* (Paris: Éditions Collections, 2000), p. 55.

2. Ben Ratliff, "Jazz Impresario Tries New Idea: Jazz. Just Jazz," *New York Times,* June 11, 2004.

3. Brierre, *Le jazz français,* p. 53.

4. Anthony Tommasini, "Making the Difficult Look Easy, Part 2," *New York Times,* May 20, 2004.

Bibliography

Encyclopedias

Kirchner, Bill, ed. *The Oxford Companion to Jazz*. New York: Oxford University Press, 2000.

Lyle, Wilson. *A Dictionary of Pianists*. London: Robert Hale, 1985.

Sadie, Stanley, ed. *The New Grove Dictionary of Music and Musicians*. 20 vols. London: Macmillan, 2000.

West, Aberjhani, and Sandra L. West, eds. *The Encyclopedia of the Harlem Renaissance*. New York: Checkmark Books, 2003.

Periodicals

Banks, Ann. "Jim Crow's Last War." Review of *Blood for Dignity* by David P. Colleys. *New York Times,* February 16, 2003.

Copland, Aaron. "Jazz Structure and Influence." *Modern Music* (January 1927).

Eichler, Jeremy. "Crossing Old World Angst with New World Music" (Review of Michael Beckerman, *New Worlds of Dvořák*), *New York Times,* January 10, 2003.

Holland, Bernard. "Recalling the Mind behind the Gears and Pistons." *New York Times,* March 25, 2004.

Kozin, Alan. "Two Yankee Iconoclasts Juxtaposed at the Piano." *New York Times,* April 10, 2003.

Meister, Barbara. "Aaron Copland: A Recollection and a Tribute." *Music Magazine* (February/March 1991).

Ostendorf, Brendt. "Subversive Reeducation? Jazz as a Liberating Force in Germany and Europe." *The American Institute* (December 2001).

Ratliff, Ben. "Jazz Impresario Tries New Idea: Jazz. Just Jazz." *New York Times,* June 11, 2004.

Rockwell, John. "No Rap but Just about Everything Else." *New York Times,* March 12, 2004.

Ross, Alex. "Revelations." *New Yorker* (March 22, 2004).

Taruskin, Richard. "Ezra Pound, Musical Crackpot." *New York Times,* July 27, 2003.

———. "Underneath the Dissonance Beats a Brahmsian Heart." *New York Times,* May 16, 2004.

Tommasini, Anthony. "Making the Difficult Look Easy, Part 2." *New York Times,* May 20, 2004.
———. "What's So Gay about American Music?" *New York Times,* October 24, 2004.
Williams, William Carlos. "George Antheil and the Cantilene Critics—A Note on the First Performance of Antheil's Music in New York City: April 10, 1927." *Transition,* no. 13 (summer 1928): 237–240.
Woideck, Carl. "Sidney Bechet: Beyond Category." *Le Jazz Hot* (University of Oregon), 2000.

Books

Appel, Alfred, Jr. *Jazz Modernism from Ellington and Armstrong to Matisse and Joyce.* New York: Alfred A. Knopf, 2002.
Baker, Jean-Claude (with Chris Chase). *Josephine.* New York: Cooper Square, 2001.
Barbeau, Arthur, and Florette Henri. *The Unknown Soldiers: African-American Troops in World War I.* New York: Da Capo, 1996.
Beckerman, Michael. *New Worlds of Dvořák.* New York: W. W. Norton, 2003.
Berger, Arthur. *Aaron Copland.* New York: Oxford University Press, 1953.
Bindas, Kenneth, J. *All of This Music Belongs to the Nation: The WPA's Federal Music Project and American Society.* Knoxville: University of Tennessee Press, 1995.
Bricktop, with James Haskins. *Bricktop.* New York: Welcome Rain, 2000.
Brierre, Jean-Dominique, *Le jazz français de 1900 à aujourd'hui.* Paris: Éditions Collections, 2000.
Brody, Elaine. *Paris: The Musical Kaleidoscope 1870–1925.* New York: Braziller, 1987.
Carmen, J., W. Gaeddert, and R. Resch, eds. *Art Songs in the United States: An Annotated Bibliography.* 2nd ed. Jacksonville, Fla: National Association of Teachers of Singing, 1987.
Copland, Aaron. *What to Listen for in Music.* New York: New American Library, 1957 (originally published 1939).
Cowell, Henry, ed. *American Composers on American Music: A Symposium.* New York: Frederick Ungar, 1962 (originally published 1933).
Crawford, Richard. *America's Musical Life.* New York: W. W. Norton, 2000.
Debussy, Claude, *Debussy on Music, The Critical Writings of the Great French Composer Claude Debussy.* Translated by Richard Langham Smith, collected and introduced by François Lesure, New York: Alfred A. Knopf, 1977.
Dobrin, Arnold. *Aaron Copland: His Life and Times.* New York: Thomas Crowell, 1967.
Dubal, David. *Reflections from the Keyboard.* New York: Schirmer Books, 1997.
Feder, Stuart. *Charles Ives: My Father's Songs* New Haven, Conn.: Yale University Press, 1992.
Fitch, Noel Riley. *Sylvia Beach and the Lost Generation.* New York: W. W. Norton, 1983.
Fitzgerald, F. Scott. *Babylon Revisited and Other Stories.* New York: Scribner's, 1960.
Fulcher, Jane F., ed. *Debussy and His World.* Princeton, N.J.: Princeton University Press, 2001.
Goddard, Chris. *Jazz Away from Home.* London: Paddington, 1979.
Hogan, E. B. *The Last Buffalo: Walter E. Potts and the 92nd "Buffalo" Division in World War I.* Austin, Tex.: Eakin, 2000.

Hoover, Kathleen, and John Cage. *Virgil Thomson: His Life and Music.* Freeport, N.Y.: Books for Libraries, 1959.

Huggins, Nathan Irvin. *Harlem Renaissance.* New York: Oxford University Press, 1971.

Hurard-Viltard, Eveline. *Le Groupe des Six ou le matin d'un jour de fête.* Paris: Méridiens Klincksieck, 1987.

Jackson, Jeffrey H. *Making Jazz French.* Durham, N.C.: Duke University Press, 2003.

Jankélévitch, Vladimir. *Ravel.* New York: Grove, 1959.

Kalisch, Shoshana, with Barbara Meister. *Yes, We Sang! Songs of the Ghettos and Concentration Camps.* New York: Harper and Row, 1985.

Kendall, Alan. *Tender Tyrant: Nadia Boulanger, a Life Devoted to Music.* Wilton, Conn.: Lyceum, 1977.

Kerman, Joseph. *Listen.* Berkeley: University of California Press, 1996.

Loesser, Arthur. *Men, Women and Pianos.* New York: Simon and Schuster, 1954.

Long, Marguerite. *At the Piano with Debussy.* London: J. M. Dent, 1972.

Meister, Barbara. *Art Song: The Marriage of Music and Poetry.* Wakefield, N.H.: Hollowbrook, 1991.

———. *Nineteenth-Century French Song.* Bloomington: Indiana University Press, 1980.

Mellers, Wilfrid. *Man and His Music: Romanticism and the Twentieth Century.* New York: Schocken Books, 1969.

Milhaud, Darius. *Notes without Music.* New York: Alfred A. Knopf, 1953.

Monsaingeon, Bruno. *Mademoiselle: Conversations with Nadia Boulanger.* Manchester: Carcanet, 1985.

Myers, Rollo. *Emmanuel Chabrier and His Circle.* London: J. M. Dent, 1969.

Nichols, Roger. *Messiaen.* Oxford: Oxford University Press, 1986.

Percival, John. *The World of Diaghilev.* New York: Harmony Books, 1971.

Richardson, John. *A Life of Picasso.* New York: Random House, 1996.

Rischin, Rebecca. *For the End of Time: The Story of the Messiaen Quartet.* Ithaca, N.Y.: Cornell University Press, 2003.

Rorem, Ned. *Pure Contraption: A Composer's Essays.* New York: Holt, Rinehart and Winston, 1974.

Rossiter, Frank, *Charles Ives and His America,* New York: W. W. Norton, 1975.

Roy, Jean. *Le Groupe des Six.* Paris: Seuil, 1994.

Russcol, Herbert. *The Liberation of Sound.* Englewood Cliffs, N.J.: Prentice Hall, 1978.

Sargeant, Winthrop, *Jazz, Hot and Hybrid.* New York: Arrow, 1938.

Schmitz, E. Robert. *The Piano Works of Claude Debussy.* London: Duell, Sloan and Pearce, 1950.

Schneider, Wayne, ed. *The Gershwin Style.* Oxford: Oxford University Press, 1999.

Schonberg, Harold. *The Great Pianists.* New York: Simon and Schuster, 1963.

Shack, William. *Harlem in Montmartre.* Berkeley: University of California Press, 2001.

Shaw, Arnold. *The Jazz Age.* Oxford: Oxford University Press, 1987.

Stevens, Elizabeth. "The Influence of Nadia Boulanger on Composition in the United States." Master's thesis, Boston University, 1975.

Sullivan, Jack. *New World Symphonies.* New Haven, Conn.: Yale University Press, 1999.

Index

BARBARA MEISTER is author of *Nineteenth-Century French Song* (Indiana University Press, 1980; paperback edition 1998). She is active as an accompanist, chamber musician, solo pianist, and lecturer on art songs. Her most recent CD for Centaur is entitled *Twentieth-Century American Music*.

———————————